The Arab Predicament

Arab Political Thought and Practice Since 1967

UPDATED EDITION

FOUAD AJAMI

CAMBRIDGE
UNIVERSITY PRESS

Published by the Press Syndicate of the University of Cambridge
The Pitt Building, Trumpington Street, Cambridge CB2 1RP
40 West 20th Street, New York, NY 10011-4211 USA
10 Stamford Road, Oakleigh, Victoria 3166, Australia

First published 1981
First paperback edition 1982
Reprinted 1983 (twice), 1984, 1985, 1986, 1987 (twice),
1989, 1991 (twice)
Updated edition 1992

Printed in the United States of America

Portions of Part 2, "Egypt as State, as Arab Mirror,"
have appeared in *Foreign Policy*, no. 35, Spring 1979.

Library of Congress Cataloging-in-Publication Data
Ajami, Fouad.
The Arab predicament : Arab political thought and practice since
1967 / Fouad Ajami. – Updated ed.
p. cm.
Includes bibliographical references and index.
ISBN 0–521–43243–X. – ISBN 0–521–43833–0 (pbk.)
1. Arab countries – Politics and government – 1945– I. Title.
DS63.1.A35 1992
320.917'4927 – dc20   92-8321

A catalogue record for this book is available from the British Library.

ISBN 0–521–43243–X hardback
ISBN 0–521–43833–0 paperback

To my son
Tarik F. Ajami

Contents

ɔɕɪɔɕ

Preface to the Canto Edition

There is a certain kind of criticism born of proximity and some sense of belonging. Michael Walzer had it right when he wrote of the critic's relation to the people he studies: "The critic need not feel kindly toward the people he criticizes. But he ought to acknowledge his connection to those people: If he were a stranger, really disinterested, it is hard to see why he would involve himself in their affairs."[1]

This book – the first edition completed in 1981, this revised Canto edition done a decade later – is not the work of a "stranger." I was born in Lebanon, in 1945, to a Muslim Shi'a family. The political tradition I hack away at here was, in the most intimate way, my own and my generation's. Years in a faraway land could never sever the bonds to that older world. The verdict issued here on the Arab condition seemed bleak to me when I probed it in the first edition. But I took no joy in the verdict: It was where the trail had led me. The book had a tempestuous career among Arabs who read it. Some saw their world reflected in it, others saw alienation and bad faith and excessive moral judgment. But Arab political history offered compliance, as it were, and confirmation beyond anything I might have imagined.

No author, however cruel or perverse, could have foreseen that "summer of Arab discontent" in 1990: Saddam Hussein of Iraq stepping out of the shadows and treating his world to a season of carnage and wrath and cruelty. But the Iraqi claimant did not emerge out of a void; he "did not descend from the sky," as one Kuwaiti put it. He walked right out of the dominant political legacy of Arab nationalism: its mix of dreams and delusions, its sins of omission and commission, its dominant political style, out of the sectarian-

ism which modern Arabs had denied and papered over but which
had grown wildly in the dark. The winds had been sown over a
long period of time; in that summer of 1990 the Arabs would reap
the whirlwind. It is with the sowing of those terrible winds that
this book is concerned.

This is a book about the grand political ideas that have swept
the Arab world in the two decades or so following the Six Day
War of 1967. I have not written a chronicle of political events.
Fernand Braudel, the great historian of the Mediterranean, was
right, I think, when he observed: "Events are the ephemera of
history; they pass across its stage like fireflies, hardly glimpsed before they settle back into darkness and as often as not into obliv-
ion."[2] There were some central themes I targeted – the balance
between the religious and the political, between Arab nationalism
and reasons of state, between the claims of authenticity and the
powerful attraction of the foreign world beyond; the place of Egypt
in the Arab scheme of things. These are the themes I stay with
here.

In this edition a good deal of the Introduction has been rewritten. I have expanded Part II at some length, to cover the assassination of Anwar el Sadat and the kind of order that Sadat's successors and inheritors put together in the aftermath of his death.
We are lucky that Egypt's police and prosecutors are as methodical
as they are. They have given us a vast amount of material about
Sadat's assassins and the underground Islamic politics they came
out of. I draw on this material here. The years that followed the
Six Day War of 1967 were, in the main, about Egypt's place among
Arabs. That question has been resolved. In the pages that follow
the story is carried to its conclusion.

Part III has also been substantially augmented. Years ago, when
the Iranian Revolution was still an audacious and novel experiment, the received wisdom was that the revolution would catch
on in Arab lands. In the first edition I had taken a dissenting view.
In this edition I follow the twists and turns of the Iranian Revolution's push into Arab politics. The struggle between the Iranian
Revolution and its Arab tributaries and the dominant order in the
Arab world (played out between Ayatollah Ruhollah Khomeini
and Saddam Hussein) is explored at some length. The larger bal-

ance between fundamentalist/nativist politics and the power of entrenched states is also given a new look and a new assessment
with the use of some illustrative new material. I probe at greater
length here the stress that secular politics is subjected to in the
Arab political landscape of today.

Some final words about personal debts: My good friend, Walter
H. Lippincott, Jr., was there for the first edition. Emily Loose of
Cambridge University Press provided the incentive and the inspi-
ration for this new endeavor.

New York City   FOUAD AJAMI
January 1992

Note to the
Nonspecialist Reader

People familiar with a particular subject often write as though their readers ought to be equally familiar with particular names, movements, and dates. What follows is a selective glossary of names and concepts that appear in the text with a brief note as to their significance.

Adonis: An Arab poet and essayist of great depth and substance. "Adonis" is the pen name of the Syrian writer Ali Ahmad Said, born in 1930. He did battle with the formalism and stiltedness of Arab poetry and writing. His concerns, like those of so many of his generation, became more political after 1967. In 1968–1969, he helped found a literary/political magazine, *Mawaqif,* which became one of the leading forums for young intellectuals. Readers interested in his poetry should consult a translated volume entitled *Blood of Adonis,* University of Pittsburgh Press, 1971.

Michel Aflaq, Sami al-Jundi, and the Ba'th Party: Michel Aflaq, a Paris-educated publicist and teacher of Greek Orthodox background, founded the Ba'th Party in the 1940s with his friend Salah al-Din al-Bitar. The Ba'th was part of what can best be described as a radical, nationalist alternative to the Communist Party. This was part of the post–World War II middle-class nationalist evolution in the Arab world. Syria was the base of Aflaq and his associates, but their horizons were pan-Arab and they developed a substantial base in Iraq. They were committed to Arab unity and to a vague and mild socialism. Much as Aflaq and the Ba'th talked about political mobilization, it was their success in recruiting military officers that gave them whatever power they knew in the 1950s and 1960s. Aptly enough, it was their alliance with the military that proved to be their undoing. After a turbulent period, Aflaq and the other theoreticians of the Ba'th were driven out of power and banished from Syria in the aftermath of a military coup in 1966. Aflaq went into exile in Beirut to lament and write; the Ba'th–military alliance turned into full-scale military rule in Syria. Eventually Aflaq was invited to settle in Iraq, home of the competing branch of the Ba'th Party, and to serve as a general secretary of the shell that remained of that party. He died in 1989.

But the ideological tale and the polemics no longer mattered. In Syria under Hafez Asad and in post–1968 Iraq, power belongs to the military. To a very limited degree, a man like Michel Aflaq could buttress Iraq's claim to preeminence over Syria and to being the true and legitimate heir of yesterday's Ba'th, but power in both countries now belongs to the military. Of the Ba'th there remains the pamphlets, the symbols, the icons. A historic footnote to their tale was provided in July, 1980, when Salah al-Din al-Bitar, Aflaq's friend during his Paris schooldays and his partner in politics, was murdered in Paris. By then Bitar had broken with his own past, dismissed the polemics of the Ba'th, declared it as dead and finished, and founded an exile magazine for which he wrote some cogent pieces about the crisis of authority in Syria and the Arab world.

Sami al-Jundi was one of the Ba'th's articulate founders and members, a colleague of Aflaq and Bitar. He left a set of remarkable books and memoirs, examined in Part 1 of this study. He left the world of politics to practice dentistry in Tunisia.

Sadeq al-Azm: A Syrian, Azm was educated in philosophy at Yale University. He taught at the American University of Beirut and wrote some substantial studies on Kant. Radicalized by the 1967 experience, he went on to write *Self-Criticism After the Defeat* (1968), *The Criticism of Religious Thought* (1969), and, later, a critical study of the thought and practice of the Palestinian movement. Azm's writings cost him his post at the American University of Beirut and made him a target of the Lebanese religious and political authorities. He came from a distinguished aristocratic Syrian family. His drift to the left and membership in one of the more radical Palestinian movements in the early 1970s were part of the broader radicalization that took place after 1967. Both those who agree and disagree with him credit him with having made noteworthy contributions to the debate after 1967. There is a novel theme to his life – novel in the Arab context of this period: It is the story of affluent young men who could have chosen acquiescence and security but instead chose to oppose, to dissent, and to lose out.

George Habash: A physician, a Palestinian of Greek Orthodox background, Habash was educated at the American University of Beirut, and now heads the Popular Front for the Liberation of Palestine. His story illuminates the Palestinian drama after 1948: first the period of individual salvation as the Palestinian refugees tried to put together personal careers and lives, assimilation into the Arab world in the 1950s and 1960s, then radicalization and the struggle for Palestinian autonomy after 1967. His political beginnings were in the pan-Arab nationalist movement of the 1950s, which drew together small groups of university teachers and students. The stirrings were those of postcolonial nationalism. Then he and like-minded Arab nationalists were drawn into the orbit of Nasserism in the late 1950s and early 1960s, only to be rudely awakened by the 1967 defeat. Habash split off from the Arab nationalist movement to lead the more radical, Marxist-leaning Popular Front for the Liberation of Palestine.

The verdict of Habash and his associates on the Syrian and Egyptian regimes was particularly harsh. Henceforth, they declared in 1967, one had to fight not only against Israel, the West, and the Arab monarchies but also against the "petty bourgeois" regimes of Syria and Egypt. Habash's group survives as a counter to the more strictly Palestinian nationalist perspective of Yasser Arafat and the Palestine Liberation Organization.

Ahmad al Shuqairi: If George Habash tells part of the Palestinians' story, Shuqairi tells a different and older one. Born to a Palestinian upper-class background, Shuqairi was active in the Palestinian politics of the 1930s and 1940s – in the struggle for Palestine that culminated in the victory of the Zionists and the establishment of Israel in 1948. The politics that Shuqairi knew were the politics of clans and notables that were hardly a match for the modern, committed politics of the Zionists.

With a gift for words, the demagogic, venal Shuqairi went on to serve as a delegate of Syria, then of Saudi Arabia, to the United Nations. When an Arab summit established the Palestine Liberation Organization (PLO) in 1964, Shuqairi was designated its leader thanks to his latest patron, Gamal Abdul Nasser of Egypt. The defeat of 1967 sealed Shuqairi's fate, and power passed to a younger generation of Palestinians who pushed Shuqairi aside and took over the PLO. Shuqairi died in Beirut, a broken and forgotten man. He is remembered for his oratory. Some students of the Arab–Israeli conflict still argue over whether Shuqairi said or did not say in 1967 that he wanted to "drive the Jews into the sea." Few others remember him. The world he knew and the politics he represented have passed from the scene and become memories.

Sulta: The term recurs throughout the text, particularly when I reproduce the arguments and concerns of Arab intellectuals. It is an evocative term used to describe political authority and power. Though used by conservatives as a somewhat neutral term, radicals and critics use it to conjure up the capricious, heavy-handed nature of political power in the Arab world. To refer to authority as *sulta* and to today's ruler as the *sultan* is to underline how little has changed over centuries in the relations between ruler and ruled.

Sunnis, Shiʾa, Alawis: Strictly speaking, *sunna* means "the custom," "the orthodoxy" (the closest approximation in English). Sunnis are the majority of Muslims, particularly among the Arabs. The first doctrinal split in Islam took place between the main body of the community of Muslims and those who became known as *Shiʾat Ali* (the partisans of Ali). Ali was the son-in-law of the Prophet; he was passed over for succession after the death of the Prophet Muhammad in A.D. 632. The battle over the succession (Ali was passed over three times in a row) became a broader split as Shiʾa served as the focus for disaffected ethnic elements and dissidents.

The Shiʾa subscribe to the doctrine of the *imamate,* the infallible leader. As their doctrine has it, the imamate belongs to what they call "the people of the House" – the descendants of Ali and his wife Fatima, the daughter of the Prophet. The doctrine of the hidden imam maintains that someday the imam will reappear to establish the realm of justice. Shiʾites suffered persecution that drove

them and their beliefs underground. Shi²a is the dominant orthodoxy in Iran and has a substantial following in both Iraq and Lebanon, where the Shi²a outnumber Sunni Muslims.

The Alawis (also known as Nosairis) are a heterodox small sect
who are mostly located in northern and central Syria. The practice
of the Alawites is a mixture of pagan, Christian, and Muslim beliefs. Alawites carry the veneration of Ali, the son-in-law of the
Prophet, to extremes that place them, as far as Sunni Islam is concerned, beyond the proper boundaries of Islam. Alawis see Ali as
the incarnation of Universal Soul, and they are said by other Muslims to make Ali either equal or even superior to the Prophet. The
practice of the Alawis is shrouded in secrecy, and much is imputed
to them by the main body of Muslims, who consider the Alawis to
be seceders from Islam.

These doctrinal differences between Sunnis, Shi²a, and Alawis
are internalized; they become part of self and history, correspond
with lines of ethnicity and class, and matter less for the hair-
splitting arguments about orthodoxy than for what people make
of them.

IMPORTANT DATES

June 5–11, 1967: The Six Day War. The defeat of Egypt, Jordan,
Syria.

Early 1968: The rise of the Palestinian movement as an independent force in Arab politics. Their early base was in Jordan.

March–June, 1969: The war of attrition along the Suez Canal. A
war designed to challenge the status quo along the Canal, to give
Egypt some diplomatic leverage.

September, 1969: Qaddafi and his fellow officers seize power in
Libya. A hitherto marginal country is brought into Arab politics.
Qaddafi throws Libya's weight and money behind Nasser and
stakes out a position for himself as spokesman for pan-Arabism
and for a radical kind of Muslim fundamentalism.

September, 1970: The civil war in Jordan between the Jordanian
regime and the Palestinian movement.

September 28, 1970: The death of President Nasser.

November, 1970: Hafez Asad seizes power in Syria.

May 15, 1971: President Sadat, hitherto a titular figure, pulls off what he calls his "corrective movement" – essentially a coup against the apparatus claiming to represent the remnants of Nasserism.

July, 1972: The expulsion of Soviet troops and advisors from Egypt. A straw in the wind for yet more drastic changes in Egyptian policies.

1972–1973: The putting together of the coalition that waged the October War based on an understanding between Egypt and Saudi Arabia and the participation of Syria.

October, 1973: The outbreak of the October War. The deployment of the Arab oil weapon.

September, 1975: The conclusion of the Sinai accord between Egypt and Israel under American auspices. The accord causes a rift between Egypt and Syria.

1975–1976: The outbreak of the Lebanese civil war, its institutionalization into a way of life for the country.

November, 1977: Sadat's journey to Jerusalem.

September, 1978: The Camp David accords between Egypt and Israel, with President Carter's participation.

March, 1979: The signing of the Egyptian–Israeli treaty.

January–February, 1979: The collapse of the Pahlavi regime in Iran. The rise of Ayatollah Khomeini.

November, 1979: The attack on the Grand Mosque in Mecca, symbolizing the troubles of the Saudi state and the appeal of religious fundamentalism.

December, 1979–January, 1980: The Soviet invasion of Afghanistan; the "Carter Doctrine" as an American response affirming the will to use military force in the Persian Gulf; deepening polarization and discord between the superpowers; an escalating ideological quarrel between the Khomeini revolutionary regime and its neighboring states.

September, 1980: The outbreak of the Iran–Iraq war; a fight between the Sunni order of states and the Iranian Revolution.

September–October, 1981: A massive wave of arrests in Egypt of President Sadat's critics; Sadat's assassination on October 6.

April, 1982: Israel's evacuation of the last strip of the Sinai Peninsula.

Summer of 1982: Israel's Lebanon war; the expulsion of the Palestine Liberation Organization from Beirut.

1983–1985: The deepening troubles of Lebanon. The Iranian Revolution finds a base among the Shi'a of Lebanon. Israel's withdrawal from the bulk of its positions in the south of Lebanon.

1983–1986: A trail of anti-Western, principally anti-American, terror. The peak of Iran's revolutionary crusade.

February, 1987: The Syrian army enters Muslim West Beirut. A turning point for the Syrians and the Lebanese. The Syrians rein in the Iranian-inspired "Party of God."

December, 1987: The eruption of the *intifada,* the uprising, on the West Bank and Gaza. A young generation of Palestinians, children of the occupation, mount a serious challenge to it.

Summer of 1988: Ayatollah Khomeini declares the end of his crusade against the Iraqi state. The waning of Iran's influence. The King of Jordan renounces his claim to the West Bank.

June, 1989: The death of Ayatollah Khomeini on June 3.

November, 1989: Elections in Jordan give the edge to Islamicists. The same outcome in Algeria's municipal elections in the summer of 1990.

August, 1990: The Iraqi conquest of Kuwait on August 2. Iraq declares Kuwait its "nineteenth province." The dispatch of American forces to Saudi Arabia.

October, 1990: Syrian hegemony is strengthened in Lebanon. The defeat of the Maronite enclave in east Beirut.

January, 1991: Joint U.S. congressional authorization for the use of force against Iraq on January 12. The beginning of an air campaign against Iraq on January 16.

February 27, 1991: The liberation of Kuwait after a swift ground war; the thwarting of Saddam Hussein's bid for primacy.

March, 1991: Shi'a and Kurdish rebellions in Iraq erupt and are then put down by remnants of Saddam Hussein's army.

October, 1991: The convening in Madrid, under American auspices, of a conference to settle Arab–Israeli claims. First direct face-to-face negotiations (Egypt excepted) since the armistice talks and negotiations over Palestinian refugees held in 1949.

Introduction

. . . and yet for aught I see they are sick that surfeit with too much as they that
starve with nothing

> Shakespeare, *The Merchant of Venice*, act 1, sc. 2.

An imitation of European customs including the perilous art of borrowing has been
lately affected: but, in the hands of Eastern rulers, the civilization of the West is
unfruitful; and instead of restoring a tottering state, appears to threaten it with
speedier ruin.

> T. Erskine May, *Democracy in Europe*
> (London: Longmans, Green, 1877), p. 29.

> What god shall resurrect us
> in his flesh?
> After all, the iron cage is shrinking.
> The hangman will not wait
> though we wail from birth
> in the name of these happy ruins.
>
> What narrow yesterdays,
> what stale and shriveled years . . .
> Even storms come begging
> when the sky matches the gray
> of the sand,
> leaving us stalled between seasons
> barricaded by what we see . . .
>
> Adonis [Ali Ahmad Said], *The Blood of Adonis*
> (Pittsburgh: University of
> Pittsburgh Press, 1971), p. 48.

THE world can be read into small events: In Clifford Geertz's imagery, winks can be made to speak to epistemology.[1] The small event into which I shall begin reading things is the death of the Lebanese journalist and publisher Salim al-Lawzi.

In early March, 1980, Salim al-Lawzi was found dead and mutilated in Beirut. He had come back to Lebanon on a personal visit from London where he had been living and working for some time. Because al-Lawzi was a critic of the Syrian presence in Lebanon, it was widely assumed that the Syrians were responsible for the deed. In the Beirut of the late 1970s assassinations and murders had become commonplace: Politics had degenerated into nihilism and violence, and there was no use trying to determine who and what should be believed.

Salim al-Lawzi had not been a particularly talented or honest journalist. Nor did he have to be. He was a great success in a world in which success was its own vindication. He mingled with the mighty; he openly spoke of and flaunted the gifts given to him by this or that Arab ruler, this or that embassy. In the time-honored tradition of Lebanese journalism (where newspapers reflected the views of particular embassies), he had served a variety of patrons and offered his services to the highest bidder. At the height of Nasser's power he had served Cairo; then he shifted his services and loyalty to Saudi Arabia.

When the Arab world found its way to London in the aftermath of the October War of 1973, al-Lawzi moved there and launched a new magazine, *Events* (the exact English translation of his Arabic magazine, *al Hawadith*). *Events* picked up where the old *Hawadith* had faltered. It catered to the Arab presence in London; it showed that men could use new garb but remain themselves. *Events* discoursed in English, but it was moved by the old spirit. It catered to the winners, to the consumers; it flattered those who mattered and displayed their life style. There was no investigative journalism, no analysis, only the banalities of what passed for truth, the version of the world dictated by al-Lawzi's latest patrons. In its pages was that unique mixture of Arab life in the mid and late 1970s – the horrors of the civil wars, the tribalism, and breakdowns together with items about banking and business opportunities, real-estate deals and speculations. One foot in the hell of the old politics re-

2

surgent, one in the benign utopia of finance. It spoke of the wounds and the incoherence and of the new possibilities. Back to back were the latest apocalyptic deeds and words of the Lebanese Phalanges and the deeds of the great Saudi financier Adnan Khashoggi. And, of course, *Events* offered a steady flow of anti-Egyptian polemics from the safety and distance of London: criticism of Egypt's "betrayal" of Arabism, its abandonment of the sacred struggle.

A few words said in eulogy by a friend of al-Lawzi suggest one reason why I open with al-Lawzi's death: "Freedom," he said, "is a plant alien to our part of the world. Whenever implanted, it dies . . . We used to blame the colonialists. Then some of us colonized others and the plant of freedom died over and over again. Each time it died a dreamer who inhabited his own world would try to revive it only to perish along with it . . . all those who made the effort rode against powerful windmills with wooden swords."[2]

This had not been a world that took responsibility for its own deeds. The invented nationalist historiography of the Arab kind had always pointed outward: It accused others — Ottomans, Europeans, and others — of causing the ills of the Arab world.[3] T. E. Lawrence had once expressed and helped spread that stereotype. The Arabs were once free; then the Turks came, who "choked the life out of the body politic." "Happiness," he romanticized, "became a dream" as the spirit of the Arabs "shrivelled in the numbing breath of a military government."[4]

But now the world the Arabs lived in was more nearly an Arab world. The Ottoman empire had become a fading memory, Turkey herself a failing society. The external scapegoats had been cut down to size. The wounds that mattered were self-inflicted wounds. The outside world intruded, but the destruction one saw reflected the logic of Arab history, the quality of its leadership. The divisions of the Arab world were real, not contrived points on a map or a colonial trick of divide-and-conquer. No outsiders had to oppress and mutilate. The whip was cracked by one's own.

In the way he lived and the way he died, al-Lawzi told volumes about what I shall continually refer to as the Arab predicament in the modern world. In the Beirut where al-Lawzi had earlier practiced his brand of journalism in the 1950s and 1960s, things seemed

3

reasonably benign and harmless. No one took seriously what his and other magazines said. Much more was said about Beirut's parties, its joie de vivre, its elegant weddings, than about its slums, about the despair of that so-called belt of misery around the city, or about the real antagonisms that separated the Lebanese. Al-Lawzi's brand of journalism reflected the place assigned to the written and spoken word in Arab politics. It also reflected the peculiar nature of that Levantine city where men lived on charm, by their wits, where "principles" were things that men could not afford, where men seemed to push things to the brink and then pull back to keep the game going, to keep things the way they were.

Then grimness crept into this world – part of the broader grimness that came into Arab life in the aftermath of the Six Day War. The sensitive could sense the gathering of the storm. In the preface to the third edition of his *The Arab Cold War*, Malcolm Kerr lamented that Arab politics "had ceased to be fun. In the good old days most Arabs refused to take themselves seriously and this made it easier to take a relaxed view of the few who possessed intimations of some immortal mission."[5] When these words were written, the ordeal of Lebanon that sent al-Lawzi to London and the unraveling of Arab society that jumbled past and future, fundamentalism and technicalism, the cultural anguish and the business deals had yet to come.

There is no "fun" in the material handled here: It is a chronicle of illusions and despair, of politics repeatedly degenerating into bloodletting, of imagined transformations followed by despair that there is some immutable core that disfigures it all, that devours all good intentions, that mocks those who would try to change things. The seemingly harmless games played by the preceding generation, the hair-splitting arguments of Arab ideologues gave way to a deeper and more terrifying breakdown. One generation had sown the wind and the other was now reaping the harvest. The stock-in-trade of men like Nasser, the Syrian Ba'thist theoretician Michel Aflaq, the braggart Ahmad al-Shuqairi of the Palestine Liberation Organization, was symbols and words. There was ample room for maneuver, a margin for errors. In the decade or so that followed the Six Day War, words were replaced with bullets, which now seemed the final arbiter. This generation, writes one observer, split into two groups: those who saw authority growing out of the barrel of a gun and those who packed up and left.[6] The young thugs roaming the streets of Beirut and the snipers on its tall and modern buildings that once stood as a monument to Lebanon's "cosmopolitanism" exposed the tribalism of a deeply sectarian country whose civilized forms were only a cover for biases and prejudices, an escape from realities intuited and known by its inhabitants.

The 1970s of Lebanon, wrote an analyst in a bitter commentary, are the 1980s of the region as a whole. Just as Lebanon led the Arab world into the bourgeois age (it was really Cairo that did so, but the writer is a Lebanese), it now leads them to the new age. It shows them the hell that lies in their future. Its storm will spread to their skies. Which country will be next? Which country will perform the "dance of death"? Will it be Turkey or will it be one of the states of the Arabian peninsula?[7]

Three great events dominate the period that concerns us: the Six Day War of June, 1967, the October War of 1973, and the Iranian Revolution of 1978–79. Men fought, worked, and reflected in the shadow of these events. In a curious way, the defeat of 1967 was better handled in the Arab world than the so-called victory of 1973. In the aftermath of the June defeat, the dominant order sought to put together an answer of its own to the defeat, as it had to if it were to survive. That it did in the form of an organized, large-scale war in October, 1973. Between 1967 and 1973, the dominant order could rely on patriotism; it had the "safety" of a limited task. Grim as its task was (for it knew that a military victory against Israel was not in the cards) it operated from givens shared by the overwhelming majority of the masses. The defeat was culturally, psychologically, and politically unacceptable, and it had to be dealt with. The managers of order patched up their differences and descended from the world of metaphysics into a more concrete world. They knew that the defeat was intolerable; they sensed the growing despair and tried to stem it. In the process they acquired some badly needed facts and rules about the way the international system worked: They learned how to speak to the outside world; they displayed some skill in a subdued coming-to-terms with the world. To be sure, the 1967–1973 interlude had its dreamers, those who thought that the world could be unmade and remade with a pamphlet, but on balance caution prevailed and the social order hung together.

The "victory" in October, 1973, proved more difficult to control, more difficult to live with. For some, that historic watershed promised an instant remaking of the world, a settling of the great score with the West, a great revenge for past injuries. The long view of this can be appreciated from the following passage by historian Bernard Lewis:

> This confrontation [between the Arab oil producers and the West] is the culmination of a long process which has been going on for centuries. It began with the expansion of Europe from both ends in the late 15th century, the Russians from the East, the Portuguese and other maritime nations from the West. This expansion, and the ascendancy to which it gave rise, eventually affected the whole world. It took different forms in different places. In some areas it led to direct colonial rule. In the Middle East this only happened in few places and for relatively brief periods. In most of the countries of the Middle East the impact of Western domination was indirect but, nevertheless, powerful enough to shatter the old society beyond repair and to initiate a process of violent social, economic, and political change which disrupted the traditional order, destroyed traditional loyalty and relationships, and engendered a deep resentment against the Western standard-bearers of the civilization from which these changes originated.[8]

The world brought about by October 1973 blew away the cobwebs of Arab society. Buffeted by mighty winds and propelled by temptations and possibilities unknown before, its cultural container ruptured. It strutted on the world stage for a brief moment; then the breakdown came. There were great victories on distant stages and paralyzing wounds at home. A world seemed to back into the past because the new terrain looked unfamiliar as old verities were challenged, old limits broken and violated. An essay written in 1978 from Cairo on the eve of the Iranian Revolution expressed my own attempt to understand the undoing of the world that the October war of 1973 had ushered in. I reproduce it here because it foreshadows my own analysis in the pages that follow:

> To those so inclined, divine will must be sending a message to the Muslim people of this region and making known its disapproval of what has come to pass in the age of affluence and "petro-power."

6

Introduction

Since the oil embargo of October 1973, the moment of that perceived great triumph over the West, there has been the tragic collapse of Lebanon, disarray in Arab politics, and of course the recent eruption in Iran. In Muslim and Middle Eastern cosmology, there is a particular emphasis on the fate of those who ride and aim too high and who come to suffer as a result of having dared to break sacred limits and having entertained false pride and ambitions. Since October 1973, the principal malady has been cultural and psychological: a growing imbalance between men and things and the rupturing of the normative order. This may sound a bit poetic and elusive, but it is not intended to be. It has to do with some very concrete things: traffic jams and inflation, growing inequalities, the wearing thin of patience and tradition, and the aftermath of an economic boom that has raised some men to new heights of grandeur and power and demeaned the dignity of others.

Five years ago, the Arabs won what seemed to be a victory over the West: The oil weapon was seen as providing the dawn of a new age of grandeur and power, a revenge for the injuries inflicted on this part of the world. The true age of "petro-power" has visited on the Arabs – as well as on Iran – great suffering and dislocation. Oil money spawned great dreams, but those were inevitably of power and "things." The recurring theme in the tales of "The Thousand and One Nights" is that of the beggar becoming king and the king a beggar. The oil victory was to be that kind of theme: a world that had structured a whole moral and social order around poverty could now do unlimited things. It could humiliate those who had once humiliated it and resurrect a great imagined past grafting onto it the power of the modern West. But the new age was not to be. Unable and really unwilling to import the West as "process" – such features as the accountability of rulers, as well as personal and cultural freedom – the oil states would import the West in the form of "things." The strategy has backfired. When it is in the West, the machinery of the West makes sense: It emerges from a larger social and political order. But imported, the same machinery poses serious problems: The narrow streets of most Middle Eastern capitals are as inhospitable to the machines of the West as are the hearts and habits of men.

The dilemma leaves those engaged in it in the midst of powerful crosscurrents. The mighty wind from the West promises power, glamour, and the possibility of doing away with what once seemed to be unbreakable bounds. But there is also the voice of authenticity and tradition with its own compelling message. It promises to sweep away injustices and troubles and to erect a more caring and true order. It raises the banner of brotherhood at a time of mounting inequalities, hence its power and relevance. Some men have pros-

7

pered in the new order and many have lost out in the boom. And the losers have not been convinced that the winners deserved all that they have accumulated. This has colored the relation between the winners and the losers both within the Arab countries and Iran and among the Arab states themselves. It is responsible for a deeply felt wound in Egypt and the widespread feeling that richer Arabs want Egypt, as one Egyptian writer put it, to starve alone, die alone, fight alone and go bankrupt alone. The sight of Arabic newspapers in London and Paris that cater to the Arab rich attacking Egyptian policies has a pathology all its own that has not been lost on Egyptians.

The phenomenal wealth of some has made a mockery of the brotherhood of man and man. One does not have to be unduly old or nostalgic to recall better times for this region – times when people had less but shared it more equitably and when the normative order had its own balance. This area's vast depths of compassion and humanity that survive and escape breakdown and violence will have to be tapped if the current malady is to be shaken off. For, as Muslim theology maintains, Allah will help and sympathize only when the believers do their part.[9]

In a useful periodization of recent Arab history, the Moroccan scholar Abdallah Laroui identified four distinct phases:

1 The *Nahda* (the Arab Renaissance) from 1850 to 1914. This was dominated by the quest to "assimilate the great achievements of Western European civilization."
2 The struggle for independence. This phase began with the collapse of the Ottoman Empire at the end of World War I and lasted until the mid-1950s: "It gave rise to popular parties that played an important cultural role by promoting the spread of democratic ideals and, to a lesser extent, of socialist values."
3 The "Unionist movement" that flourished after 1948 and found its leadership in President Nasser of Egypt and the Ba'th party in Syria.
4 The "moral crisis" that followed the 1967 defeat. This "culminated in a period of anguished self-criticism, a searching re-appraisal of postwar Arab culture and political practice."[10]

The post-1967 years of concern to us can be arbitrarily divided into three distinct phases. The first lasted from 1967 to 1973. In this phase, the Arab state system tried to clean away the debris of the defeat and worked out a reconciliation between the "radical" states and the conservative ones. The deal was worked out between President Nasser of Egypt and King Faisal of Saudi Arabia. What Malcolm Kerr labelled the "Arab Cold-War" was thus liquidated. But this cycle's early heroes were the newly radicalized Palestinians: It was their guns and pamphlets and their challenge to both radical and conservative states that dominated this cycle. This was brought to an end by the Jordanian civil war of September 1970. King Husein's army may have carried the fight to grim limits and thus frightened off those who had commissioned him to take on the Palestinians. Local grievances and offended sensibilities in Jordan forced a particularly grim battle to erupt. The Jordanian army had watched the erosion of its authority, the growth of a state within a state as the Palestinians turned Jordan into a sanctuary for attacks against Israel and into a political base. But the fight was not Jordan's alone. Save for the pariah Syrian regime (which was brought down by Hafez Asad in November of the same year), all the Arab states had either directly sanctioned the Jordanian effort or simply looked the other way: This was true of Nasser and Qaddafi and of the radical regime in Iraq, as it was true of the conservative states.

At stake was the state system's sensitivity about outsiders who play by a different set of rules. King Husein's army performed the grim service and carried it out with more zeal than some of those who had acquiesced may have wanted: As the casualties ran into the thousands, the Arab states wanted the carnage to stop. But there was no doubt as to their acquiescence in the project. The audacious radicals had to be taught a lesson; the Arab world had to be purged of Marxists; free-lance guerrillas had to be disciplined if the states were to negotiate with Israel or to respond to the diplomatic initiatives offered by outsiders. States are jealous entities: They protect their monopoly on violence and on order, and the Arab state system was no exception. The Arab states had to maintain their hold over their populations, redeem their battered pride, prove themselves to the young at home, and prove themselves to superpowers and assure them that they could deliver their constituents and make good on their promises — either promises of diplomatic deals or threats to go to war if Israel persisted in its occupation of the land they had lost.

9

By 1970, the dominant political order bounced back. Nasser's death and his replacement by Sadat in 1970, the coming to power of Hafez Asad in the same year, and the defeat of the Palestinians, gave the dominant political order a breathing spell. The states used the time to put together the trilateral alliance – Egypt, Syria, and Saudi Arabia – that waged the October War. The deed was done against overwhelming Israeli military power, in the face of the superpower detente that had pretty much frozen the status quo in the Middle East, and against mounting pressure in the Arab world for some kind of solution.

The second phase (1973–1979) involved the ascendancy of the dominant political order. There was a brief moment of elation. All, including the Palestinian self-determination, seemed possible. Great and sudden wealth spawned all sorts of dreams about development, about military power, about the resurrection of the Arab world. All this happened against a promising global background: the revolt of the Third World majority at the UN, disarray in the West, nuclear proliferation (with its promise of greater equality), the illusion that modernity and power could be bought off the rack. This was also America's moment in the Middle East: The United States was to serve as broker in the peace and as a protector of the moderate Arab order. Like all periods of euphoria, none of the troubles vanished; worse still, new and unprecedented troubles were brought about by the new wealth. There were early signs of trouble: the Sinai accord in September, 1975, concluded by Israel and Egypt under American auspices confirmed Egypt's determination to go its own way and was a harbinger of things to come. That same year also witnessed the outbreak of the civil war in Lebanon in which all Arab states were directly or indirectly involved. The great wealth was helpless to arrest the drift toward interstate discord or domestic upheaval in the Arab world. Egypt's diplomatic defection and Lebanon's collapse ended the great historic moment of triumph. Sadat's search for a separate Egyptian path took him to Jerusalem – there were no more subtleties and half-hearted measures. The bloodletting in Lebanon became institutionalized, and there was a definite drift toward de facto partition between a Muslim Lebanon and a Christian one.

The third phase is dominated by the Iranian Revolution of 1978–

10

79 and its wars. (The main war erupted on the Iran–Iraq front in 1980; there was a smaller war that raged over Beirut between its Shiʾa population and the Palestine Liberation Organization; and there were skirmishes in the Gulf between the ruling order and indigenous Shiʾa opposition.) A pied piper, Ayatollah Ruhollah Khomeini, returned home from a long exile in the shrine cities of Iraq and a brief stay in Paris to claim a vast realm and establish a theocratic state. His themes – the power of the foreigner (read the American) in Muslim life, the wicked ways of the privileged, the sanctity of the disinherited who rise up to inherit the earth free from the hold of oppressors, the right of Islam to rule and to dispense with secular governments of the monarchic and republican varieties – were explosive themes.

Khomeini was a man possessed: He had humbled and sent into exile the "King of Kings" who had strutted around the region like a rooster. The mullah had seen the delight of the crowd in the Arab world as the mighty in Iran got their comeuppance. He mixed covert sectarianism (an appeal to the Shiʾa Arabs who shared Iran's Shiʾa faith) with a more "universal" appeal to the downtrodden. Khomeini struck at a time of great confusion among his Arab rivals. Anwar el Sadat had for all practical purposes taken Egypt out of inter-Arab politics by 1978–79. An ambition now presented itself to Baghdad: It would fill the void left by Cairo. But Baghdad was a brittle city. Power and authority did not come naturally to it. An order of states that had been structured around Egyptian primacy would not take to the new claim. The Saudis disposed of considerable treasure, to be sure, but they had never put in a serious bid for dominion. They had only wanted to be spared the ambitions of their brethren. If anything the rise of Khomeini had made them more determined to seek ideological cover and to avoid ruinous ambitions.

The confusion of that large Arab world was put on display in the summer of 1982 when Israel swept into Lebanon. Labor Zionism, which had governed Israel since the birth of the state, had given way to a more militant strand: the Revisionist Zionism of the Likud Party led by Menachem Begin. A quintessential outsider to mainstream secular Zionism, Begin had ridden the frustrations of Israel's outsiders and its underclass and its religious right to power

11

in 1977. Five years later, Begin and his Defense Minister, General Ariel Sharon, were ready to reorder Lebanon's politics. The Palestinian turf in Lebanon had grown to a state within a state. From humble beginnings the Palestinians had carved up a political dominion, a substitute state. Whole regions in the country had slipped under their control. Begin was determined to put an end to the Palestinian sanctuary in that country, and to restore power to the country's Maronite community.

Israel's Lebanon War was launched against the background of Arab indifference and quiescence. Beirut had been a place of some consequence in the political geography of the modern Arab world. It was left to fend for itself. If Khomeini had been raging in the east saying that the Arabs were not pious enough or authentic enough, Israel's bid delivered a message with a different verdict: That large Arab world was not modern enough or accomplished enough in modern warfare. From the east a militant challenge of authenticity; from the west that perpetual challenge of modernity embodied in Israel and her military performance. The challenge of Israel was, of course, the challenge of an alien civilization; that of Khomeini was infinitely more problematic. The latter came from within. It was an audacious message that Khomeini bore the Arabs, a message that could not be written off because it was the message of a sectarian (a Shiʾa) and an Iranian. The full drama would have to play itself out.

Revolutionary messianism blowing from the holy city of Qom in Iran would call forth its nemesis: a chauvinistic Arab nationalism led by Saddam Hussein of Iraq. The Arab world (some of it) would draw back in horror from Saddam Hussein after his cruel conquest of Kuwait in the summer of 1990. But the Iraqi upstart had not emerged out of a void. He had emerged out of the political culture of populist Arab nationalism, out of its sins of omission and commission. He had been hailed and embraced when he did the work of containing the Iranian Revolution. The Baʾth party whose banner he carried had come to power in Iraq in 1968. The cruelty of his regime at home had been forgiven by the enthusiasts in Cairo and Beirut and Amman and in faraway North Africa. If the Kurds and the Shiʾa who constituted the overwhelming majority of the population of Iraq were sacrificed at the altar of the state, what of it? No alarm bells had gone off as the Iraqi upstart swaggered on his home turf and in the Arab councils of power. He was "the sword of the Arabs," it was said of him by his admirers. (He had plenty of them in Kuwait, it must be pointed out.) He had contained the threat from the east – Iran's threat. In time, he held out the promise that he would head west, toward the Mediterranean, to deal with Israel.

The dictator who rose in Baghdad annexed the dreams and resentments of the "Arab national movement." Large numbers of Arabs had insisted that their borders were contrived, that they were "lines in the sand" imposed by foreign powers. Homage had been paid in the Arab historical narrative to the great tale of German unification and to Otto von Bismarck, who had built with "blood and iron" a great power out of feuding principalities. The Iraqi leader who had warded off the Iranians would step forth to claim the mantle of an Arab Bismarck. The role with which the popular imagination had vested Gamal Abdul Nasser was now Saddam Hussein's. But Saddam waded beyond his depth when he overran Kuwait in the summer of 1990. Hitherto he had done well with small neighborhood quarrels. On the Saudi–Kuwaiti border Saddam threatened the American sphere of influence in Saudi Arabia. That distant power was not ready to divide the Arabian Peninsula and share it with the Iraqi claimant. Saddam's bid would be smashed with remarkable ease by an American-led military coalition. An air campaign of six weeks launched in January of 1991 broke the back of the Iraqi army. Then came a swift ground war which lasted one hundred hours.

Perhaps a hundred thousand Iraqi soldiers perished in that one-sided war, which recalled the uneven colonial campaigns of the nineteenth century. More to the point, the defeat of Iraq seemed like a replica of the Six Day War of 1967: The Egyptian rockets that did not fire, the air force that was shattered on the ground, the barefoot Egyptian soldiers lost in the Sinai desert, and above all the leader at the helm who had promised a bright new world acknowledging that his work had been for naught. A people who had lived through the trauma of defeat in the 1967 war should have been immune to another pied piper. But in a culture susceptible to legend and to the promise of a strongman there were takers for what Saddam Hussein had to peddle. A quarter-century after the terrible summer of 1967, the crowd wanted a Nasser with teeth; the Iraqi pretender had played the role. "It's a trick," said Mohammed Abu Isham, a farmer on the West Bank, of the total collapse of the Iraqi armed forces in February of 1991. "Saddam will never surrender." A legend now spread among Saddam Hussein's delirious supporters in Jordan and its Palestinian refugee camps that some 50,000 American soldiers were killed on the beaches of Kuwait and that the American leader, George Bush, had sued for peace. A wild claim spun by the imagination of a desperate crowd attributed a *hadith* (a saying, a tradition) to the Prophet Muhammad that the *Franj* (the Franks or Europeans) and the Egyptians assembled a vast force against a man named "Sadem," but their forces were scattered to the wind. Meanwhile, the road to Baghdad lay open before the American-led coalition. A quarter-century earlier, in that summer of 1967, the road to Cairo lay open before the Israelis as well. The bookends of a quarter-century: history repeats here, a cruel mixture of delusion and betrayed promises.

The Six Day War, the starting point of this inquiry, is not refought in this book. As the well-known chronology of the war has it, Nasser had mobilized his troops and moved them to Sinai on May 14 as a result of Soviet warnings about a pending Israeli attack on Syria. On May 18, his foreign minister asked the secretary general of the United Nations to withdraw the United Nations troops that had separated Egypt and Israel since the Suez Campaign of 1956. Then, choosing to push things further, Nasser closed the Gulf of Aqaba to Israeli shipping, thereby undoing the consequences of the 1956 defeat. Euphoria gripped the Arab world as the hero seemed to regain his touch.

By June 4, 1967, the hero-leader of Suez and pan-Arabism stood at the apex of a political career full of reversals and triumphs. His Ba'thist rivals in Syria, who had long taunted him about hiding from Israel behind UN troops, were now in his shadow; so were his reactionary enemies, the monarchs of Saudi Arabia and Jordan.

On June 9, the great charismatic figure acknowledged a defeat larger in scope, more dramatic in impact, than that of 1948. The

14

achievements of his reign stood in question and so did the logic
and symbols of an era of Arab political order could not go back to
business as usual. The territorial losses were too sweeping, too historically and strategically significant, the verdict of the defeat too
culturally troubling to resume the old game. Because political man
is by nature contemplative and probing, some sense had to be made
not only of what went wrong, but also of what lay ahead. Great
historic crises feed the normal desire to contemplate a nation's essence; they also open up unexpected horizons and opportunities.

Part 1 is an attempt to listen to the society's dialogue with itself,
to its anguished self-appraisal. With or without the Six Day War,
an audit of the post–World War II generation was overdue. That
generation, represented by the Nasserite Free Officers' regime in
Egypt and by the Ba'th Party/military officers' alliance in Syria,
had seized power in the aftermath of the Palestine war of 1948.
The case they had made against the ancien régime was the standard case made by broadly based middle-class nationalists against
older, more narrowly based political regimes: that they were em-
barrassingly weak and compromised, prone to collaboration, disconnected from aspiring social classes, and easily torn to shreds by
outsiders.

In rivalry and in alliance, Nasser and the Ba'th had dominated
the 1955–1967 period. This was the era of Suez, of the fight for
Algeria, of the collapse of the Iraqi Hashemite monarchy in 1958,
of the great crusade for nonalignment, and of the fight against the
West. In that battle the older, more feudal regimes were on the
defensive: The new ones had the capacity to mobilize; they could
promise socioeconomic justice, political participation, and the capacity to take on the outside world without defeat or collaboration. Like other such nationalists elsewhere, this generation's symbols had thrown young men and women into a whirlwind of
excitement and frenzy. They had stressed how radically different
they were from the old world; their experiments with state capitalism (packaged as socialism) had tinkered with the old economic
order and proclaimed the dawn of a new world. And of particular
relevance to the Arab world, this was the generation that was to
liberate Palestine and bring about pan-Arab unity. If the defeat
sustained in 1948 was due to treasonous monarchies, to feudal

orders that had kept men and women on the margins of history, the new men were bound to do better: They would create modern states and modern armies; they would somehow arrest political decline and stagnation.

Eventually, promises have to be redeemed and delivered: Sooner or later, the real limits of the experiments in Egypt and Syria would have had to be forced. What the 1967 defeat did was to force an audit during a moment of great stress and clarity. And what a spectacle it was! The normal capacity of political orders to deny and to evade, to conceal decline behind a facade of smug and hypocritical assertions that all is well, that the enemies are vanquished, that the order is sound – all those things that all political orders resort to – were denied to the heroes of yesterday. There on brutal display was the world they had wrought: They could not lie to the young and unsuspecting. In a hypermasculine political culture, a small state had displayed their historical inadequacy, had seized massive chunks of land, and had devastated the armies whose weapons and machismo had been displayed with great pride for the last decade or so. There was no place to hide; men had to contemplate where they had been and what it all amounted to. The debates and autopsy reproduced here were in many ways a unique intellectual episode in Arab thought: This had not been a society used to self-appraisal and self-criticism. Whether it was the banalities of the old custodians of tradition or the bravado of the post–World War II generation, political debate had been sterile, formalistic, and disconnected from social realities. In the harsh light of the military defeat, a younger generation came to ask tougher questions and to make greater demands upon political categories and discourse. This was a generation that was no longer sure of anything. The military defeat had rendered a harsh verdict on the world erected by the post–World War II nationalists. In the dialogue and appraisals presented here, we can observe some of the trends that were to crystallize in the decade that followed the 1967 defeat: disillusionment with pan-Arab doctrines on the part of critical populations in the Arab world – the Palestinians and, in their own way, the Egyptians; disillusionment with secularism and the turn toward Islamic fundamentalism; and, of course, disillusionment that gives up on politics and searches for personal escape and safety.

This, then, is the more "intellectual" side of the inquiry in Part 1 – an attempt to see how politically sensitive people depicted the Arab crisis, the questions they asked, the solutions they put forth. On the level of interstate politics, Part 1 deals with the political scramble that followed the 1967 defeat as the radical states (Egypt and Syria) ran for cover and sought an accommodation with the old Arab order (the oil states, Jordan) and as both sought to put down radicalism and unrest that came to rally behind the newly mobilized Palestinians. Here too can be found trends that were to become clearer with the passing of time: the deradicalization of the Egyptian state; the greater influence in inter-Arab politics of the conservative states; the fight between the dominant political order and younger, more disaffected elements; the attempt of the Arab states' system to climb out of that Arab–Israeli ditch that had partly been its own making.

Part 2 grapples with the wounds and choices of Egypt and Egyptians; it is also an attempt to see the Arab world in Egypt – hence the title "Egypt as state, as mirror." As stated there, Egypt is where Arab history comes into focus. The country epitomizes the possibilities and limits of Arab history. For the last two centuries, from Muhammad Ali to Anwar el-Sadat, Egyptians have been experimenting with statehood, with national manufacturing, with sorting out their ambiguous and difficult relationship to the West, with bourgeois ideas, with state capitalism (and its dismantlement), with large-scale wars (and their conclusion). If theirs had not been a particularly successful quest, it has been a historically gripping drama, complete with heroes, villains, tragedies, and, here and there, some solid achievements.

On Egypt's performance – sometimes a desperate trapeze act – other Arabs have been and remain fixated, applauding at times, full of derision at other times. Egypt gave the Arab world Abdul Nasser, its mass hero, during that exciting phase of populist nationalism, and it was Egypt that broke him in 1967. One side, one dimension of Egypt – its resourceful media, the security of its statehood, its stout lungs, its cultural preeminence – raised Nasser to great heights and gave the Arab world the hero it wanted and needed; then the other side – Egypt as a poor society, as a state with a weak army – brought him tumbling down. Egypt gave Nasserism to the Arab world, then treated other Arabs to a full-scale inquiry into it, a smashing of its symbols, under the label of de-Nasserization. If the first act was thrilling theater, the second left the spectators baffled: How did the worshipped hero of yesterday become the villain of today? The offer made by Qaddafi in 1980 to have Nasser's remains removed to Libya to build a shrine for the faithful in return for $500 million to be paid to Egypt is a judgment on Egypt and on Nasser as a memory and an idea. Nasser belonged to others – to non-Egyptian Arabs. And Egypt was not worthy of him. Besides, in a poor country all things are up for sale if only the price is right.

Egypt led the Arab wars with Israel and was then able and willing to say that the fight was mostly psychological anyway, that the solution that eluded everyone on the battlefields could be hammered out at peace summits.

Egypt led the revolt against the West in the 1950s – we can now begin to appreciate the impact of Suez and of Nasser's challenge to the West on the place of the Third World in today's international system – said no to foreign pacts, broke through military embargos and then succumbed to a puzzling dependency on America as the 1970s drew to a close. Was that a strictly Egyptian weakness, or was there something amiss in the Arab world that made it vulnerable to the ideas, to the wares, and to the approval of the West? Were the Arabs more vulnerable than China or India? Were they only an intermediate crossroads civilization, or did they have something uniquely theirs? Were their ideas authentically theirs, or were they, like the borrowed machines that litter their landscape, mere imports?

Egypt is both the Arab world's most accomplished state and one of its poorest – a tough combination, difficult on Egypt's pride and on those states in the Arab world that have to deal with Egypt. Egypt makes a fascinating study of the role of perceptions in politics as the world changes and power and wealth slip away to others but the memories of centrality and preeminence remain.

Finally, Egypt is a theater for an interesting dialectic between the solutions and world views of millennarians and fundamentalists on the one hand and those who want to find their way into the outside world on the other. In the Arab world's most bourgeois society there exists a nostalgia for purity that survives in every vanquished civilization that sees in the idea of return a solution for its ills.

To all these culturally and intellectually compelling justifications for focusing on Egypt may be added some practical motivations. Egypt is a highly articulate society: It thinks aloud; its intellectuals slug out the great issues of the time; its gifted novelists show us men and women trying to live in the midst of chaos, dealing as best they can with remote authority, with questions of war and peace, and, where they can occasionally afford it, with questions of individual and collective purpose. This is a society that not only tantalizes but also does something that those seeking to write and understand find irresistible: It takes the outsider in, it bares its soul and answers his questions. There is both a strictly Egyptian struggle that we try to understand here – for nations ultimately belong to themselves – and then a wider Arab drama focused on Egypt.

The main concern of Part 3 is the question of Islamic fundamentalism and return. Rather than the dark and archaic causes it is given by some interpreters, the phenomenon is rooted in two critical areas: first, in the relations between ruler and ruled. In the remarkable language of the Sudanese scholar Dunstan Wai, in the fight between those who have "fallen into things" and acquired "economic and political kingdoms," and those who have not.[11] The turning toward religious symbols is in very small measure explained by the doctrine itself, by Islam's classical teachings and its scripture; above all, it is rooted in the failure of secular elites, in the lack of alternative channels of expressing socioeconomic and political grievances.

The second principal explanation of Muslim fundamentalism has to do with the integration or malintegration of the Arab–Muslim order into the modern world system. Let me suggest the drift of my argument by citing two perspectives: The first, with which I am in disagreement, suggests a basic incompatibility between Islam and the Occident, a great binary division. In this view the revolt of Islam becomes a revolt against modernity that reflects the incapacity of Islam and Muslims to connect with others. This is the position, for example, of the great anthropologist Claude Lévi-Strauss: It is the view suggested in the aftermath of Iran's upheaval in a great deal of commentary. In Lévi-Strauss's words:

> The truth is that contact with non-Moslems distresses Moslems. Their provincial way of life survives, but under constant threat from other life-styles freer and more flexible than their own, and which may affect it through the mere fact of propinquity.

Again, deeply troubled by Islam, Lévi-Strauss goes on to say:

> This great religion is based not so much on revealed truth as on an inability to establish links with the outside world. In contrast to the universal kindliness of Buddhism, or the Christian desire for dialogue, Moslem intolerance takes on an unconscious form among those who are guilty of it; although they do not always seek to make others share their truth by brutal coercion, they are nevertheless (and this is more serious) incapable of tolerating the existence of others as others. The only means they have of protecting themselves against doubt and humiliation is the "negativization" of others, considered as witnesses to a different faith and a different way of life. Islamic fraternity is the opposite of an unadmitted rejection of infidels; it cannot acknowledge itself to be such a rejection, since this would be tantamount to recognizing that infidels existed in their own right.[12]

Less distinguished and more partisan minds than Lévi-Strauss have made and continue to make similar interpretations.

The second and more sophisticated position can be stated succinctly: Power engenders resistance. In this context, the power of the West, of an ascendent civilizational model, often forces others to look for means of resistance:

> Where there is power, there is resistance, and yet, or rather consequently, this resistance is never in a position of exteriority in relation to power. These points of resistance are present everywhere in the power network. Hence there is no single locus of great Refusal, no soul of revolt, source of all rebellions, or pure law of the revolutionary. Instead there is a plurality of resistances, each of them a special case: resistances that are possible, necessary, improbable: others that are spontaneous, savage, solitary, concerted, rampant, or violent; still others that are quick to compromise, interested, or sacrificial; by definition, they can only exist in the strategic field of power relations. But this does not mean that they are only a reac-

tion or rebound, forming with respect to the basic domination an underside that is in the end always passive, doomed to perpetual defeat. Resistances do not derive from a few heterogeneous principles; but neither are they a lure or a promise that is of necessity betrayed. They are the odd term in relations of power; they are inscribed in the latter as an irreducible opposite . . . Hence they too are distributed in irregular fashion: the points, knots, or focuses of resistance are spread over time and space at varying densities, at times mobilizing groups or individuals in a definitive way, inflaming certain points of the body, certain moments in life, certain types of behavior. Are there no great radical ruptures, massive binary divisions, then? Occasionally, yes. But more often one is dealing with mobile and transitory points of resistance, producing cleavages in a society that shift about, fracturing unities and effecting regroupings, furrowing across individuals themselves, cutting them up and remolding them, marking off irreducible regions in them, in their bodies and minds.[13]

This perspective helps capture the ambivalence of defeated civilizations: They enter the modern world, they fail, they retreat into their shells. But some things – preferences, languages learned, addictions to goods and ideas – remain with them. They play with traditions, improvise upon them as modes of resistance. Multiple identities have indeed been "furrowing across individuals" and whole societies in the Muslim world. Part of them, part of their loyalty, is fixated on a world that once was; part of them has been dragged into the outside world, leaving them ambivalent, confused – in the words of the Syrian writer Adonis [Ali Ahmad Said], "stalled between seasons." The attraction to lifestyles freer than their own draws people into the network of the world economy, into currents of world thought and culture. Then guilt asserts itself as they begin to think that the imports are not really theirs; or they experience a change of heart when their efforts to plug into the world fail, when their skills prove no match for the more polished skills of others. And it is this ambivalence, this anguish and hesitation, that is missing from much of what has lately been offered us by way of insight into the agony of the Muslim world. We have been paying attention to doctrine, to the display of militancy, and missing the hesitations and doubts of so many who continue to tell us, and above all, to tell themselves, that they wish to break with the codes of the modern world, to leave its techniques and possibilities behind. For the intense civilizational drama of the Muslim world, we have tended to substitute a smattering of easy stereotypes; to deal with it we have come up with fake geostrategic doctrines precisely at a time when so many states in the Muslim world stand indicted in the eyes of their own citizens.

Men and women have not been marching into the past because of the character of their civilization, because of the visceral passions and archaic sentiments that they have stubbornly held onto. It is in the push and pull of political life that political choices have to be situated. The detours that societies take are not to be explained by the driving habits of those in the vehicle, so to speak, but by the forks in the road they come to and by the dangers that a particular journey presents them with. That is why an interpretation of the *apparent* resurgence of Islam (my treatment in Part 3 will explain why I use the term "apparent") must make its way past the stereotypes of the millennarians in the Muslim world and then the stereotypes of those in the West ready with easy explanations that place fundamentalism on one side and rationality on the other.

As a social force, nostalgia exists in all societies. There is always a point at which societies feel that they are losing their hold on the world and begin to recall better times – times when the world was whole and reality made sense. This is true of the most sophisticated societies as it is of the most technologically backward. The past is always there as a reminder, as a weapon, as an invitation for a promising detour. As the British philosopher Michael Oakeshott so sensitively put it:

> The past in history varies with the present, is the present . . . There are not two worlds – the world of past happenings and the world of our present knowledge of those past events – there is only one world, and it is a world of present experience.[14]

Thus the interpretation of tradition and fundamentalism put forth in Part 3 of this inquiry is rooted in the present experience. It too (like the phenomenon it seeks to explain) backs into Islamic fundamentalism after an analysis of the other options resorted to in the last era – all the secular ones, the ones presented by the dominant political system, the ones presented by revolutionaries. But

22

it does so with skepticism as to how far the experiment can go, for there is, when all is said and done, a difference between apparent worlds and real ones, the worlds and systems created by nostalgia and the ones that exist.

Each political culture connects its political ideas with its practice in a unique way. Some deduce ideas from political practice; others come at the practice with ready-made conceptions and schemes and the ideas have a certain freedom from empirical realities. Some trust in the practicality of the political process – you try, and then you learn and emerge with lessons. Others begin with the scheme itself. These are ideal types and societies fall somewhere on a continuum.

The meeting ground, the relationship between thought and practice, is the thread running through this inquiry. The empirical cases, the political encounters and episodes discussed, are all approached with an eye as to that relationship and a concern that the mix between theory and practice in Arab political culture is susceptible to a recurring belief in grand schemes and ready-made doctrines. As Qaddafi once observed to a Western interviewer,

> In your gospels it's written: "In the beginning there was the word." The Green Book can destroy the world or save it. Carter can wage any war against us: to defend itself, the Third World needs my Green Book, my word. One word and the whole world could blow up. The value of things could change and their weight. And their volume. Everywhere and forever.[15]

Some of this is vintage Qaddafi style; some, however, is the long-standing dream that some doctrines, some words might do it all – exorcise weakness, make the world right again. This propensity was illuminated by Claude Lévi-Strauss in a discussion of the parallels between French and Islamic political thought:

> I am only too well aware of the reasons for the uneasiness I felt on coming into contact with Islam. I rediscovered in Islam the world I myself had come from: Islam is the West of the East. Or, to be more precise, I had to have experience of Islam in order to appreciate the danger which today threatens French thought. I cannot easily forgive Islam for showing me our own image, and for forcing me to realize to what extent France is beginning to resemble a Moslem

country. In Moslems and French people alike, I observe the same bookish attitude, the same Utopian spirit and the stubborn conviction that it is enough to solve problems on paper to be immediately rid of them. Behind the screen of a legal and formalist rationalism, we build similar pictures of the world and society in which all difficulties can be solved by a cunning application of logic, and we do not realize that the universe is no longer made up of the entities about which we are talking. Just as Islam has kept its gaze fixed on a society which was real seven centuries ago, and for the problems of which it then invented effective solutions, so we are incapable of thinking outside the framework of an epoch which came to an end a century and a half ago.[16]

Behind this "stubborn conviction" lies a desire to escape from politics, to trust it all to grand schemes – at times liberal schemes, for others, Marxist schemes, more recently, fundamentalist, restorationist schemes.

There is an apt parable by Kafka entitled "He": It shows "him" struggling with his past and future and waiting for an outcome:

He has two antagonists: The first pushes him from behind, from his origin. The second blocks his road ahead. He struggles with both. Actually the first supports him in his struggle with the second, for the first wants to push him forward; and in the same way the second supports him in his struggle with the first; for the second of course forces him back. But it is only theoretically so. For it is not only the two protagonists who are there, but he himself as well, and who really knows his intentions? However that may be, he has a dream that sometime in an unguarded moment – it would require, though, a night as dark as no night has ever been – he will spring out of the fighting line and be promoted, on account of his experience of such warfare, as judge over his struggling antagonists.[17]

But "he" of course cannot be a spectator to his own destiny, or a judge; "he" cannot step out of the fighting line. His choices and commitments do matter.

Neither large wealth nor displays of traditions will arrest the drift toward disorder in vast stretches of the Arab world. Wealth has only underlined a painful gap between what a society can buy and what it can be, between the vast means available to buy into things and the limited capacity to create a somewhat autonomous public project, a livable public order. Likewise the escape into tradition can only aggravate the crisis. The contrived past can become a narcotic. Then reality will intrude and shatter the illusion. Men cannot indefinitely live on frenzy or be kept in a trance.

Throughout that "springtime of nations," that *annus mirabilis* of 1989–1990, the Arab world seemed like a veritable backwater. The local satrapies of the Soviet Union (Syria and Iraq) seemed lost, really orphaned, after the collapse of their superpower patron. Creatures of the Cold War, the altered international order was bewildering to them. The "new thinking" of Mikhail Gorbachev seemed vaporous to them or worse – sheer abdication by a Great Power. Gorbachev had served early notice on the custodians of power in Syria and Iraq that a new world beckoned, that they better take to it. But these regimes would continue to hope against hope that the familiar world would assert itself, that the changes would blow over. These regimes could not reinvent themselves. At a time when despots were being sent packing in the most unlikely places (Chile, Argentina, Romania, Nicaragua) the Arab world's despots were still in the saddle. The Arab world snubbed the "new history." If anything, the despots in Baghdad and Damascus signaled their people that the great changes sweeping other lands would be kept at bay, that the despotic orders would remain unrepentant and unchanged.

It was not lost on the Arabs that they were being bypassed by this new resurgence of democratic politics. Of the full range of what happened during that *annus mirabilis*, it was the fall and murder of Nicolae Ceausescu in Romania that seemed to hold the attention of Arabs pondering their own condition. Romania mirrored the political order in the despotic states. Romania was in Europe, but not of it. Ceausescu was a familiar figure, and so was the large prison he had erected for his people. Ruler and ruled recognized their world in the cult of personality, the deadly *securitate*, the family and the retainers of the despot hoarding public goods and public treasure: These were things the Arabs of the "national security states" in Syria, Iraq, and Libya knew and lived with. A Syrian writer (an old Ba'thist for that matter) spelled out the clear moral of the tale of Nicolae Ceausescu: "The murder of this tyrant," he wrote, "was a vicarious way of killing other dictators who follow his method and live by his code."[18]

The states of the Arab world have driven ordinary men and women out of political life, devastated competing centers of power – the bazaar, the religious institutions, the guilds, and the labor unions. Thanks to the "command economy," the society was fully theirs. We have some revealing numbers about the dominance of the state in Arab realms when compared to other Third World countries of roughly similar levels of development. In 1985 government spending approximated 23 percent of GNP in middle-income countries, but it represented (for example) 33 percent in Yemen and Morocco, 40 percent in Tunisia, 48 percent in Egypt.[19] The ruler held the whip as in the past; he now commanded the national treasure as well. History here remains a chronicle of kings and would-be kings. A wild Islamic alternative survives on the fringe, principally among the young, to be sure. But its inspiration is the millennium, not democracy, its motivating forces are wrath and the search for purity. And at the end of the day, the very extremism of this fundamentalist current has tended to play into the hands of the rulers and to enable them to pose as the only dike against disorder.

Better sixty years of tyranny than one day of anarchy, goes an Islamic maxim, better the sultan you know than the one you don't. Thus it has been easy for the rulers. The self-confidence and the imagination societies need if they are to reinvent themselves are nowhere to be found in Arab political life. So there it is, the world of Araby, in close proximity to Europe, a veritable dumping ground for the high-tech weaponry and pop culture of the West, but a world stubbornly impermeable to any democratic stirrings.

During that "Arab Cold War" in the 1950s and 1960s, when an ideological struggle raged between the monarchies and the republics in the Arab world, the latter held out the promise of more open, more participatory politics. But now that struggle has been settled, and in an ironic sort of way. The officers and the soldiers who usurped power became kings in their own way. And the cruelty of their regimes – particularly in Syria and Iraq – made a compelling case for the old order of dynasties, for its manners and relatively benign rule. Say what you wish about the dynasties and the monarchies, this much should be granted them: Saudi Arabia, Jordan, the small principalities of the Gulf, all are held together by a social contract of sorts between the dynasties and the societies they rule. And Jordan aside, there is enough wealth in the other dynastic states to buy off the disgruntled and to strike a time-honored bargain between ruler and ruled: The ruler keeps the peace, the citizenry minds its own business.

The "national-security states" in Syria, Iraq and Libya rest on entirely different foundations: political terror, a primitive cult of personality and an unyielding notion of the state as a virtual possession of the man at the helm. After all the pamphlets and the ideological smoke screens, it came down to the rule of the soldier and the despot. Modernity only means that the ruler's weapons of destruction have become more deadly, his means of surveillance more refined. And the men in power play for keeps. There is no need for guesswork as to whether the armed forces of these regimes could be enlisted in large-scale carnage against dissidents and rebels at home. They have done it before. In early 1982, Hafez Asad's army went at the rebellious city of Hama with abandon. Thousands perished, and Hama became a metaphor for official terror. The regime's "Hama Rules" (the term was coined by the American reporter Thomas L. Friedman) were unusually stark and simple: It was "rule or die."[20] After Hama, nothing stirred in Syria. Cruelty of an even greater magnitude was unleashed by the army of Iraq in March of 1991, when the Shi'a in the south and the Kurds in the hill country of Kurdistan responded to the American call on the people of Iraq to "take matters into their hands" in the aftermath of the campaign against Iraq. No mercy was to be shown the rebels or the cities they hailed from. It was indiscriminate terror, made easier, no doubt, by the antagonism that separated a predominantly Sunni Arab political class from the two disaffected communities. Here, too, it was "rule or die," the state of one universe, the compact communities of another.

It has been hard for the Arabs to escape from a deep historical dilemma: prison or anarchy. Damascus and Baghdad tell the story of imprisonment. Beirut tells the other story. In between, in a place like Cairo, the hand of political power doesn't suffocate quite as much as it does in Baghdad and Damascus. But there, too, it is military autocracy with the army as the final arbiter. And everywhere in that large Arab world, the political discourse is a monologue. It conceals and smothers reality, runs away from it. It conjures up enemies at the gates. It celebrates the "children of the stones" on the West Bank and Gaza while the powers that be reduce their own citizens to frightened spectators behind the shutters.

Amin Maalouf, a Lebanese writer living in France, has recently published a remarkable novel, *Leo Africanus*, set in Granada and the Mediterranean world in the last years of the fifteenth century, before the end of Muslim rule in Al-Andalus, southern Spain. The novel is clearly and transparently allegorical. Granada is made to carry much of the contemporary Arab political reality. "This city," a character in the novel laments, "is protected by those who seek to despoil it, and governed by those who are its enemies. Soon we shall have to take refuge beyond the sea." Before the fall, there was great disorder in Granada. The sultan found a way out, or so he thought: war against the Castilians. And we know how that turned out. The Castilians won, and the people of Granada fled, taking the keys to their houses with them. Each of these exiles lived on the assurance that one day, thanks to Providence or some great savior, he would return and find his house again, "with the color of its stone, the smell of its garden, the water of its fountain, all intact, unaltered."[21]

1

One's World As It Really Is

❧❧❧❧❧❧❧❧❧❧❧❧❧❧❧❧❧❧❧❧❧❧❧❧❧❧❧❧❧❧❧❧❧❧❧

The flute and the lute
do not secure victory;
our pompous speechifying
has cost us 50,000 new tents.

Blame not circumstance, no,
blame not heaven if it forsakes you;
for God, who grants victory to whomsoever He wishes,
is no smith forging spears for you.
It pains me to hear the news in the morning,
to hear the dogs bark.
The Israelis conquer not our borders,
but thrive on our shortcomings.

Nizar Qabbani, *Comments on The Notebook of Defeat,*
in Leo Hamalian and John Yohannan, eds.,
New Writing from the Middle East
(New York, New American Library, 1978), p. 74.

How can a thought melt away before anything other than itself? Generally speaking, what does it mean, no longer being able to think a certain thought? Or to introduce a new thought?

Michel Foucault, *The Order of Things*
(New York: Vintage, 1970), p. 50.

PEOPLE read into the world what they are inclined to: There is in great events, defeats, and revolutions something for nearly everyone. No sooner had the Six Day War ended than a war of a different sort erupted in the Arab world: a conflict over the defeat. Who was responsible for it? What did the defeat say about the basis of Arab society, the quality of the Arab as an individual? How should the Arab world be organized to cope with the defeat and its consequences?

The traditional plea in such historical moments to keep the doubts and questions within reasonable limits was shunned. Some, as expected, made that plea, but an intense wave of self-criticism swept the Arab world, mocking the ways of an era, and beyond it, the burden of history; trying, as it were, to go to the roots of the defeat. And inevitably the search for answers ranged beyond the strictly political. We heard from some who wanted a total break with the past and from others who saw redemption in a tradition that had once supplied order and meaning.

The notion that societies in crisis have no choice but to leap forward is an arbitrary judgment. In our age this notion is fostered by the liberal imagery of stages of growth and evolution and the Marxist imagery of revolutionary transformations. But the temptation to retreat into one's own tradition in a moment of historical stress can be far more powerful than the tendency to leap into uncharted territory. There are many conceivable interpretations of a stressful condition. For a defeated society, the victorious enemy can be many things, its victory attributable to many factors. This is poignantly illustrated by one Arab intellectual's commentary on the June defeat:

> The Imam came forward repeating that we lost because we deviated from morality . . . The opposition leader insisted that we lost because the men in power monopolized total power . . . The engineer came forward asking for new machines and new factories . . . all found in the enemy what justified their argument. The theologian found justification in the theocratic orientation of our enemy; the politician in the fact that our enemy had a parliament; the engineer emphasized the abundance of the enemy's technical schools. Only few were able to observe that the religious faith of the enemy, his democracy, his technology, were all useful instruments but that the principal factor was the enemy's social organization, his sense of

30

individual freedom, his lack of subjugation, despite all appearances, to any form of finalism or absolutism.[1]

The enemy, then, was many things; victory entailed adopting the path that appealed to whoever was passing judgment: democracy, science, return to tradition, Marxist revolutionary transformation, or, of course, a slightly revised version of the pre-1967 status quo. An era in Arab politics had ended, and the struggle for the shape of the Arab order had begun. In the ideological war that erupted we heard the expected apologies of men who had blundered and were now looking for a way out and the recriminations of opportunists who said how much better they themselves would have done. But beyond all that lay a more profound and interesting set of developments: the honest soul-searching of intellectuals for the roots of the Arab ailment; the quest of a younger generation for a new political truth and for concrete solutions to harsh realities; changes in political and intellectual substance and styles; and the desperate attempt of the men in power to deal with altered realities.

Yesterday's radicals – the Ba'th Party and President Nasser – were the principal victims of the defeat: Whereas they once had stood for revolt against an older, more traditional, more compromised leadership, they themselves were now on trial. A younger generation was to see, in the full light of the defeat, the shortcomings of that brand of radical nationalism that had held sway from the early 1950s up to 1967. Some would naturally conclude that a deeper revolt than the one attempted by the Ba'th and Nasser was in order, that the massive dislocations of the June defeat presented an opportunity to effect a radical transformation of society, a break with the past, and the construction of a revolutionary social order of the kind that emerged in China, Cuba, or Vietnam. Short of that kind of conscious commitment to revolution, there was an inchoate groping for something new, a relentless attack on most facets of Arab life, a desire to go beyond Arab nationalism's rhetoric, to transcend the ideological and intellectual framework within which preceding generations had worked. It was suddenly easy to see – by those who were so inclined – that the men who had been yesterday's rebels had just not gone far enough.

31

THE RADICAL SENSIBILITY

For an articulate and sensitive segment of the intelligentsia and students, Nasser's explanation, given in his first statement on the defeat, that "the enemy we expected from the east and north came from the west"[2] and that the defeat was an error that could have been avoided, was not enough. In the eyes of a large number of radical activists, the defeat was an indictment of an entire way of life, proof not only that some deep realities had eluded yesterday's radicals but also that those radicals themselves were part of the problem. Thus, all facets of Arab life were subjected to a ruthless assault: Islam, the Arabic language, the capacity of the Arab as an individual, the record of the radical Arab states.

Among those who wanted to get to the deep structure behind the defeat there was a consensus that the heroes of yesterday had made too many compromises with the past, that they had given in to that frustrating, hopeless body of attitudes and habits, that immutable thing called tradition. Adonis, one of the most articulate spokesmen of the new radical sensibility, declared in the first editorial of the lively magazine, *Mawaqif,* that he and a group of radical intellectuals launched in 1968, that henceforth there would be nothing sacred and beyond discussion, and that – borrowing from Marx – it was no longer enough to interpret the world but to change it.[3] Over the next few years, the radical intelligentsia would leave very few stones unturned. They were convinced that the millennium was around the corner, that enough fire, skepticism, and clear theory would plunge the Arab world into genuinely revolutionary politics.

Nothing so clearly illustrates the commitment of the radicals to get to that deep structure behind the defeat as the radicals' attack on the Arabic language. The 1950s and 1960s had been immensely verbal times in Arab politics. The gripping language had been one of the principal weapons of the pan-Arabists in Cairo and Damascus: It intoxicated and created an impression of great power and accomplishment. The 1967 defeat created a backlash against the old style of expression and underscored the need for a more living, more honest language.

"Even the politicians' phraseology was borrowed largely from

32

the books they read; it was cluttered up with abstract words, gaudy flowers of speech, sonorous clichés and literary turns of phrase."[4] That was de Tocqueville's depiction of eighteenth-century France. But the crisis of "sonorous clichés" was far more acute in the Arab world than it was in the French context. Probably the case most comparable to that of the Arab world was China in the early years of the twentieth century, where the collapse of the Confucian order was followed immediately by an attack against the classical literary language. In both the Chinese case and the Arab case half a century later, style of expression became an issue between different generations; in both cases reformers attacked the classical style out of conviction that the dominant mode of political and cultural discourse enabled old interests to structure the political and cultural universe, to conceal decay, to flatter. It was an inevitable process: impatience with tradition and rejection of it leading to a rejection of the medium through which a political culture expressed and maintained itself.

The Chinese attempt at literary reform was launched in 1917 by the intellectual Hu Shi and a group of associates, who saw the dominant ways of Chinese literature and discourse as the root cause and expression of China's decline. Hu Shi dismissed most of China's written output as "dead stuff written in a dead language." A colleague of his linked political reform and the reform of the language by attacking the so-called forest, or esoteric literature: "These types of literature are both causes and effects of flattery, boasting, insincerity and flagrant disregard of truth and facts. Now that we want political reform we must regenerate the literature of those who are entrenched in political life."[5]

The connection between political reform and the reform of language was to become one of the prominent concerns of those who wanted to get to the roots of the Arab defeat. The Ba'thist Sami al-Jundi, whose experience and insights I shall closely examine, was to root the troubles of the Ba'th Party in the rhetoric and poetry of the party's founder, Michel Aflaq. To read Aflaq's main contribution to the post-1967 debate, a book entitled *Nuqtat al Bidaya* (The Starting Point), is to perceive fully the bankruptcy and incoherence of the politics of the Ba'th. Nearly three hundred pages of text yield no insight, on his part, into what went wrong and what needed to be done; there is only the visible infatuation with words and Aflaq's summons to the party to renounce power and go back to its "pure essence." Some men had "stolen" the party and its symbols from Aflaq, and the party's redemption lay in its regaining its soul.[6] Disaffected Nasserites were to see in the polemics of Mohamed Heikal, Nasser's spokesman, the predicament of Nasser's ambiguous experiment. The parallel Palestinian predicament would likewise be seen in the bombastic oratory of Ahmad al-Shuqairi, the head of the Palestine Liberation Organization, who made and unmade the world in a speech.

This language, observed one social analyst, had provided catharsis and relief and had enabled the Arabs to run away from their weakness: "Our wars have so far been verbal wars"; Arab society was basically an "expressive verbal society."[7] Another serious writer's inquiry into the renewal of Arab society took him straight to the Arabic language as the root cause and expression of Arab decline. Arabic, he observed, was not so much a means of expression but an end in itself: A great writer was not measured by the worth of what he said but by his mastery of the language. The language – its nuances, its rhythm – was an instrument of entertainment rather than a medium for transmitting thought and information. Unless liberated from the spell of the language, the Arab would remain a captive of a sterile system of thought.[8]

The classical language had been the pride of the Arabs. Like classical Chinese, it had become esoteric at a particular juncture of its history, when repression by the dominant orthodoxy forced thinkers to resort to dissimulation and concealment to escape persecution. In the tenth century, concealment became "a general pattern for all thinkers who did not conform to the narrow range approved by the official ulama scholars."[9] Much had changed since then, but the style had remained static.

Contemporary discourse suffered from the burden of the past – was stultified by the spirit of a Thousand and One Nights, according to several harsh critics – because the historical experiences that had transformed other languages had not taken place in the Arab world. Nationalism had, if anything, compounded the problem: Essentially romantic, it added to the pretensions and the delusions and hence to the escapism of the language. The defeats that nationalism came to suffer meant that analysis would have no hope and that expression would alternate between melancholy over setbacks and delusions of grandeur.

Bassam Tibbi, a Syrian scholar educated in Germany, took to task most of what had been disseminated in the Arab world: Written work, whether produced by university scholars or by ideologues, he found wanting in precision, depth, and quality. "Contemporary Arabic writing," he observed, "is speculative, non-revolutionary, non-scientific."[10] In his view, the men who had elaborated the political doctrines of Arab nationalism had inflicted on the Arab world superficial thought and endless slogans because they were second-rate thinkers mired in polemics and out of touch with the experiences that give political thought honesty and relevance. The pan-Arabist publicist Sati al-Husri, who had played an important part in the dissemination of pan-Arabist thinking in monarchical Iraq and then throughout the Arab League, had, according to Tibbi, offered only a hodgepodge of abstractions, an apology for nationalism rather than a serious inquiry into it. It was Tibbi's contention, moreover, that al-Husri's reliance on German sources was not really authentic: Al-Husri made things up and attributed them to Fichte and others to support his polemics on behalf of Arab nationalism. Michel Aflaq, of the Ba'th Party, offered only vague metaphysics. The most eminent theorist of a party that came to power in two countries never wrote a serious book. Tibbi said that Arab Marxists had fallen into the same trap: It was easy to tell from their writings that they had never understood Marx. Tibbi's scathing critique was both a plea for a "living language" that breaks with the past and an expression of what the younger generation thought of the men and the ideas of the preceding generation.[11]

Underlying the torrent of radicalist criticism in the post-1967 years was a simple message: We must confront our heritage, our tradition; we must slay the past if we want to liberate the present. An address by President Nasser at Cairo University in April, 1968, in which Nasser paid lip service to freedom of thought, gave Adonis an opportunity to comment on the responsibility of the intelligentsia and their relation to the dominant tradition: "We must realize that the societies that modernized did so only after they rebelled against their history, tradition, and values . . . We must ask our religious heritage what it can do for us in our present and future . . . If it cannot do much for us we must abandon it."[12]

According to Adonis, such a confrontation was inevitable, for God and religion permeated all aspects of social life: God was not solely a religious matter; the religious message was an "economic, sexual, and political problem in addition to being a spiritual supernatural problem." The supernatural ideas of "paradise, resurrection, hell and the angels" were not strictly religious; they had something to do with "the land, hunger, war." The attitudes and beliefs of popular culture had not radically changed; the "progressives" in power had not been willing or daring enough to challenge the tradition. "Our masses," Adonis lamented, "are not up to the level of the revolution. When the revolution surrenders to them it betrays itself, when it abandons them it dies."[13] He did not say which of the two fates the Arab revolution had met, but it would seem in keeping with the general thrust of his conviction and the conviction of his fellow radicals that the Arab revolution had committed both sins: It had surrendered to popular beliefs and reflected them; it had also abandoned the masses and failed to impart to them new beliefs and attitudes. The progressive Arab states had, as Adonis pointed out in a different essay, talked revolution but done very little about it: Half a century after talking about the revolution and years after the establishment of regimes that described themselves as revolutionary, Arab society was still the same; people did not think for themselves but still succumbed to supernatural thoughts; they were not free agents but followers. True revolution, Adonis wrote, would make human beings the center of the universe; they must above all be free before they can believe in "homeland," "nationalism," "socialism" or "humanity."[14]

In the view of the new radicals, whether or not the Arab revolution had taken place was now beside the point. For some the revolution had aborted; for others it was betrayed. In Adonis's words, the revolution turned out to be "a means to a different kind of end": The end was political power and control, authority, *sulta*. Adonis of course assumed that real revolutions aim at a different kind of end. In so thinking, he was hardly alone. The fear that revolutions will end in betrayal or, short of that, in routine, that yesterday's energy and idealism will end either in terror and oppression or in bureaucracy and routine, has haunted and worried others committed to revolutionary politics. Because the danger of betrayal or routine is ever present, the critical difference presumably lies in whether the revolution, before it settles down, manages to do some radically new things to people's thoughts and habits, to the economic system, and to the distribution of power. The tragedy of the Arab revolution was that it had done none of those things.

Frustrated with the failure of the men in power, Adonis called for a separation between the regimes and the revolution. The revolution, he said, would have to dissociate itself from radical-sounding regimes if it were to succeed. The regimes had robbed their people of initiative and spirit and so overwhelmed them with authority that submission and obedience had become second nature. There was no living, dynamic relation between the citizen and the state, between the individual and society. The most that individuals could hope to do in a culture of that kind was simply to look after their own safety.

The concerns of the new radicals were best expressed in a book by Sadeq al-Azm entitled *Al Naqd al Dhati Ba'd al Hazima* (Self-Criticism after the Defeat).[15] Written in 1968, this book must surely go down as one of the most impressive and controversial pieces of Arabic political writing in recent times. Malcolm Kerr rightly describes it as "the most scathing of all indictments of Arab society and culture."[16] Azm, an American-educated Syrian intellectual then teaching at the American University of Beirut, captured and expressed the new radicalism and dissatisfaction hovering in the air. His courage in confronting such sacred facets of Arab life as Islam and his manner of presentation – direct and to the point – attest to the radicals' commitment to a sharp break with the past and to their determination to succeed where their predecessors had failed. On the level of ideas, they were rebelling against the dissimulation and polemics that had afflicted so much of Arab political writing. On the level of practice, they were outflanking Nasser and Nasserism from the left.

Azm's *Self-Criticism after the Defeat* belongs to a species of political analysis that major military defeats or great upheavals occasion in a society. Azm's point of departure is military defeat and material weakness: A society fails to stand up to its enemies, to catch up with others. But the "crisis of power and energy" soon takes on another dimension, as a critical segment of that society comes to question the worth of the social order, its capacity for order and justice, its right to survive. The book's initial complaint is that the Arabs failed to win the war, but its central concern is with the inadequacy of the Arab social and moral order. Azm begins by examining the weakness of the Arab as a soldier, but he ends up by evaluating the Arab as an individual – his quality of thought, his capacity to make decisions and to shape a viable social order.

Azm's analysis of the June defeat begins with a telling historical analogue: the defeat of tsarist Russia by Japan in 1904. In the victory of the numerically smaller Japan and Israel over the massive but lethargic Russia and the Arab world, Azm sees the triumph of energy over mass, of dedication and work over pomp and ceremony and the rituals of power. The devastating defeat of the Russian navy is an analogue for the destruction of the Egyptian air force.

Tsarist Russia and the Arab world were both essentially backward but smug societies, sure of victory, contemptuous of their respective enemies. The officialdom of both tsarist Russia and the Arab regimes insisted up to the last moment that they could overwhelm their enemies. Their defeat served a harsh judgment on them: They had failed to modernize and to reform; they had fallen behind, could no longer generate power, and were unable to secure the loyalty of the populace. Azm considers that Russia made the best of her defeat: Defeat triggered the revolutionary events of 1905, fostered radical politics, and set the stage for the Bolshevik revolution.

Ideally, the 1967 defeat should have led to a similar process in the Arab world. But Azm, writing one year after the defeat, saw little reason for hope. He noted the tendency among Arab officials, spokesmen, and even some critics to lay the blame for defeat elsewhere instead of accepting responsibility. Some were quick to explain away the defeat by pointing to American and British participation in the war. Others went further and accused the USSR of plotting the Arab defeat. Finally, there were those who declared it was Allah's will.

Azm finds an extreme illustration of Arab fatalism and of the wish to escape individual responsibility in the statement of the mufti of the Jordanian kingdom: The Arab defeat was divine will, a punishment inflicted by Allah "as a result of our abandoning our religion." The notion of people as actors, as masters of their own destinies, is, as Azm and his fellow radicals argue, still alien to the Arab world. Arabs remain the objects of history. Their supernatural explanations of social phenomena betray their passivity. They are more spectators than actors. The very term used by the Arabs to describe their defeat in Palestine — *nakba* (disaster) — connotes the absence of human will and responsibility. Azm is convinced that the choice of terminology was not an accident: It reflected the weakness of Arab society, its desire not to face up to its backwardness.

Azm carefully shows how the dominant Arab conceptions of politics and war were at odds with contemporary thinking and practice. First the Arab states pushed things to the brink, then they expected an easy way out. When war came, they complained of Israel's aggression, of the ruthlessness of its military assault — as though war was supposed not to be grim. In their conduct of the war and their justification of the defeat, the Arabs seemed saddled with ancient codes of chivalry, with nearly tribal ways of warfare. Azm singles out two statements, by President Nasser and the Jordanian prime minister, respectively, that exonerated the Arab armies. Nasser's statement was that Arab soldiers fight bravely and well in face-to-face combat with the enemy and that defeat was attributable to the fact that they did not have a chance to encounter the enemy. The Jordanian prime minister said that the Israelis know the bravery of the Jordanian soldier when the battle pits soldiers against one another, but that, in this instance, the confrontation was between soldiers and fire that "descends upon them from the skies." Is it possible, asks Azm, for a people to wage war with such obsolete notions? Is it possible to enter a modern war that requires movement and initiative when the society is permeated by passivity and reluctance to initiate decisions?

The intimate connection between war and citizenship lies at the heart of the modern state. The 1967 defeat revealed the failure of the Arab states to train and create modern citizens, to inculcate men with the will to fight and die for the state. Remote and hostile, the Arab state is disconnected from its citizenry. The latter wish only to be left alone, and they shelter themselves from the capricious will of the state. The state – as in the case in oriental despotism – reigns but does not rule. When push comes to shove, that state falters, because it lacks the support of its populace. It is not to the state that Arabs owe loyalty, but to their families and clans. And if there is an indisputable verdict rendered by the history of the last two centuries, it is the incapacity of tribal orders to stand up to modern states.

The failure of public politics was demonstrated by the hoarding of goods on the eve of the war, the panic and flight before the Israeli army. Privatized, loyal only to their families, careful to protect the honor of their women, the Arabs were all too willing to flee. For Azm, such behavior does not indict the individual citizen but the Arab state system as a whole. The absence of modern institutions and meaningful bonds of solidarity left individuals at the mercy of their fears. Demoralized, disconnected from others, they took the understandable option of escape, of saving their own skins and the lives of those who form their primary social unit.

Having entered and lost the war, the Arabs conducted postwar diplomacy in the same spirit: They now wished to shame Israel before the court of world opinion; it was believed that their case should move the conscience of humanity and force Israel back to its prewar boundaries. World opinion, wrote Azm, is a factor of some importance; however, there is natural sympathy for Israel in both the capitalist and the socialist worlds – both see Israel as an extension of the Occident, as an embodiment of what human energy and will can accomplish.

No amount of crude propaganda will substitute for the more difficult path of entering the modern world, of making a contribution to the scientific and literary output of mankind. Azm's admiration for energy is readily apparent; it is the Faustian aspect of Western civilization, its capacity to move people and matter, that appeals to him. And precisely because the West is built on energy, Azm finds limited utility in the Arab appeals to Western opinion.

40

The view that the West is deceived and that if it were only to understand the Arab case it would see where justice lies and would change its ways is an extension of a simplistic view of politics into the world of international politics. Azm cites the work of Kamal Yusif al-Hajj, a Lebanese professor of philosophy, as an example of this kind of thinking. Hajj had written that the Arab people were mistaken in blaming the West, because the West was merely deceived by Zionism. He argued that it was up to the Arabs to save the West from the hold of the Zionists. Once that was done, "the formidable powers of the West would then be under our influence instead of the influence of the Zionists."[17] Here, in a nutshell, is the great illusion: The innocent West would be liberated from the hold of the Zionists; the Arabs would then become its manipulators. Demonic powers are at work; one spell is broken and another one takes hold. This explains why the Protocols of the Elders of Zion were taken seriously by some Arab writers. In the Protocols, too, the world is a dark conspiracy; diabolical schemes for control and myths are seen to move the world. If the Protocols are believed, then the Arab defeat would make sense: The Arabs would simply be another deceived, dominated people, and what overwhelmed them would be not a small state but a vast conspiracy.

The brunt of Azm's criticism is focused upon the so-called progressive Arab regimes rather than on the reactionary ones. Not much could be expected from the latter. It is the failure of the former that highlights the backwardness of Arab society, its stubborn resistance to change, and the weakness of the human element that guides it. The progressive regimes had produced a barrage of noise; they had openly declared their allegiance to the strictures of revolution and socialism. What the defeat did was to show that the Arab revolution was neither socialist nor revolutionary: The Arab world had merely mimicked the noise of revolutionary change and adopted the outside trappings of socialism; deep down, under the skin, it had not changed.

Like radical intellectuals elsewhere, Azm is frustrated with the persistence of tradition, with the fact that the past simply refused to go away. It is when he compares the Arab revolutions to the socialist revolutions he admires that the Arab experiment seems particularly defective and flawed. Unlike the great experiments that

41

worked – China, Vietnam – the attempts of Egypt and Syria were half-hearted and ambiguous. The Arab attempts were afflicted with a middle-of-the-road orientation: They never decided what they wanted – socialism or state capitalism, limited land reform or an agricultural revolution. Did the Arab revolution want to keep the life of the Arab individual under laws codified fourteen centuries ago and to stress values derived from the past, or did it want "a new legislative order derived from scientific, socialist thought"?[18] Did it want a new educational system to replace the inadequate hodgepodge of antiquated programs and stale imports from the days of the Third Republic?

Clarity and commitment are the hallmarks of revolutionary experiments. The absence of those ingredients damned the Arab experiment. Stripped of their mystifications, their noise aside, the Arab socialist states turned out to be traditional orders. This explains the energy these regimes devoted to sheer sophistry, to hair-splitting arguments about the compatibility of their version of socialism with Islam and about their indigenous, authentic form of socialism that dispenses with class struggle in favor of a cooperative path to socialism. Phrases like "Arab application of socialism," constantly repeated in Cairo and Damascus, were a travesty of the notions of socialism. Lacking the will and the determination to wage socialist politics, the Arab states made socialist noises while the bases of their societies remained largely traditional.

There comes a time in the life of societies when they must choose among rival social systems. Penetrated, cross-pressured, and timid, the Arab states were simply unable to choose. They prided themselves on their capacity to integrate different world views. But, as Azm argues, no society, however proud of its capacity to synthesize, can escape difficult choices, all of them having different costs. The Arabs cannot pose as brokers among rival systems; sooner or later they must make real choices. Some choices are irreconcilable. The Egyptian claim of having achieved a so-called Arab–Islamic–Scientific form of socialism demonstrates the depletion of a culture. If all things go together, what then distinguishes one social order from another? The Egyptian slogan, "We must not sacrifice this generation for future generations," served to keep intact the privileges of old vested interests: Inequalities remained, and the whole thing boiled down to putting old wine in new bottles.

Influenced no doubt by Marxist analysis, Azm believes that a strictly political revolution is impossible, that meaningful political change rests upon moral and cultural transformations. This is a crucial issue on which Arab revolutionaries seem to have faltered. There is considerable consensus among young intellectuals of Azm's persuasion that Arab revolutionaries — when they really existed — confined their revolution to the strictly political domain. Young Arabs may rebel politically, but their social relations, family ties, judgment on public and private matters, and attitude toward work all derive from traditional sources.

Because the rebels are unable and unwilling to tackle the cultural and psychological obstacles that impede revolutionary politics, the strictly political rebellion ends either in failure or in state oppression. The state may manage to survive with the help of the whip, but that is a far cry from the revolutionary goals of bringing about a new order and creating the new Arab.

If revolution and socialism became disembodied forms or were disfigured when in Arab hands, it is Azm's judgment that science encountered and is bound to encounter the same fate. In the period immediately following the Six Day War, Nasser and his spokesman Mohamed Heikal seized on the theme of science and modernity and made it their new cause. Azm said that the cause was bound to fail, due to the peculiar view of science held by the men in power: For them science was a veneer, a wrapping around an essentially unscientific culture. It is not enough to stockpile weaponry and modern machines; to be scientific requires a particular frame of mind. Here again it is the human element that decides. The Arabs, says Azm, have been importing the products of science, but this falls short of the dynamic relationship between human beings and matter that a scientific orientation requires. "We have made room in our lives for the refrigerator, the television set, oil wells, MIG airplanes, the radar . . . etc., but the mentality that uses these imported products remains the same traditional mentality that belongs to bedouin, agrarian supernatural stages that preceded the industrial revolution."[19]

The rhythm of Arab life has yet to accommodate itself to the scientific age. Arabs import the fruits of science to increase their power, but the same machines increase their alienation. Others produce and they merely consume. They come in contact with the secondary products of science, but they are far removed from the social process that made scientific breakthroughs possible. How else, asks Azm, can we explain the statement made by one religious thinker in Lebanon that the Arabs were destined to prevail over Israel because the angels that came to the help of the Prophet in one of his battles will descend "to help us today and to secure our victory in our battle with the enemy"? Such a statement may be dismissed by the sophisticated reader, but, contends Azm, it closely reflected the prevailing mentality. It was not merely popular culture that stood between the Arabs and science, but also the nature and orientation of the regimes in power, which had lagged behind the times and were still unmoved by "reform and change." Nor did universities measure up to the task: "For all of us know that our national universities are in reality institutions for administering final examinations at the end of the academic year rather than institutions for preserving, renewing, and transforming human knowledge and putting it at the service of the nation and the people."[20]

Azm's critique expresses the standard radical contempt for tradition: Tradition must be overthrown if people are to overcome their anxieties and inadequacies. Audacity, will, and dedication will liberate people from their chains. Like alienated intelligentsia in other backward societies, Azm embraces the radical notion that the destruction of tradition and the creation of the future are inseparable: Unless the first is accomplished, all ends in futility. So much, Azm concludes, was proven by the record of the regime that had tried more than any other regime in the Arab world to bring about a new political order. The Nasser regime was far too circumspect in its approach to tradition: It made too many compromises, it viewed too many things – religion, popular attitudes – as outside the domain of revolutionary politics; it left largely unchanged the deference of the lower orders to the upper ones. In short, it left standing all the main pillars of a traditional order, and thus in defeat was forced to capitulate to the will of the conservative states and to that stratum of Egyptian society that never accepted the radicalization of politics.

With the post-1967 détente between the progressive and conservative Arab regimes more or less a fact of life, it was clear to Azm, Adonis, and their fellow radicals that the revolutionary claims of the progressive states were a thing of the past. So clear, indeed, that some would go so far as to deny a distinction between the two types of regime. The issue, said Adonis, was no longer the kind of regime that the Arab lived under but the rebellion against one's conditions and weakness. In the conservative as in the radical states, people were disenfranchised and history was made from above. If Arabs continued to submit to their lot, there could be no hope that they could engage in the decisive battle, because submission breeds fear and cowardice. Writing in 1969, Adonis expressed his growing disenchantment with the Nasser regime and his doubts as to the existence of Arab will and power to undertake a serious military effort against Israel.[21]

After 1967, there was a widespread sentiment that unity was no longer the issue. It was not a frontal attack against pan-Arabism, but a deeper agnosticism that saw no utility in banding together so long as the fundamental issues of Arab society were unresolved.

An older Saudi writer, Abdullah Qusaymi, who had long been settled in Beirut, commented bitterly that the single large state that the pan-Arabists wanted would only be a vehicle for bringing to power a new version of the Abbasid Caliph Harun al-Rashid.[22] Instead of wasting the people's bread and money on "maidens, singers and poets," as the old caliph had done, the new sultan would waste people's dreams and lives on "adventures, conspiracies, and armies which would not engage the enemy and if it did would not win." The pan-Arabist dream was a search by proxy for a new tsar: The large unitary state exists only to produce the tsar whose authority derives from the authority of Allah and the Prophet. The new tsar would have all the inclinations of the old ones – "Bedouin habits and values" – with all the trappings, inducements, and instruments of modernity. Why then bother with the large unitary state? It is a frightening possibility rather than a source of hope. The state would enslave without generating power; it would aggrandize the power of one leader at the expense of mass suffering. "The story of the big state and the big empire has never been the story or idea or hope of the masses. It has always been the story of men who wanted to be great men or tyrants by diminishing others." Furthermore, why worry about progressive and reactionary states and indulge in make-believe distinctions? Like Adonis, Qusaymi is obsessed with that immutable core. The Arab remains the same regardless of the differences in regimes; his "vision of himself, of his enemy, of the world, of things around him" has not changed. So much had amounted to so little.

This agnosticism, which we shall fully encounter in the memoirs of Sami al-Jundi of the Ba'th party, was to deliver to pan-Arabism as serious a blow as the frontal attack of separatists. Under otherwise normal conditions, the radicals – by age, sensibility, and education – would have provided pan-Arabism with its faithful crop of believers. They would have gone on to spread the word on behalf of pan-Arabism against Islamic fundamentalists, communists, Marxists, or believers in separate Egyptian or Lebanese or Syrian destinies. The weakness of pan-Arabism, which was to become more obvious a decade later, could already – more so with the brilliance that hindsight always endows – be seen in the attitudes of post-1967 radicalism. At the time, however, the myth of pan-Arabism was still strong enough for the break with pan-Arabism to be made in a conscious and forthright manner.

Two other reasons precluded a frontal attack against pan-Arabism at the time. First, the radical intellectuals themselves had a wide elite audience dispersed throughout the Arab world; they spoke of issues that transcended the boundaries of individual countries. Second, the Palestinian question that was to emerge after 1967 provided another barrier against localism. Where the intelligentsia and activists happened to be Palestinian, they gave themselves a leading role and special responsibility, but they still wanted to engage the energies of other Arabs lest their quest seem too isolated. Where those concerned with the Palestinian question happened to be non-Palestinians, they wanted to rein in extreme Palestinian nationalism – not only to give themselves a role (and that motive was, understandably, present), but also to make sure that different Arab states did not go their separate ways, accept a peaceful settlement with Israel, and solidify their positions (military regimes in

Egypt, Syria, and Iraq; traditional monarchy in Saudi Arabia; a peculiar blend of pluralist and feudal politics in Lebanon at home). The new radicals had sufficient contempt for nearly all Arab states that they did not want to see these states try to retreat within their own boundaries to tend to their own problems. The Palestinian question was seen as a catalyst for radical politics, an antidote to the defeatism and conservatism that the radicals believed was all around them.

But the sentiment behind the Palestinian quest, while transcending localized and parochial concerns, would nonetheless differ from the pan-Arabist assumptions of the preceding era. For some new radicals, the Palestinian question was a vehicle for bringing about social and political change; for others it was a confrontation between the larger forces of imperialism and antiimperialism, between an insurgent Third World guerrilla movement and an established state sustained by the West. From the intersection of the Palestinian movement and the new radicalism emerged two currents: One was for Palestinian nationalism that rejected wider Arab trusteeship over the Palestinians; the other was for a broad revolutionary movement of the kind popular in the mid and late 1960s, comprising guerrilla warfare, Third-Worldism, antiimperialism, and commitment to socialist change. In other words, one was narrower, the other more encompassing, than pan-Arabism. Whereas the former dismissed the right of established Arab states to make decisions for the Palestinians, the latter dismissed pan-Arabism as an empty shell – too narrow, too chauvinistic, devoid of socioeconomic content; captured, as the radicals were to state repeatedly, by a petty bourgeois element incapable of bringing about social change at home and of understanding the nature of the international system. If one group was saying, "We are Palestinians first and foremost," the other was saying that the "We-are-all-Arabs" slogan of pan-Arabism was a holdover from the past, that it had done nothing to rid the Arab world of the burden of tradition, to bring about social change, to generate power vis-à-vis other states, to build a viable order at home.

If pan-Arabism had failed, and if the prior attempt to incorporate the Arab world into the liberal order of the West had come to naught, then why not turn to the methods that worked elsewhere

– in Cuba, Algeria, Vietnam, China? The radicals would now seek in the translated writings of Guevara, Debray, Marx, Lenin, and Giap what the liberals had sought earlier in the nationalism, the legality, and secular politics of the West. The sentiment was the same as was the frustration and impatience that gave rise to it. What differed were the books that people read and the models they admired.

Thirty years earlier, the distinguished Egyptian writer Taha Husayn had expressed the consensus and the yearning of a generation of liberals when he called upon Egypt not only to partake of Western civilization, but to become European.[23] Now a younger generation – for whom liberalism had become anathema, another word for Western colonialism – would seek a different inspiration. The politics that struck at the base of old social orders and constructed new ones was clearly more appealing than yesterday's liberalism. Here and there some liberal voices were heard after 1967, but this was not to be a liberal era. Long before 1967, the liberals had lost power and self-confidence. None of what happened after 1967 improved the prospects for liberal politics. Indeed, the political milieu was to become less hospitable to liberal politics and ideas. If people looked outside the Arab–Islamic tradition for models, it was to the radical examples of revolutionary change.

THE BA'TH PARTY: A RETROSPECT

People do not always rebel or follow new orthodoxies after old ones play themselves out. Some get discouraged and give up. Having tried one thing and dedicated their lives to it, they become disillusioned, turn inward to contemplate their own experiences, try to put together shattered lives and careers. For them the positive choices made by others are premature, not appealing enough, or too optimistic. Some experiences are searing enough that they leave in their wake nothing but bitterness and disillusionment. When these experiences are deeply felt and fully lived and those who live through them are sufficiently honest and articulate, the revelations can become unique human and political documents, a way of seeing history through the eyes of sensitive participants who felt the ela-

tion of momentary success and then witnessed the betrayal of once-
bright ideals, the incompetence or the greed that distort or undo
political quests.

The writings of Sami al-Jundi capture the experience and tragedy of Ba'th rule in Syria. The four books he published after 1967
tell his personal story, and, perhaps more important, the story of
his generation of Syrian pan-Arabists.[24] Jundi grew up in the interwar period and was one of the earliest members of the Ba'th –
the party that came to think of itself as the vanguard of the national movement and in whose name the military was to rule in
both Syria and Iraq. He rose to prominence in Ba'thist politics in
the early 1960s, becoming Syria's ambassador to France and serving as a minister in several Syrian cabinets. He also experienced
the capricious side of national politics: the cruelty of the torturer,
the loneliness of the prison cell, the evanescence of so much that
his generation had believed in and done.

The troubles and irresponsibility of the Ba'th had played no mean
part in the malady of the pre-1967 years. The Ba'thists had urged
unity but had conspired against it after it materialized. Their stout
lungs and rhetoric had helped push Nasser into a corner and pre-
cipitate the Six Day War. While in power in Syria and Iraq, they
had plotted, conspired, murdered, and made a mess of things. (The
antics of the Ba'th have been denounced in a book by a former
secretary-general of the party, Munif al-Razzaz. He had been imported from Jordan to Damascus presumably to head the party,
but soon discovered that he was a mere puppet of the military,
who brought him to Syria because they opposed the party's principal ideologue, Michel Aflaq.) In November, 1967, the co-founder
of the Ba'th, Salah al Din al Bitar, resigned from the party, declaring that a "counter-party" had been established within the Ba'th,
and that from 1963 onward he had been living in a state of "internal exile," alienated from the workings of the party and the military men who came to dominate it. The party, he said, had come
to suffer from "anemia and the hardening of its arteries"; it was a
"backward" party that had become "captive of a demagogic mentality and bureaucratic authoritarianism."[25] But Bitar's statement
was too brief and uninformative. It remained for Jundi to write

the obituary of the Baʾth and to express the disillusionment with politics and nationalism felt by those who, in the aftermath of 1967, saw no hope for the future and no way out.

Jundi's account has the power of a genre of African fiction produced by writers such as Chinua Achebe, Ngugi Wa Thiongʾo, and Peter Abrahams. The theme is the bright nationalist vision ending in betrayal. The main characters begin as aspiring young men full of promise; they turn into tormentors and murderers who end up being tormented and murdered by others. Along the way, they act incoherently, become corrupt and violent; one compromise leads to another; they betray their fellows and are in turn betrayed. The outcome is all the more tragic when juxtaposed with the "beautiful beginning" – the moment of nationalist innocence, the fervor of youth.

The young men who came together in 1940 to form the Baʾth were rebels with a compelling vision. They believed they were the dawn of a new age – "We were strangers from our society, rebels against all the old values." All the leaders of the time were condemned by the new idealists, dismissed as expressions of tribalism that must be destroyed to make way for the future Arab state. The young men saw themselves as "idealists who based social relations on love." They found in European doctrines – mostly German – of nationalism the answer to the decadence of the Arab world. No one who lived through those beginning years would have believed that the Baʾth party would end up as a group of "informers, torturers, murderers." The founders of the party did not believe that they would actually achieve political power. Circumstances enabled them to get there. And once in power, they turned out to be "strangers with new mentality and old methods, with neither experience nor ideology. We believed that the centuries of decline ended with our predecessors, the politicians, and that we were the great beginning of a new culture. But we were the latest version of backwardness, a tragic expression of it. We wanted to be a resurrection of honor and heroism but nothing was resurrected with us – in power – but the age of the Mamluks."[26] While others of their generation tended to personal matters, the young men of the Baʾth lived like true believers. They wasted their youth, as Jundi bitterly remembers, on political work: "A lesson that we would recite to young students, a new member for the party, a talk in a distant village with the peasants, and how generous and attentive they were and how pure was their friendship." The experience of the Ba'th turned out to be "rich and tragic": It yearned for a new world but it was seized by the lure of power.

Jundi's work is an honest and sad portrayal of what has befallen many national anticolonial movements in the Third World. From a distance, nationalism was all glitter and promise. The age of colonialism was destined to exaggerate what people thought they would do when they took matters into their hands. As Clifford Geertz notes in a commentary on nationalist revolutions in the non-West, independence was to show that it was different to live in a nationalist world than to imagine it.[27]

A whole literature of disappointment has been coming out of the Third World; cumulatively it tells what has become of yesterday's nationalist dreams. The ruled now share the pigmentation of their rulers, speak the same language, pray to the same deity, but the new rulers crack the whip with unprecedented zeal, and the ruled have come to wonder what has become of the nationalist promise. This is not to say that they yearn for the days of colonialism – a curious argument often implied and sometimes openly stated by apologists for the colonial order and some critics of Third World politics – but only to note the discrepancy between what the anticolonial struggle visualized and the state of many Third World polities today.

Disappointment with what political power had wrought, imprisonment, torture, and then exile from Syria give Jundi's memoirs a fatalistic tone: Not much can be done to spare societies the agonies of change; no ideology will make the Alawites and Sunnis of Syria forget their primary loyalties. There is a sense of bewilderment and frustration with an inner core that defeats or disfigures ideologies. In one passage, Jundi writes of the "tribes" or the "clans" of the Ba'th. The press may have given the more modern name of "factions" to the groups that battled for power in Syria, but they were simply "primitive tribes."[28] The Ba'th began with youthful idealism, then surrendered to the intrigues and brutality of the military. It wanted a shortcut to political power, and the military gave it the chance to wield political power, but the bargain demolished the party; the men in uniform used the slogans of the Ba'th and gave some prominent positions to its ideologues, but it was the military men who ruled and eventually pushed the civilians aside.

The civilian ideologues had words and pamphlets and could endow a ruling regime with revolutionary legitimacy. But power rested with the military, which grew increasingly weary with what Jundi calls the "poetry" of the Ba'th and struck out on its own. The military men themselves caught the Ba'thist infatuation with ideology and verbiage; they too were to repeat the term "revolution" until it lost all meaning. In the turbulent 1960s, people got used to the movement of tanks from barracks to government buildings whenever the military announced the rise of a new order and the end of a decadent one. First the people would rejoice, then all hope would vanish and the tanks would reembark on the same journey to take over the same places and repeat the same words. These are the ways of the military and the teachings of their civilian mentors – a degradation of ideology and a demeaning of revolution.

Jundi attributes the Ba'thist infatuation with words to the character of Michel Aflaq, the intellectual founder of the Ba'th party. Aflaq was more an artist than a leader and politician; he had the artist's propensity for escape from reality to a world that exists only in his imagination. "To him [Aflaq] the party was an artistic creation that took the place of a novel or a poem; he wanted the party as his novel or glorious epic and he loved it as an artist would love his own creation."[29] But politics and art are different things. Aflaq's creation turned into a tale of horror – bloody coups, repression, disillusionment and, finally, the loss of the Golan.

Neither the party's civilian ideologues, with their abstractions, nor the military men were capable of competent, dedicated governance – they were too busy conspiring. Domestically their rule led to economic ruin; their foreign policy led to war and a catastrophe for the Arab world. In both domestic and foreign policies, the Ba'thists were obsessed with one idea: "We must be ahead of Abdul Nasser." Land reform and nationalization of industries were ill considered; the economic dimension hardly occurred to the Ba'thists. Local feuds and rivalries dictated the course of land reform. Slogans determined the issue of nationalization and helped bring about the economic ruin of the country.

No one in the top leadership bothered to say – or even managed to understand – that war and peace and an orderly state required a sound economic base. The tribes of the Ba'th were immune to such considerations; all they cared about was the securing of public jobs for their relatives. Salah Jadid, the quintessential conspirator, the Alawite officer who shunned the spotlight and was at one time the real power in Syrian politics, had every person in his family over eighteen years of age on the public payroll. Clans battled for advantage and conspired to eliminate one another. The state remained an extension of that tribal mentality. Jundi reports an exchange he had with Salah Jadid in which the latter asked what could be done to deal with the "sectarian problem." Jundi suggested that the Alawites, a minority sect shrouded in mystery and accused by the Sunni population of deifying Ali, the son-in-law of the Prophet – hence of being unbelievers – make public their secret books and beliefs so as to remove the Sunnis' suspicions once and for all. "He [Jadid] said, 'If we did so we would be destroyed by the Shaykhs.' I answered, 'You are a revolutionary and you fear the Shaykhs? How then will you deal with the big problems?' He did not answer, but from then on my problems with the regime began and I later learned that he was paying *Zakat* [alms] to the Shaykhs and that he was endearing himself to them."[30]

Incompetence and irrationality in domestic matters were paralleled by erratic conduct in pan-Arab and Arab–Israeli politics. In these spheres, the Nasser complex was a more powerful obsession. As Jundi tells it, the Six Day War ended in tragedy because the civilian demagogues and the military men in Syria miscalculated: They thought Jordan would stay out of the war, Egypt and Israel would exhaust and destroy each other, and they themselves would come to the rescue, inheriting the Jordanian monarchy and emerging as the true leaders of the nationalist movement.

While the Syrian army was in disarray, paralyzed by conspiracies and counter-conspiracies with hundreds of officers either in prison or on diplomatic missions abroad – regardless of whether they spoke the language of the country to which they were sent – the Syrian head of state, Nur al Din al Atasi, gave ringing speeches of fire and bravado. "We shall feed the Sixth Fleet to the fish of the Mediterranean," was one of Atasi's typical statements. In the Ba'th's distorted and romantic view, the Soviet Union was an instrument at the disposal of the Syrian regime – a giant that appears when one rubs one's ring to one's command. When these delusions turned to ashes – King Husein entered the war, Syria shared in the defeat and had neither prestige nor overthrown monarchies to inherit, and the Soviet Union could not change the outcome – the Ba'th had a choice between the survival of its regime and land – the Golan Heights. Thinking that land could be regained but that the order could not, it chose the latter. And in so doing it destroyed itself.

Jundi's generation had thought that their predecessors lost Palestine because of treason and betrayal – King Abdullah's duplicity, King Faruq's treachery, Iraq's rivalry with Egypt. Now there was an unflattering comparison between the record of the monarchies and that of the pan-Arabists: "What is the difference between stupidity and treason if the result is the same?"[31]

That was not what the young men who had pinned their hopes on the Ba'th thought back in 1940 when they declared war on tradition and committed themselves to Arab unity. They believed that they had put the past behind them, that they had once and for all brought to a close the age of decline. But the generation that was to be the savior bequeathed to its successors impotent thought, a mountain of words, and a legacy of defeat: "We accomplished all the wishes of imperialism while we were shouting against it." Jundi notes that freedom is needed if the Arab world is to make the life or death choice that faces it, but the "world of defeat" does not look kindly upon those who dissent and rebel: "I am sure that the world of defeat will not forgive me, for it rejects the rebellion of the solitary individual. My books are banned in most Arab countries; whether reactionary or progressive, the men in power in these countries prove that rebellious thought is their most dreaded enemy."[32]

Others may see nothing particularly profound in the conclusion that the behavior of a particular nation reflects the substance and style of its historical experience and the durability of its cultural patterns. But it has always been the tendency of revolutionary imagery and ideology to claim novelty and to stress the breaking of chains and the forging of new relationships. In such situations, the discovery of the past emerges as a theme only after a particular experiment overreaches itself, suffers defeat, and fails to build the new Jerusalem.

Discontinuity with the past had been the hope and claim of the Ba'thists of Jundi's generation. But the experience of nearly three decades was to impress upon Jundi the haunting power of the past. Like so many others who examined the 1967 defeat, he was eventually to raise questions about the weight of the past and the burden of Arab history. The discovery of the past underscored the extreme pretensions of novelty and radicalism that had been part of the ideological baggage of the self-styled radical nationalists.

Al-Jundi's discovery of the past leads to a set of remarkable, sober, and insightful excursions into Arab history that break with the dominant nationalist historiography of his time. They warrant attention because they constitute an honest attempt to grab hold of a particular tradition, to see Arab history for what it really is without the cant of nationalism or the glorification of apologists.[33] History was not to be read into a sacred text or to be inferred from examining a society's ideals, but to be derived from the actual push and pull of events, from the compromises made, from the wounds suffered, and the way in which people went about consoling themselves and reconciling noble claims with dismal realities. For Jundi, the thrust of Arab–Islamic history was the attempt to evade the decline of a once ascendant and successful order, to run away from an unflattering and cruel reality to a mythical view that explained away failure and held out the promise of redemption.

During centuries of decline, the Arabs kept alive the image of past greatness. Backwardness and decline were attributed to deviation from religious teachings and to the disappearance of belief. "The image of the past becomes a heroic myth which the Arab compares with his desperate situation."[34] This, in Jundi's view, accounts for the sense of melancholy and tragedy discernible not only in Arab music and literature but also in political theory. "Roving poets" went from village to village telling "innocent listeners removed from the influence of European civilization and of the machine" about the past, with many embellishments and an abundance of imagination. Their stories helped create a heroic model – the Savior who will appear to restore the glories of early classical Islam. The model was a simple popular image that embodied all the traits that the Arab – the imagined one, that is – had lost along the way. Thus history intermingled with myth and produced a "primitive, simple ideology removed from the necessities of the modern age."[35]

The ruthless assaults of the world engendered even greater escapism as well as largely futile attempts to stave off further decline. After the Napoleonic invasion of Egypt, the Arabs came to feel that the world they lived in was only a distorted reflection of the real world. The grave violations to their psyche, values, religion, and sense of historical and cultural integrity inspired a handful of men, such as Muhammad Ibn Ahd al-Wahhab, the founder of the Wahhabi movement in Najd, Jamal al din al Afghani, Muhammad Abdu, and Rashid Rida to attempt to revitalize Islam, to make it capable of resisting the assaults of the modern world, to integrate parts of the heritage with what they judged to be the least disruptive features of modernity. These men, says Jundi, mixed religious doctrines with nationalism. This confusion persisted until the Young Turks tried to impose national Turkish dominance upon the Arabs at the turn of the twentieth century. The secular zeal of the Young Turks, the inducements of the West, and the inspiration provided by new nationalist doctrines finally broke Muslim universalism and enabled the Arabs to rebel against the Ottoman Empire and to support the cause of the Allies. But the Arabs soon learned that they were not considered allies but "one of the targets of the war." "They were deceived and were sold like slaves." The scars of that period made the Arabs "doubt the worth of human values."[36] As a result, many thinkers came to propagate the logic of force in the world, to argue that the rule of the strong is the only truth, and to push their nationalist doctrines in chauvinistic directions. German doctrines of nationalism – romantic, militant – seized the imaginations of a number of intellectuals. These doctrines seeped down to a small number of activists and would-be intellectuals anxious for a new recipe for glamor and power. Jundi provides a vivid reconstruction of the ideological climate of the period. He and his fellow radicals read with great admiration Nietzsche's *Thus Spake*

Zarathustra, Fichte's *Addresses to the German Nation*, and Chamberlain's *Foundations of the Nineteenth Century* and were the first to want to translate Hitler's *Mein Kampf.*

How did this exalted view of nationalism work in the Arab world? It presumably filled the ideological void caused by the collapse of liberalism and the growing disaffection with traditional institutions. Where there was weakness, it promised power and glamor; it supplied an anticolonial framework; it gave alienated young men a sense of purpose and mission. But, in retrospect, did it not contribute, among other things, to the extremism of the Ba'th? Is there no connection between the glorification of the nation and the trampling upon the individual that Jundi observed all around him? What of the romanticism, the noise, and the metaphysics that had characterized Arab nationalism? Can they be explained, at least in part, by the Germanization of so much of Arab nationalist doctrine? Jundi does not directly take up these questions, but this much can surely be read into his historical narrative: The exalted theories of nationalism popular in the interwar period and during World War II were to come to fruition in the post–World War II years. The discrepancy between the exalted claims and the dismal realities was only to lead to greater frustration and incoherence.

The Germanization of Arab nationalist thought occurred at a time when liberal notions of nationalism were on the wane in the Arab world. If liberal nationalism was too individualistic, associated with domestic privilege and with the colonial powers, then why not an integral, collectivist notion of nationalism? Long before Arab nationalists were seduced by Germanic doctrines, the intelligentsia and the politically zealous in other nations had felt the almost mystic appeal of those doctrines. Did not the Russian intelligentsia in the nineteenth century find in Germanic thought the answer to the problems of a decaying order? In nineteenth-century Russia, Germanic thought "impose[d] its prestige on minds torn between their desire for vengeance and justice and the realization of their own imposed isolation." Even in France, as Camus reminds us, the nineteenth century was, thanks to thinkers like Michelet and Quinet, "the century of Germanic thought."[37]

Surveying the wreckage all around him, Sami al-Jundi tries to find slivers of hope. More out of despair than conviction, he identifies three signs of hope. The first was Palestinian resistance; the anger of the fedayeen reassured him that the Arabs were still a living people, capable of doing more than simply devouring themselves: "Little by little," he said, the Palestinians were separating themselves "from the world of the defeat."[38] Men are numb in the age of decline, and the capacity of the Palestinians for some action was perhaps a sign of some life. But even they, Jundi prophetically warned, exhibited some traditional ailments: machismo, failure to organize, exaggerated claims, and a bit of escapism. The second hopeful sign was what he judged to be a different Nasser: a man deepened by tragedy, determined to correct his own errors and the errors of an entire generation.

The third sign may reveal the extent of Jundi's despair but may also include some deeper wisdom about the groping for change in post-1967 Arab politics – it was the suicide in mid-September, 1967, of the Egyptian commander Abdel Hakim Amir. Jundi saw that act as a harbinger of a new world. Many, he said, saw the suicide of Amir as an "ordinary event but I saw in it the beginning of a new world of anger and the eradication of old beliefs so that new ones would arise in their place."[39] For Jundi the suicide of Amir revolved around the question of personal responsibility. In the old world, men acted, and when they failed they laid the blame on others or on divine will. Amir, however, in choosing suicide, chose to make a different statement; he saw himself as responsible for

> the defeat of his army, for an occupation of part of his country and then for a conspiracy against his boss, leader and friend, so he tried and convicted himself and passed on himself a death sentence . . .[40]

This may seem like a "normal chain of events to a European," but it is something entirely alien to the Middle East. Muslims, he rightly observed, rarely commit suicide. Amir, although an observant Muslim, chose to kill himself; his sense of personal responsibility overpowered his adherence to Islam. Few notable suicides can be found in the history of Islam – the only case known to Jundi was the suicide of Abu al-Qasim, the conqueror of the Indian kingdom of Sind who was reported to have commanded his victorious army at the age of sixteen. That Amir chose to kill himself may suggest that Arabs were now willing to see the world as a product of their labor and sacrifices as well as of their errors.

The illusions entertained in a more youthful and innocent period were shattered; men could no longer hide behind slogans. The pessimism of Sami al-Jundi goes beyond the boundaries of Syria and the Arab world. A life of political struggle and then defeat led him to rethink the achievements and the failures of his generation of nationalists in what he calls "backward countries." That generation, he says, tried to close the cultural gap with Europe, but the harvest of so much effort was a good deal of repression and perhaps an aggravation of backwardness. Trying to do so much in a short period of time, Jundi's generation saw salvation in political power; it made many attempts — some sincere, some desperate and clumsy — to organize backward societies and push them toward modernity. Troubled by the slow progress of things, it

> thought that power would enable it to fulfill its historical role, so it tenaciously clung to it and depended on it and forgot its starting point and good intentions until power became its goal rather than its means.[41]

Sami al-Jundi's memoirs re-create the desperate search of the intelligentsia for a system of thought that would smash tradition, drive out Western colonialism, build up the nation, glorify it, and unite it, as Prussia united the German nation. But as Jundi was to learn, tradition persists, and theory — imported, immoderate, lacking a sense of proportion as to the costs, means, and ends of political action — can create plenty of noise without altering the substance and bases of politics. Worse yet, it can destroy the sensibilities of a hitherto dominant tradition without imparting new standards and values. Then there is a change in mood: The earlier confidence in the easy destruction of tradition is dissipated, and tradition is seen as an unchanging core that will defy all remedies, mock all solutions, and use as garb anything new that is proposed. But moods are conveyed in Sami al-Jundi's reflections and review of his past: first, the desperate escape to books and doctrines; then, three decades later, the discovery of self, the loss of all hope. With enthusiastic, messianic politics there is always the risk that men's belief that everything can be done will vanish, that men will be left with nothing but defeated spirits.

THE ISLAMIC RESPONSE: RADICAL
FUNDAMENTALISM

In both liberal and radical analyses, religion is denounced as the dead hand of the past. Because both systems of thought seek to liberate humanity and harness its energy for the reconstruction of the social order, the hold of religious sentiments is seen as a reactionary force. Modernization puts religion in an unfavorable light; religion becomes an obstacle to social change. The bias of secular ideologies is that people must discard their religious faith if they are to make progress. This is not an analytical judgment on the part of secular ideologists, but, paradoxically, an article of faith that is adhered to with the same intensity with which religious beliefs are said to be held. In the imagery and folklore of secular ideology, religious individuals are caricatures: men obsessed with other-worldly concerns, surrendering to divine will, immune to science, exploited by a religious hierarchy, willing to forgo struggle for this world in order to gain the other. The details of the caricature may vary from one religion to another, but the composite is the same: Instead of attending cell meetings, participating in electoral politics, or giving body and soul to the nation in arms, a religious man would pray, fast, spend his money on a pilgrimage, trust in the will of Allah.

For many secular Arab ideologists, the defeat was another dramatic illustration of the crisis of Islam: lethargic, backward Muslims defeated by a modern enemy.[42] The debate about the relation between Islam and the modern world is of course an old one; it preoccupied the intelligentsia in the nineteenth century. During the age of Islamic decline and European ascendancy, the twin issues of internal reform and external defense engaged Arab intellectuals and men of public affairs and divided their ranks. By its very nature, this debate did not lend itself to a resolution. Different people went different ways, and some, as usual, juggled many systems of belief. Thus it was only natural for the debate about Islam to reemerge in the aftermath of the 1967 defeat.

The defeat provided radical secularists with an opportunity to express their frustration with the persistence of Islamic sentiments. In the era that preceded the defeat, secular nationalism, seemingly radical politics, and the tempo of social change had somehow created a set of expectations that Islam would wither away and lose its hold on the believers. That view was never sturdily based but rested on the alienation of the intelligentsia from religious belief, on the easy assumption that religion and nationalism were incompatible and, finally, on the fashionable global assertion of the time that people were killing their deities and that religion as a social force was living on borrowed time. The secularists had read their own alienation from religion into the society at large. To be sure, a certain segment of the population had rebelled against religion but the overwhelming majority of people had not. Nor did the presumed incompatibility between nationalism and Islam hold for the Arab world. The more popular nationalism became, the more it identified with Islam. The separation that the secular Arab intellectual made between Arabism and Islam was not made by the less educated citizen; for the latter, the two were overlapping, almost identical forces.[43] The power of Islam was attested to by the fact that the regimes that professed their adherence to socialism had dressed their socialism in an Islamic garb and justified their version of socialism by saying that it emanated from Islamic sources. If Islam could survive nationalism and be grafted onto socialism, the secular intellectuals were no longer sure of the withering away of Islam.

In the aftermath of defeat, the turning of the masses to religion for solace and consolation and the continual appeal, couched in religious terms, for faith and patience on the part of no less a figure than President Nasser, served as a reminder that God may be dead elsewhere – particularly in existential European literature and in Marxist tracts read by Arab youth – but was alive and well in the Arab world. The attempt of the radicals to link Islam with the defeat did not go uncontested. Indeed, Islamic fundamentalism made an eloquent and moving case of its own and turned defeat into advantage. Fundamentalists argued that the Arabs had lost the war not because they were busy worshipping – as the radical caricature would have it – but because they had lost their faith and bearings: Disconnected from a deeply held system of beliefs, the Arabs proved an easy prey to Israeli power.

The argument made by thoughtful fundamentalists was similar

to the one made by the radical critics: The latter, too, had argued that a society needs a system of beliefs, an ideology, to guide it. The fundamentalists' contention was that Islam offered that system of belief, that it could do what no imported doctrine could hope to do – mobilize the believers, instill discipline, and inspire people to make sacrifices and, if necessary, to die.

Muhammad Jalal Kishk's *Al Naksa Wa al Ghazw al Fikri* (The Setback and Cultural Invasion) is the work of a prolific writer with Muslim Brotherhood affinities. The notion of cultural invasion seems to be the cornerstone of Kishk's outlook; the term appears in the titles of four of his books – one on general cultural penetration, two volumes on Marxism and nationalism as variants of cultural penetration, and one on the connection between cultural penetration and the Six Day War.[44] Kishk's writings belie the notion that Muslim fundamentalists are reactionaries fixated on the image of a theocratic past that has to be restored. In Kishk's world view, cultures clash for preeminence: Some rise and conquer, and others surrender and are subjugated. An old-fashioned thinker, Kishk has no appreciation for what he sees as a fraudulent kind of cosmopolitanism propagated by the West and subscribed to by fifth-column Muslim Arabs. For Kishk there is no such thing as a world civilization; cosmopolitanism is the pretension of the ascendant culture "that asks others to abandon their identity and sovereignty, to dismantle their culture," and gives them a choice between adherence to its postulates or extinction.[45] According to Kishk, what we are witnessing now is the third crusade against the Arab people. The first crusade, using the sword and the cross, realized some victories but was eventually overwhelmed. The second crusade – the age of imperialism – began with Napoleon's invasion of Egypt in 1798 and succeeded in destroying the self-confidence of the Muslim world. The third crusade picks up where the second left off: It accommodates itself to political independence; instead of using armies, it seeks to penetrate the mind of the Muslim and to rearrange it. Once the Muslim accepted the "supremacy of the West – not just material supremacy but cultural and spiritual supremacy as well – the Muslim's resistance would collapse; he would become like an open, defenseless city, vulnerable to every plunderer and invader."[46]

That civilizations clash in a Darwinian manner for preeminence and survival is fully realized by Westerners. Why, asks Kishk, do Muslim Arabs fail to refuse to accept that overwhelming historical fact? In part, they have been lulled into complacency by the West, which spreads the myth of cosmopolitanism. Then there is the role played by an imported ideological doctrine, such as Marxism, which postulates a fake universalism of its own. Afraid of looking old-fashioned before their liberal and Marxist mentors, Muslim Arabs succumb to the process of cultural invasion and come to accept the myths propagated by the West about the decline of religious fervor and the unity of cultures. Meanwhile, the West brings to its encounter with the Arabs a *ruh salibbiyya* (crusading spirit); it is as hostile to the Muslim world as ever.

Sincere people cling tenaciously to their beliefs. Mimics go whichever way the wind blows. They translate others' works, accept the latest fads, live through others' experiences, try to shed their biases, apologize for their particularism, adopt the ways of others. In Kishk's analysis, Muslim Arabs are neutralized, paralyzed by false doctrines of universalism – both liberal and Marxist – pitted against one another by sham ideological divisions concocted by the West. Meanwhile, underneath the sound and fury of ideology, behind the hair-splitting arguments, the eternal clash of civilizations goes on, the dominant civilization parading as globalism and subjugating other civilizations. Kishk holds up for his readers the Sino–Soviet split as an example of the transparency of ideology. No amount of ideology can bridge the gap between an Oriental country and an Occidental one, the old rivalry between China and Russia.

Kishk argues that cultural and ideological penetration are to the twentieth century what gunboats were to the nineteenth. Marxism, which has succeeded in seducing Arab intellectuals, is but another weapon in the West's ideological assault. For Kishk, it is the westernism of Marx that matters, not his opposition to capitalism. In the duel of civilizations, Marx is clearly on the other side:

> Marx did not call for a new civilization: he is a faithful son of Western civilization who formed his theory out of German philosophy, French socialism, and English political economy . . . Marx believed in the values and the history of Western civilization; he was proud

of that history which he considered as a triumph for humanity on its way to its final victory. He considered the crimes of Western civilization a historical necessity and did not trace those crimes to the philosophy of that civilization but, rather, to economic necessities.[47]

Marxism was not the only European affliction forced upon the Arab–Muslim world: Another, earlier one was secular nationalism. Kishk is even more contemptuous of secular nationalism than he is of Marxism, more certain of its disruptive consequences. Arabs were so convinced of the power of secular nationalism, so taken by its mystique, he says, that they were willing to set aside their religious beliefs in pursuit of the nationalist dream. But the history of secular Arab nationalism was a chronicle of defeat and setbacks. It does not strike Kishk as a paradox that the force that generated power for Europe brought weakness to the Arab world. Europe needed secular nationalism, which provided an effective way of organizing a community. But things were different in the Muslim world. Under the banner of Islam, disparate populations and ethnic groups had long been organized into a community. A unique kind of socialist ethos had been part of this community's creed and practice. At the height of its glory, it had laid siege to Vienna and outstripped Europe in the realms of science, philosophy, and culture, as well as war. Then the Muslims caught the germ of nationalism. The Ottoman Turks were the first victims of nationalism; the Arabs were next. The house of Islam was now divided, and Europeans could easily subdue the Muslim world. Minorities were now warring against one another. The concept of nationality, held in check by Islamic universalism, had shattered the basis of the community.

All this, it could be said, is the remote background of the June defeat. Had the Arab states waged the war along the only true lines – religious lines – victory would have been theirs, Kishk argues. Certainly the Israelis had seen their conflict with the Arabs along these lines. Kishk's image of Israel allows of no ambiguity: It is a religious state through and through. In Kishk's account there is grudging admiration for the clarity with which the Israelis saw the war, for the fact that young Israeli soldiers prayed behind their rabbis at the Wailing Wall after their capture of Jerusalem. Why did Muslims fail to exhibit the same religious zeal? Kishk believes that they were too embarrassed to do so: False doctrines about the class struggle and progressive nationalism had blurred their vision. He blames the regimes in Syria and Egypt for leading their people astray, for making cowards and inept soldiers out of a community that had a history of glorious victories.

A war society should organize itself in a roughly egalitarian manner: Bread and hardships should be divided in such a way that men are convinced of the justice of the social order. Such was not the case in the Arab military regimes, in which class arrogance and social stratification precluded a fighting society. The military class, placed at the apex of a social order of inequality, appropriated the public wealth for its own privilege and edification. The Arab armies were too busy living off the public treasury to stand up to the enemy. Furthermore, the military was riddled with factionalism; officers spent far more time watching and plotting against one another than they did thinking about the enemy. The Arab officer, according to Kishk, costs his society far more than does his American counterpart, but he hardly gets a chance to put to practice what he has learned. Sooner or later he finds his way to prison, or he becomes a corporate director, or an official responsible for fouling up industrial production in some factory, or someone who sabotages politics in some embassy.

Unimpressed with the ideological claims of the military and their advocacy of socialism and revolution, Kishk finds in medieval dynastic history an apt explanation of the military in power. These men, he says, are "socialist Mamluks." The new men, like the Mamluks before them, consider the land and those on it the property of the sultan.[48] For the military establishment, socialism means the military's dominance of the wealth of the country. None of this is new or modernizing. Kishk was exposed to Western writings that, in the early 1960s, saw the military as an instrument of modernization, as a vanguard of social change. In alluding to the Mamluks, he places the ascendancy of the Arab military in proper historical perspective. It is not a new, modernizing phenomenon but a retrogression, a resurrection of the politics of dynasties and intrigue. In the age of Islamic decline, " military gangs" assassinated, usurped power, and established dynasties that were subsequently

65

overthrown by other soldiers of fortune. A keen student of Islamic history, Kishk can see through the claims of the military who proclaimed themselves – and were accepted by many analysts – as a repository of the national will. He can find the thread that connects the new military with its predecessors.

The new Mamluks have misunderstood and distorted the meaning of revolution. For them revolution is mere seizure of power; they see no difference between a coup d'état – *inqilab* – and a revolution – *thawra*. Had they appreciated the difference, they would have realized that revolution does not occur with a mere attack on a radio station. In a practice of the military, the sole determinant of revolutionary politics was control of the radio station. Whoever controlled it was a revolutionary socialist, and whoever lost it was denounced as a reactionary agent of imperialism. None of this of course had anything to do with war and preparation for war. The military cliques were disinterested in it and unprepared for it. And when they lost in 1967 their main concern was to rush back from the front to hatch new conspiracies and prepare for the coming purge.

Kishk does not consider the military officers the only culprits. He also blames the radical intellectuals who hammered at the foundations of belief, imported false doctrines, and unleashed the moral confusion that paved the way for the defeat. The radical intellectuals put their faith in concepts such as world peace, brotherhood among nations, and humane socialism, but such beliefs put nations that take them seriously at the mercy of aggressive ones. In this world, the eagle and the sparrow cannot coexist; there can be no brotherhood between the killer and the victim. Human history is built on strife. Islam recognized this truth. The Muslim battle cry *"Jihad"* was the only thing that frightened the Europeans; it drew the boundaries between belief and unbelief, setting Muslims apart from other men. But Islam has long been on the defensive, and in its own house men preach its obsolescence and inadequacy and call for its destruction.

Each society must analyze its own predicament; each people must proceed from its own reality. For Kishk, the overwhelming reality is the existence of Muslim people who want to be true to themselves and to withstand the assaults of outsiders. Thus, Islamic movements that proceed from the objective social conditions of the Muslim world are the only ones that can claim to be authentic. Movements that attempt to read into the Islamic world the predicament and the solutions of other societies can lead only to estrangement and mimicry. Kishk's opposition to the radical intellectuals is based more on utilitarian concerns than on concerns about heresy. Our soil, he says, is Islamic; a nonnative plant is destined to die. Nor will attempts at cross-fertilization work: The plant will not survive.[49] Revolutions, Kishk insists, must be authentic. For all its polemical output, he points out, Arab radicalism has yet to produce a single volume, like Mao's, that analyzes local realities independent of the thoughts of foreign masters. No translators have ever transformed societies.

Kishk singles out as an example of the output of the radical intelligentsia Nadim Bitar's book on the 1967 defeat, *Min al Naksa ila al-Thawra* (From Setback to Revolution). Bitar, a Western-educated sociologist, proposed a typically radical argument about the defeat. He saw Islamic loyalties as the primary factor behind it. He also called upon the Arabs to revolt against their religion and adopt a truly revolutionary ideology: Arabs had to "stand naked before history" if they were to break through their dismal situation; they had to recognize that Islam and the traditional thought from which it emerges and that it sustains had led to a stagnant, superstitious society that looked for guidance in a classical text and in the lives and thoughts of men who inhabited a different world.

Other modern revolutions, Bitar argued, understood that the first revolutionary act was to liberate society from the hold of religion. The French Revolution was unambiguous in its denunciation of religion; it understood and taught future generations that the notion of divine transcendence was a pillar of a reactionary political order. Brissot, Chalier, and Saint-Just had set an example for others: To sanction a new order one must slay the God that had long sanctioned old arrangements. Bitar urged Muslims to do the same, for Islam too, in his view, had served as a pillar of reaction.

Kishk spotted a paradox in Bitar's presentation. The latter had chided the ordinary Muslim for surrendering to a system of authority outside his will. But, asks Kishk, what is the difference between a traditional Muslim who says that we lost the war because we disobeyed the will of Allah, and Bitar, who asserts that we lost it because we disobeyed Marx's teachings and the teachings of the other messengers whose testimonies he has showered on us? Different people, different prophets: The Muslim looks to the Hadith of the Prophet; Bitar finds truth in Marx's writings. Bitar is as much a captive of a closed ideological system as he presumes the Muslim to be.

That authenticity alone can secure victory is confirmed for Kishk in Algeria's struggle against France. Where others see in Algeria's triumph a victory for a radical ideology, Kishk sees the triumph of Islam. Islam alone, he maintains, preserved the integrity of Algeria and gave it the will to survive. The French had succeeded in seducing the intelligentsia, in remaking that layer of Algeria in France's image. Shelter, escape, and resistance were provided and made possible by Islam. Islam was one fortress that the French could not conquer and the rock on which their plans for integrating Algeria with the Metropole faltered.

The Algerian case and Kishk's views of it substantiate Clifford Geertz's depiction of the role of Islam as a language of refusal. Because the colonial encounter had been, in Geertz's words, a "clash of selves," religion became a safe haven, a way of defending one's integrity, for the "only thing the colonial elite was not and, a few ambiguous cases aside, could not become was Muslim."[50] That was why Muslims increasingly became oppositional Muslims at the height of the anticolonial struggle: When other routes of escape and resistance were cut off, religion provided the will to revolt and the language of dissent.

The many faces of the Algerian revolution were examined in this and countless other exchanges that took place in the Arab world after the June defeat. For the radicals, the Algeria that had triumphed was the Algeria of Frantz Fanon – guerrilla struggle, militant Third Worldism. They believed that the Arabs of the mashriq (the Arab East) had only to emulate the heroic resistance of the Algerians and adopt their ideological commitment. For Kishk and other fundamentalist writers, Algeria's triumph was a vindication of indigenous tradition, the triumph of militant, anticolonial Islam.[51]

Fundamentalists as well as radical critics held up the example of Algeria, not only because it was a case of Arab success on the battlefield, but also because it signaled their opposition to the politics of compromise and to the pursuit of a diplomatic settlement with Israel. Both groups reasoned that the Arab world had no bargaining power, that negotiation was tantamount to surrender. World politics is not decided by appeals to the court of world opinion, warned Kishk; the system of stages is a cruel one, and Western thinking is particularly Darwinistic. This was not a theoretical discussion as much as an attack against the view that what was lost on the battlefield could be recovered at a peace conference, that world public opinion would arbitrate the matter in a spirit of fairness and justice.

Kishk's analysis, which takes as its premise the clash of civilizations, has very little patience with appeals to the conscience of humanity. The edifice of Western civilization, he observed, was built largely through violence and through the near extinction of many native populations. The Arab stands vis-à-vis the Israeli in roughly the same manner as the native American stood vis-à-vis the white settler. It is folly to expect sympathy for Arabs suffering from Western civilization – "the civilization of Tarzan and the cowboy."[52] For two thousand years, Jews grieved over their treatment by the West. That brought them very little sympathy; indeed, it invited greater persecution. The enemy is again an example of how people should struggle to alter their situation, a reminder that the world feels no sorrow for the losers, that it accepts the realities created by the victors.

The Arabs, once winners, are now losers and their capacity to survive is at stake. In an interesting appropriation of Israeli imagery, Kishk sees Muslim Arabs threatened with extinction. More than a century ago, European imperialism denied the Arab world the opportunity to enter the modern, industrial system. Since that time, the gap between civilizations with power and those without has increased at an alarming rate. The pace of growth threatens to widen the gap; it may make the gap impossible to bridge, something akin to the gap that separates man from the ape. Israel is part of an ascendant, powerful Occident; the Zionist invaders will try to subdue this part of the world in the name of white civilization. This is the central challenge to the Arab world, a threat to its foundation. If the Arabs are to continue to misinterpret their predicament, their survival will be called into question.

Kishk's diagnosis of the Arab ailment and his prescriptions cannot be dismissed simply as reactionary, fundamentalist, or theocratic. Kishk's quest is not just the resurrection of a lost and ideal past. For some time, indigenous Third World traditions have been on the defensive against Western analysts and young intellectuals in Third World societies who openly ridicule indigenous traditions and assert that these traditions are incompatible with the needs and issues of our time. Indeed, the consensus on the obsolescence of traditional orders has been so overwhelming that those who hold it have felt no obligation to supply proof or to look into the tradition in question. In simplistic fashion, tradition and modernity are seen as two radically different worlds. The supremacy of modernity is an article of faith. It has never been fully explained how and why traditions should be shed or whether they can be shed. The intellectual who asks people to stand naked before history perpetuates a false myth: He or she fosters the illusion that such a thing can be done and that others elsewhere have done it to get where they are today. But Kishk and those like him are perceptive: They not only reject the intrinsic moral worth of such an act; they know that it is impossible.

The radical Arab intellectuals whose ideas I have sampled had an undifferentiated view of tradition, and their view was that tradition should be smashed. Daniel Lerner's once-influential book *The Passing of Traditional Society*[53] took for granted the supremacy of modernity over tradition. Lerner was sure that modern man was a superior species and that tradition was doomed to extinction. On the whole, what has been missing from both radical and liberal perspectives on traditional orders is the appreciation that fundamentalism of any kind comes with variations, that traditions have multiple usages.

The virtue of Kishk's analysis was to demonstrate that traditionalist thought can be penetrating and unapologetic and can be turned onto social and political problems without excessive piety. For a society that came to doubt itself after a massive defeat, Kishk's brand of fundamentalism offered a vision of the future out of a certain reading of Islam.[54] And the product that emerged was far from reactionary or static. In an oft-cited passage, Wilfred Cantwell Smith, a leading student of Islam, speaks to the multiple usages of traditions and the potentially radical impact of the kind of fundamentalism represented by Kishk and the Muslim Brotherhood:

> To regard the Ikhwan [the Muslim Brothers] as purely reactionary would, in our judgment, be false. For there is at work in it also a praiseworthy constructive endeavour to build a modern society on a basis of justice and humanity, as an extrapolation from the best values that have been enshrined in the tradition from the past. It represents in part a determination to sweep aside the degeneration into which Arab society has fallen, the essentially unprincipled social opportunism interlaced with individual corruption; to get back to a basis for society of accepted moral standards and integrated vision, and to go forward to a programme of active implementation of popular goals by an effectively organized corps of disciplined and devoted idealists. It represents in part a determination to sweep aside the inactive reverence for an irrelevant, static, purely transcendental ideal; and to transform Islam from the sentimental enthusiasm of purely inert admirers or the antiquated preserve of professional traditionalists tied in thought and practice to a bygone age, into an operative force actively at work on modern problems.[55]

This is why radical fundamentalism has posed so formidable a problem to ruling regimes and why it manages, despite repeated crackdowns, to survive in a country like Egypt. The shock of the military defeat created a deep need for solace and consolation, and Islam provided the needed comfort. That phenomenon was strongest in Egypt, but the same thing happened throughout the Arab world. Sensing the new mood, the previously more or less secular pan-Arabists began to display greater piety: The officially guided media in both Egypt and Syria recalled the great achievements and adversities of Islam and the deeds of the Prophet and his early followers.

In Egypt, this may have begun as early as June 6, as soon as the defeat had sunk in. A cable from President Nasser to King Husein giving Nasser's consent to the evacuation of the Jordanian troops from the West Bank had a heavier dose of religiosity than was

71

customary in Nasser's statements: "We believe in Allah and it is not possible that Allah will abandon us and perhaps the coming days will bring us a victory from Him. May Allah help us and let his will be a guide for us."[56] A mere two months after the defeat, the Egyptian press reported that booklets explaining the meaning of *jihad* and recounting the campaigns of the Prophet had been distributed to the armed forces. A fundamentalist writer noted the change of heart on the part of the Egyptian regime, which, on the eve of the war, had reported that one hundred and sixty thousand pictures of an old musician, a matinee idol, and two popular actresses had been sent to the soldiers at the front "as though the faces of these singers were going to secure victory."[57]

The same change of heart could be observed in Damascus. Despite the homage Michel Aflaq paid to Islam – as a Christian what else could he do? – the Ba'th had been, on the whole, either hostile or indifferent to Islam; it was committed, as its theorists repeatedly stated, to the destruction of "tradition," and tradition in the Arab world was deeply and ultimately Islamic.

Only a few weeks before the outbreak of the Six Day War, the official magazine of the Syrian armed forces, *Jaysh al Sh'ab*, had published an article by a military officer that stated that belief in the old values, both Islamic and Christian, was in vain, that these values had made the Arab "a fatalist, a defeatist" who submits to his destiny, and that the only way to build Arab civilization and society was to create a new socialist man who would believe that God, religion, feudalism, capitalism, and the old values that dominated Arab society are nothing but "mummies in the museum of history." This new socialist man would reject heaven and hell; he would accept that man had to toil for his nation and humanity and that his toil would be an end in itself and not something he had to do in return "for a small corner in paradise."[58]

Popular outrage within and outside Syria over the publication of this article forced the government to dissociate itself from the statement and to punish the writer and the editor of the magazine. But the article's appearance confirmed the schism between the predominantly secularized official class and a deeply religious popular culture. Defeated on the battlefield, the official class would now retreat and show greater deference to popular sensibilities. Rather than leave the religious sentiment to be turned into protest by fervent fundamentalists, the regime would try to do what ruling regimes had done throughout Islamic history: coopt the religious sensibility, identify it with the interest and the stability of the nation, and channel it into less destabilizing endeavors. And as had been the established norm, the official religious hierarchy that had long made its peace with the men of the sword would be ready to pitch in: bless the men in power and urge believers to trust the men who had it within their power to order and presumably change things.

But this is not the Islam of the Muslim Brotherhood. Coopted Islam and populist Islam are radically different. The first has always been willing to compromise: When soldiers usurp power, it accepts the supremacy of the sword. It asks men to obey their rulers or at least to refrain from rebellion against them. It also counsels patience in the face of material inequalities, for they are Allah's will, part of His design for the universe.

Populist Islam of the kind represented by Kishk and the Muslim Brotherhood is an activist, militant brand of belief, however. It keeps alive – and takes quite seriously – the notion that legitimate rule must be Islamic rule, and – to the discomfort of the dominant order – it preaches opposition to corruption and inequalities.

Much of what is attributed to Islam by radical Arab critics is easier to hang onto official coopted Islam than onto the populist strand. At any rate, it has always been official, traditional Islam that troubled the radicals. It is easy to understand why this is so if one keeps in mind not only the radical propensity for wholesale, innate condemnation of religion, but also the balance of power between the populist strand and the official, coopted one. What worried the radicals and the ruling elites in Damascus and Cairo was that the official conservative strand of Islam was claimed and manipulated by the monarchies. As interpreted by the monarchies, traditional Islam became a pillar for their kind of order, a prop for the monarchies that had been warning against wild men, imported ideologies, and subversive movements. The struggle over the role of Islam was an extension of the profane struggle for power.

CONSERVATIVE FUNDAMENTALISM

The power of traditional Islam was one of the weapons that the traditional states brandished against Nasser's regime. This was the Islam that King Faisal of Saudi Arabia invoked against the pan-Arabists at the height of the Arab cold war. (Faisal called for an Islamic Pact in late 1965 to combat the radical pan-Arabists. Its leitmotif was clearly not Islamic piety, for the pact included the Shah of Iran and Habib Bourguiba of Tunisia – men not particularly known for their observance of Islam.)

Nasser and the Ba'th could brush aside King Faisal's brand of Islamic solidarity before 1967, but they found it harder to do so in the aftermath of their defeat. Traditional Islam was heard from as soon as the dust of the battle settled. King Hassan of Morocco lectured the rulers of Cairo and Damascus about the error of their ways, attributing the radicals' ineptness to their deviation from religion.[59] That peculiar institution, the Moroccan monarchy, saw in the defeat of the upstarts and the ideologues divine confirmation of the rectitude of its own position: The Arabs had turned away from God, and God had turned away from them. On a less exalted plane, the Moroccan monarch volunteered that the Arabs had been defeated because they were divided by ideologies and because they relied upon the Soviet Union.

Among some diehard traditionalists the failure of the radical Arab states was taken to mean the bankruptcy of the entire framework of secular politics. In 1969 one fundamentalist writer called for the extreme solution of resurrecting the Islamic caliphate and bestowing it on King Faisal. As the call had it, a traditional *bay'a* – the acknowledgement of a new caliph and a pledge of loyalty to him – had taken place in Saudi Arabia, and Muslim scholars and *ulama* now had to spread the word to the believers that obedience was due King Faisal as the new caliph.[60] When a radical critic stated that this showed that Islam was a handy instrument at the disposal of the traditional Arab states, the same fundamentalist writer responded that it was a legitimate way of taking on communist influence and ideas, and that opposition to this move was based on the communists' full awareness that "the call for an Islamic Caliphate in the Kingdom of Saudi Arabia meant putting Muslims beyond the reach of Western or hostile currents and the mobilization of the Islamic community on a worldwide basis to liberate it from socialist and capitalist systems that have engulfed the world."[61]

That call died out – the caliphate was not restored – but it was an important statement on the mood and the climate. Sa'd Jumah, who was serving as Jordan's prime minister at the time of the Six Day War, issued his own independent call for the resurrection of Islamic rule with the aim of saving the Arab world from "barbarism and unbelief." There was, he said, a "contemporary living experiment" that could serve as a model for the Arabs – namely, the Pakistani experiment, which was, in his view, a full and living Islamic system. Arabs had to return to their cultural sources "to eradicate class and sectarian differences, to realize the justice, freedom, and equality decreed by our *Shari'a* eleven centuries before they were known to Europe."[62] Secular nationalism, Jumah insisted, was forced upon the Arabs and not really suited to them; it was imported by minorities that had erroneously believed that Islam looked down upon them. The revolutionary socialist and nationalist slogans were motivated by a desire for self-improvement on the part of ambitious, misguided minorities and by the schemes of the West. Bad intentions aside, the very model of the state system developed in the West, with its separation between church and state, was inherently unsuitable for the Muslim world: The separation might have made sense in its original habitat, but it did not in the Arab–Muslim world because of a fundamental difference between Christianity and Islam – the first was a system of morality, but the second was a complete social, political, and economic order. Christianity, Jumah said, was born at a time when the Roman Empire was politically at its zenith and required only moral reform – hence the ethical thrust of Christianity. Islam, however, emerging as it did out of a backward, bedouin setting, had created from scratch an entire social order in which the separation between secular and religious realms made no sense at all.

From such lofty considerations, the former Jordanian prime minister descended to the grubby details of inter-Arab politics that concerned him by advancing conspiracy theories about revolutionaries and minorities. He was told – by whom he does not say – that the ambassador of a great power (he leaves no doubt that it was the Soviet Union) met with a Syrian official on the first day of the war to convey a message from Israel. The message sought to reassure Syria that Israel had sympathy for "Alawite Ba'thism" and that, if Syria stayed out of the war, power and leadership in the Arab world would pass to Syrian hands after the defeat of Egypt and Jordan. The innuendo was all too clear: Revolutionary minorities would not fight; only true Muslim believers rallying under the banner of Islam and inspired by the cry *"Jihad"* would do so. The revolutionary state had been a total failure: It had torn asunder the fabric of the social order and was cowardly and treasonous in war.

These and related conservative Islamic themes coalesce in *Amidat al Nakba* (The Pillars of the Disaster), a widely read book by Salah al Din al Munajjid, a pamphleteer working in Beirut. Munajjid, as we shall see, is a bitter critic not only of radical nationalism and of the Soviet Union but also of those who restrict "freedom of commerce and industry."[63] His vision of what is properly Islamic differs from the more radical and egalitarian outlook of Muhammad Jahal Kishk. Munajjid's Islam inveighs against those who nationalize the people's wealth and make them dependent on a parasitic, godless version of socialism and on the capricious desires of the state. In Munajjid's discourse, property – sanctioned by Islam – would do what Milton Friedman claims it is able to do: give the individual citizen leverage vis-à-vis the state, limit the power of government, and thus expand the domain of freedom.

Thanks to the revolutionary socialists, al Munajjid says, the Arabs have reverted to the age of *Jahiliyya* – pre-Islamic ignorance. Armed with Islam, they had accomplished miracles, conquered kingdoms, enlightened souls, and turned "the solitary individual fighter into a thousand."[64] Islam had once made heroes out of weaklings; it had defeated two powerful empires, the Persian and the Byzantine, despite their superiority in numbers and weaponry. By instilling belief in the hearts of men, it enabled them to fight and die for a just cause. Its power lay in the believers' certitude that Islam was the best message for the world and that the Muslims were "the best community ever raised up for mankind."[65] Today's Arabs have lost all this: Instead of teaching others, they have become followers of the unbeliever Tito and of "imported ideologies" that are destructive and evil. The West and its local fifth column destroyed the foundations of the community. Nationalism and Marxism are responsible for Arab decline: The first turned fellow Ottoman Muslims into alien occupiers, and the second, so unattractive to the Arabs, was imposed by military rule in Damascus and brought chaos and repression.

No normal, well-adjusted, integrated Muslim would have succumbed to such false and divisive doctrines, asserts al-Munajjid. The people who took the lead in propagating alien doctrines were individuals with "resentments and psychological complexes."[66] Some of them wanted to seize political power; others wanted to destroy Islam. A prototype of the former is Salah al-Din al-Bitar – he loved power, and wanted to rise to the top "even though he was not a Damascene."[67] An example of those whose aim is the destruction of Islam is Michel Aflaq. In both Cairo and Damascus an entire generation systematically embarked upon the Bolshevization of Islam. Even before that misguided generation – Nasser and the Ba'th – others were paving the way for the disaster with their subversive call for nationalist politics. Fifty years of Arab life were wasted on two unsuccessful experiments – nationalism and socialism. Revolutionary socialism was a devastating disease, "more harmful than cholera or the plague."[68]

Munajjid indicts the revolutionary regimes for restricting commerce and industry and reducing to starvation those who were once prosperous, for destroying the spiritual bases of the community (for the first time since the invasions of the Tatars, the sanctity of mosques was violated in Ba'thist Damascus as soldiers entered the mosques with their shoes on and stained the walls with the blood of the believers), and pitting individuals and classes against one another. Particularly objectionable to al-Munajjid is the way the revolutionary socialists had manipulated the masses. They had appealed to emotions instead of reason, and, because the masses are a "willing obedient flock" with no critical faculties of their own, the once stable order that supplied people with meaning and made sense of life and social relations was nearly destroyed: Subordinates began challenging superiors, the young dared challenge the old, and the uneducated demagogic element would no longer honor the notables of the community or the men of intellect. And,

77

presumably, radical officers who defied monarchs and the established order of authority could be included among those who no longer knew their place and no longer played by the rules. To cap all this, the revolutionary socialists then surrendered to the Soviet Union, which stabbed them in the back and abandoned them in their moment of need.

Munajjid's view that the Soviet Union betrayed its radical allies — encouraged them to go to war and then left them to fend for themselves — was a modern, contemporary one. But there was another view of the Soviet Union that was popular among some zealous, traditional Islamic writers and that subsequently seeped down to the public who read their commentaries: The Soviet Union as the incarnation of evil. In this more extreme, diabolical view, the world is Manichean, conspiratorial, a battleground for the forces of good and evil. And in that world, the Soviet Union's Communism and Israel's Zionism are twin evils.

The same publicist who defended the caliphate of King Faisal saw the Six Day War as a Soviet *mukhattat* (plan). He argued that there was an intimate connection between Zionism and Communism: Marx, the founder of Communism, was a Jew, and his solution to the Jewish question was a world-wide socialist revolution. Zionism and Communism were slightly different means for solving the Jewish question and for serving Jewish interests. The guiding force behind their unholy alliance was the desire to destroy the Muslim world. America supposedly acquiesced in this design, but it was more naive than sinister. All the quarrels about strategy and ideology were merely a cover for the old standing duel between Islam and the West.

The subtleties of international politics and the limited objectives of the state system have always seemed unconvincing to some people. In the Arab world, as elsewhere, conspiracy theories of history in which evil forces scheme and distort have always come in handy: They simplify a complex world and justify ancient and visceral quarrels. Far more important than ideas themselves is the climate that makes some ideas more persuasive than others or more persuasive at one point in time than at others.

The ideas of al-Munajjid and of the former Jordanian prime minister had been around prior to the Six Day War, but they were defensive ideas then, the ideas of a discredited past. Pitted against them was the power of charisma, the apparent success of a secular and nationalist ideology that prided itself on its accomplishments and its modernity, and the smug assurance of a younger generation that was in power and that believed that the future was on its side. With the unexpected outcome of the war, the secular pan-Arabists lost their self-confidence and the traditionalists recovered theirs. The latter no longer seemed as anachronistic as the former had said they were. In the minds of the traditional leaders, the modern world had in a sense betrayed those who had made so much noise about their capacity to master that world. To the diehard traditionalists, the defeat of their adversaries was a message, an omen: Radical leaders had turned things upside down and now divine will had made known its disapproval.

Modern human beings are far more superstitious than they think they are. Success seems like a vindication, a confirmation that what individuals and nations are doing makes sense, conforms to some higher law – which, depending on one's inclination, may be the dialectics of the class struggle, the stages of economic growth, or divine will. Conversely, setbacks are warnings: Something is not going well or not going according to schedule. People begin to feel that they are swimming against the current, that they are trying to do too much, or that they are on the wrong track. Without the daring they once possessed, leaders and movements suddenly discover the limits that exist in the world, all the obstacles that stand in the way of what they are trying to do. The superpower that yesterday was told to go drink the ocean becomes an awesome reality whose will you cannot defy. The power that you were going to feed to the fish of the Mediterranean becomes an unassailable entity. The monarchs who appeared so vulnerable and doomed to extinction become formidable rivals to whose will you must bend if you are to survive. And the arguments that were previously mocked as reactionary or xenophobic or archaic become believable.

It is not sufficiently appreciated that the images and doctrines that people and movements manufacture are more for internal consumption than for persuading others. Failure or weakness relative to others is usually preceded by loss of self-esteem, by inner doubts: People cease to believe their own utterances before others doubt them. We know the phenomenon quite well – aristocracies lose their belief in their inherent superiority; colonialists begin to doubt their right to empire; ideologues are no longer confident that their doctrines have the capacity to explain and order the world. Something like this was to happen to the rulers of Cairo and Damascus in the aftermath of the June war. Their traditional rivals gained a new lease on life while they themselves stood exposed. The Ba'th became a shell of its former self after the desertion of the party's founders, the revelations of men like al Razzaz and Jundi, and the doubts raised everywhere about Syria's participation in the war. The region was no longer hospitable to the poetics of Michel Aflaq. A regime claiming the Ba'thist label did survive in Damascus. One year after the Six Day War, a clique of officers calling themselves Ba'thists seized power in Baghdad, and, as if to underscore that they were serious about their claim, imported the ideologue Michel Aflaq, who had been banished from Syria.

Over the course of the next few years, the two Ba'thist regimes battled one another more than anyone else, and there was an intense struggle over who represented the Ba'th. Their polemics were, as usual, passionate, but there was no longer an audience to take their exchange seriously. Soldiers seizing power and proclaiming revolution no longer fooled that many people. Michel Aflaq wrote a few more articles and gave a few more speeches, but people wearied of his style and of his kind of politics. The game became far too serious and grim for slogans such as "Arabism is love" to catch anyone's attention. Three years after the Six Day War, another Ba'thist officer, Hafez Asad, toppled the Syrian regime, but his stock in trade was not the ideology of the Ba'th. Asad was a shrewd man with a remarkable instinct for survival, but he had not read the books that the earlier Ba'thists had read. His instinct was for the center of Arab politics as he sought to govern what has traditionally been an ungovernable society.

Each political order has its own kind of political style and expression. The style and expression of the pan-Arabists gave way to a subdued language that was more in line with the sensibilities of the conservative states, more deferential to the heritage, less threatening to the prerogatives of wealth and power. The political discourse of the established leaders now emphasized inter-Arab solidarity rather than ideological splits and assigned a more central place to Islam than had been the case in the previous era. The style reflected the change in the material distribution of power: The traditional states were no longer defensive and off balance; their new power would make respectable their style of discourse, their symbols, and their language.

The discourse of the traditional Islamic view was laced throughout with a greater emphasis on Israel's religiosity. This point is essential to an understanding of the resurgence of Islamic sensibility in the aftermath of the Six Day War. The Arabs had been poorly informed about Israel: In the dead language of the preceding era, Israel was only a bridgehead of imperialism, a gathering of Zionist gangs. Israel was mostly seen as a technological, scientific power, and a whole generation in the Arab world had been taught to believe that religion and modernity were mutually exclusive.

The Israeli capture of Jerusalem and its significance for the Israelis gave Muslim believers ammunition in their debate with Arab secularists: Modernity and religion can be brought together; man can fight for religion just as well, if not better, than he can fight for the modern state – and definitely much better than he can fight on behalf of cosmopolitan ideology such as socialism, whose slogans can be repeated without great feeling or authenticity. The principal lesson that the religiously inclined Arabs drew from Israel's victory was that people can both go to the laboratory *and* worship. Israel combined what an entire generation of liberals and secularists had assumed to be incompatible things. It was both more religious and more scientific than the Arab states. Israel, writes Ahmad Baha'a al-Din, one of a handful of Egyptian establishment journalists, poses a "strange challenge" to the Arabs: it challenges in them "the ancient and the modern, the past and the future." In Israel's arsenal are modern weapons and technology as well as ancient visions and claims. What are the Arabs to make of such a challenge? How are they to reconcile the modern side of Israel and the ancient one, which "indulges in archaeology not to write a history but to plan a future"?[69] It was probably no accident that the Nasser regime began after its defeat to pay homage to the modern scientific state and urge greater adherence to Islam at the same

81

time. Israel had demolished the easy superficial distinction, taught by a generation of Arab liberals and embraced as well by younger radicals, that religion is a reactionary force, that the scientific state is built on the debris of an extinguished religion.

But hard as they tried to identify themselves with the resurgence of the Islamic sentiment, the regimes in Cairo and Damascus could not really hope to claim it as their own. This was a battle that the traditional states were destined to win. The matter would not be decided on grounds of true Islamic piety, for some symbols lend themselves to certain individuals and groups more easily than they do to others. The people who benefit from the symbols need not necessarily honor them, at least not fully; they need only honor them more than their rivals are seen to do. Most ideologies and belief systems are not savored for what they are; they are more appreciated for what they do, for their utility in taking on others who manipulate other symbols. Giant corporations thrive on the myth of private enterprise – they feed off attacking bureaucracies and red tape, conveniently forgetting that they themselves are giant bureaucracies and that a corporate technostructure has replaced the brave creative hero of the private enterprise story; they dwell on the myth because they want to have a lofty vision of themselves – the individual entrepreneur taking risks and facing narrow-minded bureaucrats. Moreover, they need the myth as a weapon to use against other bureaucratic systems, such as labor unions and governmental agencies.

As it is with the corporate technostructure and the myth of private enterprise, so it is with the traditional elements of society and the banner of Islam. It is not so much that those who brandish Islam have to be good Muslims, rather, it depends on the day and the issue. What the myth does is raise one's self-esteem and then turn it against others – religious minorities, self-styled radicals, Marxists who in a religiously steeped culture foolishly dismiss religion as the opiate of the people, secular regimes that allow the sanctity of mosques to be violated.

For men who wage political struggles, as well as for those who are brave and curious enough to try to interpret the struggles, the ideas that are thrown around are less important than the material struggles that underpin them and give them value and importance. The tangible issue that arose immediately after 1967 was the new balance of power between the traditional conservative states and their rivals, who had just suffered a major defeat. With or without the issue of Islam, a fight to determine the postwar configuration of the Arab system of states was next on the agenda. The radicals' loss was bound to be the conservative states' gain: The latter had the money, and the former had been in error, had lost the war and the land, and had to worry about their survival at home. But few struggles for power are ever waged without pretensions to ideological or normative stakes. The protagonists drag ideas into the game both because they take the ideas seriously and because they wish to invest their quest with moral worth and to provide a cover for what otherwise would seem to be narrow and selfish goals. The oil states could not have stated openly that the fight was about stability, that they were on some level relieved that the people who had disrupted stability for so long had paid for their sins, that as a result of the defeat they could now enjoy a period of relative peace. They might have said that they felt more secure because the radio stations and the media that had blasted them daily and accused them of treason and reaction had finally lost whatever credibility they once had, that Israel's victory – though painful on one level – had worked to their advantage.

But of course they would not say so. Like all others engaged in such struggles, they would wrap their interest with what E. H. Carr called "convenient morality."[70] In their case the convenient morality was Islam – a particular kind of Islam, to be sure. The monarchs of Saudi Arabia, Libya, and Morocco and the emir of Kuwait were – as far as they saw it and as far as they wanted others to understand it – engaged in an attempt to reconstitute a community that had lost its bearings, to liberate a people from imported doctrines, to correct the errors of a misguided generation, to exorcise the region of the irresponsibility of pan-Arabist doctrines. That in dong so they would protect their own dynasties and interests went without saying, for political struggles are not waged by individuals who renounce the world in favor of transcendent ideals. The transcendent ideals that the monarchs would put forth were the *turath* – the heritage. And in their reading of it, it was a conservative, cautious *turath*, which upheld the authority of elders and notables and kept individuals and classes in their places.

At this point, the conservative states had a choice: They could either push their victory too far in order to avenge the injuries and the abuse of the past and try for a full restoration of the ancien régime, or, sensing the new storm – far more militant enemies than Nasser, Marxist Palestinians, embittered youth had been – they could accept a reconciliation with a former rival in the interest of overall stability. The revolution that the Arab radicals waited for after 1967 did not take place, largely because – as we understand with the benefit of hindsight – the conservative states took the second option and because the man at the helm in Cairo would swallow his pride and adapt himself as best he could – and that was not easy, given his own personal makeup – to a new set of realities.

Several factors were to bring about an alliance between the traditional states and the Egyptian regime: the radicalism of the new revolutionaries (George Habash of the Popular Front for the Liberation of Palestine, and young men who were far more relentless in their opposition to tradition than the regime in Cairo had ever dreamed of being), the emotional appeal of the slogan "a war of national liberation," and the dangers to a totally discredited Arab system of states of a military outcome that had dishonored all the regimes and ridiculed all those in power. The regime in Damascus would continue to snipe at the system, but the arrangement that mattered would be worked out between Nasser on the one hand and King Faisal on the other. A frightening generation gap developed in the aftermath of the defeat: The language, the symbols, and the world view of the men in power were losing their grip on the young, who were now marching to a different drum. In the circumstances, Nasser no longer seemed as much of a troublemaker as he once had – or, more accurately perhaps, as he once had been. With the threat posed by the new radicals, it was easier for Nasser to work with King Husein than with someone like George Habash, who was declaring to receptive young men that Nasser's experiment was "petty bourgeois" and no revolution at all and that the answer lay in a popular war of liberation and not with armies that had proved their incapacity to fight.

It was at this point that the logic of the state system – limited resources and capabilities, and the knowledge, to which outsiders are immune, that great and popular crusades must be checked against messy and sobering constraints – asserted itself. Faisal, Nasser, and Husein headed established states, and they wanted some control over what they saw as a situation of great danger. Their adversaries were free from governmental responsibility: They could agitate; they could ask for the impossible; they could endlessly cite Debray, Fanon, and Giap; they could hijack airplanes and make a mockery of the regimes' standing in the eyes of the citizenry. The men in power operated from vastly different premises, but they would, to the extent possible, patch up their differences to ensure that turmoil, frustration, and radicalism did not go beyond reasonable limits.

De Tocqueville's classic discussion of the French intelligentsia rooted their totalism in the marked separation between precept and practice in French political life: "One group shaped the course of public affairs, the other that of public opinion."[71] This separation between precept and practice was to become a particularly severe problem in immediate post-1967 Arab politics. The intelligentsia, who shaped public opinion, were for the most part radical outsiders: They gave precept a revolutionary tone, and they wanted total and bold solutions – nothing less than a new society and a new human being. The people who shaped public affairs were far more cautious and restrained: They had economies to keep afloat, defeated armies that had to be reequipped, two superpowers that had to be appealed to for weapons and diplomatic support, and a more powerful enemy holding occupied soil and showing every sign that it was digging in for a long stay. The radical outsiders were a more impatient, younger breed who thought a war of national liberation would do it all – transform the domestic order and defeat their more powerful enemy.

It should be recalled that post-1967 radicalism began with a profound rejection of the unfulfilled, empty slogans of the previous generation. But the radical intelligentsia and activists soon

85

succumbed to a typically intellectual affliction: conviction that revolution was imminent. Whether they rallied to the cause of the new revolution – the Palestinian movement – or simply believed that the dominant order was about to collapse from its own weight, their talk of revolution came to dominate the political and intellectual marketplace. Was history repeating itself? Were the radical intellectuals and activists playing the same game that the Nasserites had played in Egypt and the Ba'th in Syria? The radical intellectuals would have objected to such a portrayal. They knew that they were different and that they would escape the errors committed in the preceding era. At any rate, it was their belief that they were living in a situation that was soon to give rise to revolutionary politics: Out of the debris of the defeat would emerge new people and new politics.

That wars and defeats can speed up the dissolution of a social order is received wisdom that is underscored by great revolutionary upheavals. But a revolutionary outcome is neither inevitable – as Arab politics were to show in the years that followed the Six Day War – nor even the norm. A revolutionary situation has to be appropriately defined and seized upon if the potential inherent in it is to be realized. Extreme situationism is unpersuasive, for there is always a range of outcomes inherent in a particularly fluid situation.[72] This is where circumstances, luck, clear thought and, above all, gifted leadership can make a difference. If the gifted leadership is on the revolutionary side, it can activate the processes that conduce to the collapse of a reigning regime. If the gifted leadership is in the saddle, it can outmaneuver its opponents, seize the initiative, and offer a more compelling justification and a way out of a particularly acute crisis. Whatever revolutionary potential existed can thus be defused as the dominant order is given a chance to correct its previous errors.

Fear of uncertainty and chaos can help the established order: In a dismal situation, a familiar voice and face can be soothing and reassuring. Particularly gifted leaders can rise above the ashes of regimes that they had ruled and promise a new beginning. In a dark and frightening hour the old order can bounce back with new slogans and promises: Give the leader another chance and he will find, as he did in the past, a solution of some kind, an honorable way out; he will renew himself and the nation. To lose the leader at this particularly traumatic moment is to plunge into the dark and to be set adrift. This is the way events evolved after the June defeat: Faith in the imminence of revolution collided with President Nasser's determination to survive and to keep the Arab system of states from taking too radical and dangerous a turn; the talk about the bankruptcy of traditional orders and the revolutionary nature of the masses met its test in Jordan when the Palestinians faced King Husein's army. It is one thing for a political order to face military defeat and loss of credibility; the capacity to push it over the brink and replace it with a new order is an altogether different endeavor:

> And was all that . . . intoxication, delirium? Perhaps – but I do not envy those who were not carried away by the exquisite dream. The sleep could not last long in any case: the inexorable Macbeth of real life had already raised his hand to murder sleep . . .[73]

The writer was the great Russian publicist Alexander Herzen, the dream that of the European revolutionaries in 1848. On a far lesser scale, to be sure, there was "intoxication" and "delirium" in the Arab world during that radical interlude that followed the June defeat. But here too the "Macbeth of real life" would appear to slay the dream, and we would see all the standard ingredients that devour dreams: "revolutionaries" who turn out to be far less radical than they presume themselves to be; a dominant order that turns out to be more powerful than it looks; an international system that hems in radical movements and reiterates the fact that nationalism is a far more real question than revolutionary delirium.

2

Egypt As State, As Arab Mirror

There was but one dominant discussion at Al Karnak [a Cairo cafe]: Day after day, week after week, month after month, year after year, we had no other topics to discuss. Exhausted by boredom one of us would say: let us choose another topic. We would show enthusiasm for that suggestion, raise some topic, deal with it with carelessness and then go back to our old topic, devouring it and it devouring us, without interruption and with no end:

- "The war, there is no option but war."
- "No, it is the Fedayeen [guerrillas] struggle."
- "A peaceful settlement is also possible."
- "The only possible solution is that which is dictated by the great powers."
- "Negotiations mean surrender."
- "Negotiations are a necessity. All the nations negotiate – even America and China and Russia and Pakistan and India."
- "Peace means that Israel would dominate the entire area."
- "Why should we fear peace? Were we swallowed up by the English and French?"
- "If the future proved that Israel is a 'good state' we would coexist with her and if it proved the reverse we would eradicate her as we eradicated the crusaders' state before."
- "The future belongs to us. Look at our numbers and our wealth . . . "
- "Our real battle is a civilizational battle. Peace is more dangerous to us than war."
- "Let us then demobilize the army and rebuild ourselves."
- "Let us declare our neutrality and ask other states to recognize it."
- "What of the Fedayeen? You ignore the real catalyst in the situation."
- "We have been defeated and we must pay the price and leave the rest to the future."
- "The real enemy of the Arabs are the Arabs themselves."
- "Everything depends on the unity of the Arabs in the effort."
- "Half the Arabs . . . were victorious on the fifth of June [1967]."
- "Let's begin then with the internal situation. There is no escape."
- "Great. Religion, religion is everything."

Najib Mahfuz, *Al-Karnak* (Cairo, 1974), pp. 95–96.

Egypt is neither the beginning nor the end . . . If the Arab nation is great with Egypt, Egypt cannot be great but with the Arab nation.

The Tripoli Summit Communique, in *The Middle East Reporter*, December 10, 1977, p. 17.

B URSTS of enthusiasm have a way of sweeping away things that have been around for a long time, defying incredible odds, challenging time-honored traditions and continuities. Then the enthusiasm fades or is thwarted by the superior resources of others, by incompetence or an overwhelming defeat: The old doubts and fears return, and the old battles have to be refought; paths once abandoned or thought unworthy in the revolutionary movement are rediscovered, as societies hemmed in by difficult circumstances reach out for solutions and possibilities.

Nasser's Egypt lived a revolutionary moment, or so it believed. Its defeat in 1967 broke that revolutionary wave; it added a new wound to a deeply scarred civilization; it threw new constraints in the face of a society whose history has been a frustrating struggle to push back − or to ignore and avoid − what seemed to be eternal constraints. And because the new constraints had to be dealt with, the attempt to deal with the 1967 defeat forced upon Egyptians yet another encounter with their classical themes and vulnerabilities. It threw out questions that the revolutionary order had confidently declared to be obvious and settled.

Egypt's centrality in the Arab world made it inevitable that Egyptian thoughts and second thoughts and Egyptian choices would become wider Arab concerns and dilemmas. The Palestinian question may have been the public issue of post-1967 Arab politics; but there has been an equally serious concern with the Egyptian question. The latter may not have generated the sound and fury of the former, but it has been a deadly serious matter that has touched upon fundamental civilizational sensibilities and fears. And just as the Egyptian struggle with the pan-Arab identity was in a way an internal debate about one's own society and civilization, so too was the wider Arab speculation about Egypt a proxy debate about the harvest of Arab history, about the capabilities of the Arabs and their place in the world.

The people who in the aftermath of the Six Day War denounced Egypt's incapacity to rebel, to become another Cuba or Vietnam, to win a war, and to build an austere society were really debating what they saw to be the frustrating incapacity of the Arab-Muslim order to shake off a stultifying legacy. A decade later, the concern with Egypt's despair and surrender was yet another debate about the failure of the Arab world either to win its fight with Israel or to come to terms with it. No other question – not even the Palestinian question – raised for the Arab world as a whole the magnitude of cultural and political issues generated by Egypt's agonizing struggle with herself, her search for a way out of military stalemate and economic breakdown, her attempt to deal with far-off powers that have the means, and the illusions that tempt them, to shape Middle Eastern realities.

Other Arab states may have derived some satisfaction from Egypt's troubles. Egypt's crisis – dwindling resources, military defeat, loss of energy, economic and political stalemate – may have given other Arab states added room for maneuver, and a greater chance to neutralize Egypt's demographic weight, cultural lure, and traditional political preeminence. But there is more to the world – even the world of politics – than the harsh calculus of power. In civilizational and psychohistorical terms, Egypt's crisis was a trauma to other Arabs. If Egypt was faltering and its society was falling apart, what then was to become of the Arab world? If Egypt was the hub of the Arab system, its decline and hardships at a time of Arab affluence and its surrender to the West are damning indictments of the state of the Arab world. Then there was the conflict with Israel: If Egypt were to disengage from that conflict, what hope was there for seeing that conflict to some kind of honorable solution?

Latecomer as it was to pan-Arab politics, Egypt was slated to head that movement once the nation entered it. When pan-Arabism had an anti-Ottoman thrust, the Egyptians, who were then worried about the British occupation of their country, had low regard for a movement that was not only anti-Ottoman but also burdened with a British connection. Early advocates of pan-Arabism moved between Damascus and Baghdad, but it was in Cairo that the league of Arab states was headquartered when it finally came into being in 1945. It may be true that Egypt simply waved an "Arab flag which fell into its hands,"[1] but there is no denying that it was Cairo's leadership that gave Arab nationalism the concrete reality it came to possess. This may strike other Arabs as peculiar, but Egyptians have generally taken for granted their preeminence in the Arab system. In the first half of the twentieth

91

century, bourgeois Egypt could rightly feel that sense of preeminence: It had a relatively developed economy and sophisticated cities, its exposure to the liberal ideas of Europe had put it decades ahead of the rest of the Arab world and its literary and cultural output far surpassed the achievements of other Arabs. And when it shifted leftward during the Nasser years, it became the Mecca of Arab radicals and progressives. Whatever his domestic faults, Abdul Nasser was an Egyptian, and his hold over the masses of Syria and the young of Saudi Arabia and Beirut was another confirmation of Egypt's preeminence. In the view of the Egyptian middle classes and the politically conscious, Egypt's centrality to the Arab world was natural and inevitable. Whether Egyptians were dealing with liberal ideas, building a modern army, making movies, writing books, exporting revolution, or conducting diplomacy with Israel, they were convinced that they of course excelled and led and that other Arabs would follow.

But preeminence has its risks and price. There are responsibilities to be shouldered; the allies and dependents one acquires can limit one's freedom and drag one into all kinds of troubles. Precious resources can be wasted in vain attempts at securing the gratitude of others. One ends up fighting others' fights only to be denounced when one grows weary of a long-drawn-out battle. Preeminence can also distort the view of the leading member of a community. Weariness has a way of rewriting history, as the emotions and interests that led people to fight are forgotten and the preeminent see the fights in hindsight as selfless sacrifice on their part in pursuit of others' dreams and in defense of others' interests.

The scarcity of material resources can make things particularly difficult for nations − as well as individuals − whose ambitions, memories, standards, and claims to preeminence overreach their power and resources. Others who have more resources at hand are seen as crass newcomers who either cheated or were lucky or grubby enough to succeed. The imbalance between one's cultural achievements and one's pretension is a nightmare for individuals as well as nations. Behind Egypt's struggle with its sister Arab states is the all-too-familiar human rejection of downward social mobility. Egypt's power and wealth vis-à-vis other states in the Arab world have declined; the world outside interfered in October 1973 and played havoc with the Arab order and its ranking; it conferred immense riches on those who had historically been in Egypt's shadow. In so doing, it challenged the geography of the mind within and outside Egypt: it left gloom and a sense of betrayal in Egypt, but among the lucky states, there were the dreams of a new order and unlimited possibilities.

This jolt to the mental geography and sense of self must be seen against the background of a deeply held Egyptian belief in Egypt's centrality to the region around it. Nasser had given the Egyptian claims a radical thrust, but the material with which he worked predated him – Egypt's belief in its supremacy and its urge to pursue its destiny in places such as the Sudan, Syria, the Arabian peninsula. The same urge that had taken Muhammad Ali, the builder of the modern Egyptian state (ruled 1805–1848), and his son Ibrahim to Syria and the peninsula would operate on the radical Abdul Nasser. There may have been deeper historical roots than were suspected in Saudi Arabia's response to Nasser's thrust into Yemen. After all, Muhammad Ali had undertaken a similar expedition in the early nineteenth century against the Wahhabi forefathers of the present dynasty.

Currents borne by the wind and the constant of geography underpin what may seem like modern ideological contests. Egypt, long an established state, saw it as its burden and privilege to lead others around it. In a seminal and rich study on Egyptian personality, culture, and ecology, the Egyptian scholar Jamal Hamdan expressed that kind of innate belief in Egypt's centrality: Leadership in the Arab system was not open to debate and speculation but has been once and for all determined by geography and location – once Egypt entered the house of Islam, it was destined to lead.[2] Even when other Islamic empires arose elsewhere, they were transient. They collapsed because they were built on the periphery of the Arab–Muslim order. In Hamdan's mental geography and reconstruction, the Umayyad and Abbasid empires were marginal: The first ended in the escape of Umayyads, and the second was vulnerable and susceptible to destruction, as seen in its fate at the hands of the Mongols in the thirteenth century. Centrality belonged to Egypt, and that is why ambitious dynasties and rulers sought to make their home in Egypt and why repelling the crusaders had to be launched from Egypt by the Mamluks and Saladin. Geography placed Egypt between the Asian part of the Arab world and Arab Africa. Egypt introduced the two parts to one another and was a magnet for the talented, the ambitious, the dissatisfied, the oasis of the Arab world.

Hamdan's view is partly warranted by the objective facts of history; it is partly myth and imagery. But myths have their own power and reality, and in the years that followed the Six Day War both the reality and the image of Egypt's ascendancy were to be tested – sometimes consciously and openly, sometimes in the deep recesses of the mind, where things are more sensed and intuited than seen. Few Arabs stated this with the clarity that the Egyptian writer Muhammad Jalal Kishk did when he wrote that the June defeat marked the end of the Egyptian myth in Arab life.[3] The objective inter-Arab struggles and the cumulative Arab debate of more than a decade – all the way form the polemics of the intellectuals after 1967 to the Arab diplomatic conferences of 1978 and 1979 that sought to bring Egypt back into the fold – revolve around Egypt's pride of place and the imbalance between her material resources and her psychological esteem of herself – between her old glory and current poverty – and around the attempts of other Arabs to sustain, limit, or oppose Egyptian choices.

All the currents in the region battled to win Egypt over, to save it from itself or from others. The Arab radicals wanted Egypt to go beyond itself and become genuinely revolutionary; the Palestinians first wanted it to step aside and accept that there was a new revolution on the Arab horizon and then to commit itself and its resources to the creation of a Palestinian state. The third bid came from Qaddafi, offering Egypt redemption through radical fundamentalist Islam – return to the sources – and a cure for its poverty through a union with Libya. Then there was the bid by conservative Arab wealth offered by Saudi Arabia and the smaller oil states: Arab wealth was willing to help, and in return it wanted from Egypt an expulsion of the "atheistic" Soviet Union, a dismantling of the public sector, greater deference to Islam, an end to the pan-Arabist zeal, and the patience and willingness to abide by collective Arab will in diplomatic matters. Finally, there was the duel of the two superpowers in the region, which culminated in the eclipse

94

of one and the engagement of another.⁴ Here too Egypt was a coveted prize and a main arena. The Soviet Union had to concede its incapacity to comprehend, let alone control, this costly and peculiar ally, while the United States moved from being a friend of the enemy to President Sadat's and Egypt's full partner. The United States had tangible interests to protect, but there were intangibles – the desire to be wanted, the excitement of a new frontier – that played a part in Sadat's successful courtship of America. Ancient civilizations (witness America's attitude toward China) stir the imagination: They have a kind of malleability that enables others to read into them what they want; they can be hotbeds of revolution or fragile entities ready to be courted and redeemed. They invite those who have a sense of destiny. From Napoleon to Kissinger, powerful societies and leaders have seen Egypt as a natural zone of their influence: "It is proper for this country (Egypt) to attract the attention of illustrious Princes who rule the destiny of nations," wrote Jean-Baptiste Joseph Fourier, the secretary of Napoleon's Institut d'Egypte.⁵

Lesser figures than Napoleon had equally vivid imaginations, and Egypt was sufficiently ambiguous to allow them all their moment. For commissars, it was a candidate for socialism to be imposed on from above; for an Arab–Muslim soldier like Qaddafi, it was home of the Arab–Muslim world's leading university, and it was there more than anywhere else that Islam fashioned a civilization, made its peace with the world, built a great city, and debated the issues of the day. For a bourgeois, cosmopolitan liberal, Egypt was the place where the West as process left its deepest marks as well as its most durable scars in the Arab world. For those states with wealth – either a faraway superpower, a militant soldier next door, or a nearby conservative dynastic state – Egypt's poverty stimulated the imagination. It suggested the possibility of conquest and conversion, of buying into a major undertaking. In having Egypt see it one's way, there is a tangible interest to be served – stability or revolution or a base in a turbulent region, depending on the viewer – and the intangible gratification of having an ancient civilization on one's side.

Throughout that turbulent passage, all the way from militant pan-Arabism to its embrace of American power, Egypt's path was

95

navigated by two men, and there is a temptation to see the choices the two men made as idiosyncratic, personal ones. Both men have been the subject of a great deal of speculation. Nasser was a hero, a tragic figure who occupies a special place in recent Arab history; Sadat was an enigma who surprised the Arab world first with a remarkable deed in October, 1973, and then with a psychohistorical shock in November, 1977, with his journey to Jerusalem. But a king, wrote Tolstoy, "is the slave of history. History, that is, the unconscious common swarm of life of mankind uses every moment of the life of kings as an instrument for its own ends."[6]

That is why the temptation to go after the personalities of the two "kings" in order to explain Egypt's path must be checked, for there were constants that both men had to deal with: (1) an unacceptable military defeat that both men had to try to break out of; (2) a revolutionary legacy that had generated a great deal of noise and that now had to come to terms with the world. In the case of Nasser, the revolution was his own work; in the case of his successor, it was an inheritance that he had to pay homage to and then try to transcend. There was also the question of growing economic dependency: One leader faced it in 1967 and the other capitulated to it; and there was the difficult matter of Egypt's relation to the Arab system of states, both during the stalemate years of 1967 to 1973 and, later, at a time when the oil revolution had created new realities and rival centers of power. The last question was the old issue of the Arab–Muslim order and the West. Where Nasserite Egypt once led the rebellion against the West, Sadat was to move all the way to a special relationship with the United States. Some of the drama can be understood by focusing on the two "kings." But it is important not to let their performances and the passions about them overwhelm us, for even in one of the most centralized of cultures – a place where men once worshipped rulers as deities – the logic of a society's history and its predicament can use the life of kings for its own ends.

THE LEGACY REASSESSED

Great charismatic figures have, as it were, two careers: one while they live, and another after they pass from the scene and their legacies are fought over by their followers. The fight over what they leave behind is often more intense than the fights they generated when they were alive. The great leader is more flexible than those who seek to emulate him; he has no text to follow, no chapter and verse to cite; he can make up the text as he goes along. Different claimants to the great leader's legacy pose another problem: Are the real heirs the ones who fill the institutional void he left behind? Or are there more legitimate claimants who, although removed from the position once held by the great leader, may nonetheless be able to claim his mantle? Finally, there are the endless problems posed by concrete policies: Would the great man have handled it that way? Have his successors deviated from his path?

Eventually these debates are transcended. The leader ceases to be remembered with the same passion and intensity; once-timid successors go on to assume power in their own right; one faction decisively wins, and it either turns the legacy into an incantation that loses its evocative power or it slays it. But before that occurs, there is that critical period when the legacy is a potent weapon and a real issue, when people talk about the memory of the leader but have something else in mind: their own interests, the distribution of power, this or that compelling issue on the agenda.

Nasser's legacy persistently haunted and troubled Sadat; it became a weapon brandished by his rivals in the Arab system and by his critics at home. But legacies can become inflexible when they are brandished as weapons and when they are remembered by those who want something to hold up against what they see as a compromised world. Qaddafi's Nasser is a hero, a rebel, a modern-day Saladin who in time would have redeemed the Arab world; Sadat's post-1967 Nasser is recalled in Sadat's autobiography as a "living corpse."[7] That is why legacies have to be rescued from true believers and harsh critics and why we need a basic reconstruction of what the "great man" left behind and how he responded to the wounds inflicted by the June defeat.

Part of Nasser no doubt died on June 5, 1967, but the "living corpse" somehow survived for another three years at the helm, assumed his role as a "resister," was given a new mandate of sorts with the popular demonstrations of June 9 and 10, and went on

97

to preside over the redefinition and transformation of Nasserism. The charismatic relationship between him and the masses formed during the bright youthful days of Bandung and Suez was shattered with the defeat; another variant, born out of despair and a sense of loss, sustained him until his death. He would stay in power not as a confident, vibrant hero, but as a tragic figure, a symbol of better days, an indication of the will to resist.

Sadik Abdul Hamid, a character in Najib Mahfuz's *Al Maraya*, conveys the way in which the leader manages to survive: Sadik Abdul Hamid was an educated man who believed in the "July 23 Revolution" and was willing to overlook its errors. When the "thing" happened on June 5, he was overcome with grief and despair; he wondered why no one was going mad or committing suicide. But then he recovered his composure and came to believe that the continuity of the revolution was the central issue: "The more he heard of the enemies' wish to liquidate the revolution the more firmly he became committed to it until he sincerely believed that the continuity of the revolution was more important than the recovery of the occupied Arab land, for what good is it to recover the land and lose ourselves?"[8]

Nasser's genius and the popular need for belief in someone, in anything enabled Nasser to rise above the defeat. The leader was dissociated from the defeat and invited to go beyond his political apparatus and to purge the elements that had supposedly captured and undermined his revolution. For the true believer, the Egyptian defeat was easy enough to explain. There were really two states in Egypt prior to 1967: One was the state of revolutionary Nasserism with all its accomplishments; the other was the state of power centers, which was doubtless an obstacle in the way of greater accomplishments by Nasserism. The state loses, but the leader rises from the ashes of his regime, supposedly to go on and deepen the revolution.

Beneath that level of metaphysics and belief, Nasser's game was to become purely defensive: how to deal with his own legacy and previous ambitions; how to shore up the popular will in the face of despair; how to absorb the frustrations and anger of youth; how to tackle Israeli occupation, inter-Arab matters, and the frustrations of international diplomacy. All this he had to do while his own health continued to falter. His own health was a metaphor for what had gone wrong – his revolution was, like him, exhausted and finished, the daring of youth had ended in tragedy and an incentive somehow to redeem himself before death caught up with him.

Egypt was Nasser's principal arena, but he had also to worry about the wider Arab theater. The immediate need was to secure the economic help of the oil states; more remote was the need to check the radicalism that erupted in the volatile Fertile Crescent. The first task required a deal with a former rival, King Faisal, and the deal was negotiated by the Sudanese Prime Minister Muhammad Ahmad Mahjub and concluded during the Khartoum summit conference that met in August, 1967. As Mahjub recalls it in his memoirs, he told King Faisal that as a "noble Arab," Faisal should refrain from killing a wounded rival but should instead nurse him to health and offer him a choice between a duel and an understanding.[9] The Egyptian "revolution" was on the defensive; the Arab cold war that had generated so much sound and fury had become banal and irrelevant.[10]

The radical delegates to the Khartoum summit conference – Algeria, Iraq, the PLO delegation headed by Ahmad Shuqairi – had come to the meeting expecting a fight with the conservative oil states, but they now had to contend with Nasser. Their radical proposals were lamely withdrawn: "The Arabs' petroleum," wrote Ahmad Shuqairi with his usual rhetorical flourish, "triumphed over the Arabs."[11]

Nasser's course at Khartoum was novel: He read the situation correctly. While in Khartoum he was to concede privately to Mahjub and Shuqairi that Egypt was on the verge of breakdown, that there were plots and schemes in the military and dissatisfaction among the population, that he was not sure he could keep things under control. "Exporting revolution" and "supporting the progressive forces" were the luxuries of a more youthful era. The Egyptian state was face to face with its limits, and it had to fight for its survival. The notion that revolutions are born out of despair is a naive stereotype (de Tocqueville had devastated it long ago in *The Old Regime and the French Revolution*, but it is still a popular dictum). Pushed against the wall, devoid of hope and resources, men and societies do not rebel: Instead, they give up, they surrender, they make compromises. And that is what Nasser had to do, as much as his history and personality would allow him to. Egypt, he was to tell President Boumedienne of Algeria and the Sudanese Muhammad Mahjub, was the "big fish" of the Arab world and was now "on the hook"; it could die slowly or try to break free. A dialogue with the United States – the United States, he said, had proven a skilled fisherman – was hopeless.[12] The best he could do was set the stage for his successor, someone who might be able to initiate such a dialogue. Meanwhile, he had to keep the troubles and the doubts within Egypt from tearing the country apart.

The confusions and frustrations of the country found expression in a deep generational split between the custodians of the regime on one side and the students on the other. The youthful revolution had been tarnished; the seemingly invincible leadership suddenly looked vulnerable, and there were all kinds of demands. There were communists on one extreme and Muslim Brotherhood adherents on the other; there was a world of difference between those who wanted to liberalize the economy and those who wanted to make sure that the populist gains were not lost, between those who wanted an all-out war of national liberation and those consumed with the understandable human desire to be left alone to pursue normal lives.

Whatever else they did or did not do, the popular demonstrations of June 9 and 10 had given the citizenry a sense of their own power. Spontaneous or not, they had become part of the regime's self-defense and, hence, directly and indirectly sanctioned popular initiative. The protests that erupted in February and November of 1968 and that were to become a recurring feature of 1967–1973 Egyptian politics served notice on the regime that it had to change its ways, that it was no longer omnipotent, as it used to be. In both of the 1968 demonstrations, trouble erupted over a particular issue, sparked latent discontent, and turned into a full-scale confrontation between the regime and the students.[13] The immediate pretext that touched off the February demonstrations was the light sentences, given to the accused officers by a military tribunal that had been looking into the June defeat. The issue was symbolic: the military class that had led the nation for fifteen years and dragged

it to defeat would persist in protecting its members. No crime –
not even wasting the lives of thousands of Egyptians, losing Sinai,
and blocking the Suez Canal – would be adequately punished. In
November, 1968, demonstrations started in the city of Mansura,
after a clash between the students and the police took the lives of
several students, spread to other cities, and escalated into a major
confrontation in Alexandria. In both Mansura and Alexandria, the
army had to be called upon to put down the riots. The two erup-
tions shook the self-confidence of an already traumatized regime:
In a traditionally deferential and stable society, neither deference
nor stability could from then on be taken for granted.

The regime tried to put forth the best possible interpretation of
what gave rise to youth unrest. Nasser explained it away as the
"urgency of youth" and youth's understandable desire for reform.
The organs of the regime played up youth unrest that was then
sweeping other societies – France, the United States, and so forth.
The implication was that there was a worldwide groping among
the young and that Egypt was just another society confronted with
angry, confused youth trying to make sense out of their own lives.
The first outburst was explained away as a spontaneous response
to the verdict of the military tribunal – a verdict that the regime
quickly proceeded to overturn. But neither this limited explanation or the phenomenon of worldwide student unrest really came
to terms with the predicament of Egyptian youth. One explanation
was too limited, the other too cosmic.

The verdict of the military provided the spark, but the fuel had
already been there. One account by a participant observer, then
an engineering student at Cairo University, shows that the verdict
of the tribunal was one of eight issues raised by the students and
that it was of low priority. The common denominator of the other
seven demands was the question of authority and freedom: the
regime's style, the rights of youth and other groups in society, the
arbitrary power of the state. Two of the demands called upon the
state to rein in the power of the police; one called for an independent legislative assembly with real political power; one asked for
freedom of expression and for a free press. This last demand, as
the engineering student reminds us, was to reappear in all the student declarations of the succeeding years.[14] The semiofficial *Al-*

Ahram was one of the student's continual targets, and, under Nasser, there was a particularly deep hostility to his spokesman Mohamed Heikal. The editors and the spokesman were to change under Sadat, but the hostility persisted. At issue was the moral responsibility of the written and spoken word. The spread of mass education and literacy, greater exposure to the outside world, and the June defeat itself as a great teacher, had made it more difficult for the rulers to get away with what they had gotten away with before. A generation that had been systematically lied to, and told that a new world was in the making, was in effect saying, "We have had enough of your distortions, and because we will have to pay for your errors and decisions, you'd better tell us the truth, no matter how difficult and painful."

A message was being delivered to people like Mohamed Heikal: The audience was no longer as gullible as it used to be; it could see through the apologetics and distortions, it wanted a new language and a new style of discourse – one that dispensed with hypocrisy and pretensions. The old school had lost its hold on the symbols, its pretensions had become transparent, its memories almost irrelevant. For fifteen years, it had insisted that it represented the wave of the future, that it broke with the defeat and betrayal of the old world. But now it was clear that this was mostly illusion, that the new forms were empty shells, that the slogans were hollow. So deep was the split between the old school – how bitter it must have been for the youngsters of 1952, for the new nationalists to age before their time! – and the new sensibility that it often seemed that the two sides were using two distinct languages and mental frameworks, inhabiting two radically different worlds at war with one another. As the testimony of the engineering student puts it: "I used to feel that I lived in a different society from the one inhabited by the people outside the college. Here we are free and they are the slaves; we are the judges and they the accused; we are the truthful ones and they the liars."[15]

The political tradition itself was on trial in the encounter between the rulers and the young dissenters. The men in power thought that the state belonged to them and that outsiders could not be trusted with the truth and were not entitled to it. The students wanted the state to trust others and mobilize them, to shed its fears and suspicions. This sentiment was reflected in a remarkable statement made by a student leader in a session of the Arab Socialist Union, the country's legal political party, chaired by President Nasser. Youth, said the student leader, still believed in Nasser, they were still with him. The President was suggestively reminded that the young stood by him in the "darkest hours" of the defeat when he was defenseless, that they were the ones who turned the "shifting sands" beneath his feet into "solid ground" on the days of June 9 and 10, that nothing stood in their way then had they really wanted to undermine him and his order.[16] In other words, the state need not always be on the defensive: Liberate individuals from the tyranny of state power and engage them in a common effort if you want the political order to stand on its feet and to stand up to the outside world. A worker from Suez struck a similar note: Involve the young if you want them to fight and die, inform them of the decisions that affect their lives. The young used to hear about the battle but not directly experience it: They would hear about clashes across the Suez Canal as though they were remote events in Vietnam.[17]

The individual had all along been a subject of history; people had been and remain spectators to their own destiny. The sultan was being asked to share political power, and the daring needed to ask him was supplied by the great defeat of a few months ago. Israel's success lent courage to those who could now insist that people who witness their own destiny, who stand idly outside history applauding when sham political parties ask them to do so and trusting that a seemingly masterful and heroic figure can do it all on his own, will be prey to others.

Economic concerns and anxiety over careers and private lives gave to the encounter between the regime and the students a grim and desperate dimension. Mass university education made possible by the regime's populism had produced a glut of university graduates who had to be employed and whose expectations surpassed the capacity of the economic system. The regime had had a difficult choice to make: It could restrict access to university education, it could expand the educational system but make the graduates fend for themselves in the marketplace, or it could guarantee both university education and employment. For obvious political reasons, it had chosen the third option, and the result was an inefficient, bloated public sector that guaranteed economic survival but engendered deep frustrations and a sense of uselessness. At a time when patience was wearing thin, when the seeming verities began to unravel, the inequity of the system could be more clearly seen and became more difficult to defend. The privileged economic position of the officer corps had been an obvious but more or less tolerated fact of life.

In defeat, the socioeconomic ascendancy of the military became unbearable, and the dormant resentments of the civilian graduates toward their military counterparts came to the surface. Because the military officers held such an ascendant position in the public sector, there was now an undercurrent of support for the private sector among the students. The motive was not so much a revolt against socialism but a simple desire, born out of frustration, to encourage a competing system of production wherein the deck was not as heavily stacked in favor of the military. If socialism had degenerated into a rule of the Mamluks, then why not try something else?

The wind was blowing from all directions: On one extreme was the call for domestic austerity, a war economy, and a people's war of liberation. On the other were the enemies of the regime, who saw in the defeat an opportunity to roll back the changes of recent years. In between was the bourgeoisie, whose support the regime had to bid for. This Nasser understood, and he made an offer to share political power – that was the meaning of his so-called March 30 Declaration. He was willing to change the symbols and style of the regime that had alienated them. Instead of the language of revolution, he would now speak of efficiency and science; where he had previously appealed to emotions and instincts he would use more sober, technical language. Instead of making noise about justice and equity, he would pay homage to efficiency, productivity, work.

Together with the change in symbols went some economic concessions: If the regime could not engage in a full-scale war, it could lower the barriers to imports, bring in more cars and other consumer durables, give the middle-class peasantry more incentives. Whereas the Yemen war had been financed out of consumption – private consumption had declined from 72 percent to 68 percent of GNP during the Egyptian intervention in Yemen – a critical political decision was made after 1967 to keep private consumption stable. Rearmament was to be financed at the expense of the investment sector, which dropped from a high of 18 percent of GNP prior to the Six Day War to a low of 13 percent in its aftermath.[18] This was a decision with awesome consequences in the years ahead: Consumption levels had to be maintained while the infrastructure continued to deteriorate. The moment of reckoning was postponed, and others – Russians, Arab oil states, Americans – were to help keep things from coming apart. The dependency that Nasser had found so repugnant was to become a fact of life. The choices available to the men in command would be reduced to a choice among different backers.

The economic concessions to the middle class were one side of the regime's response to its crisis; the war of attrition across the Suez Canal was another. Whereas the first sought to create a sense of normalcy and to preempt the potential opposition of the middle class, the second appealed to the patriotism of all Egyptians. Moreover, the fight across the Canal served to underline Egypt's role as the critical Arab actor. When the Palestinians struck out on their own in early 1968 and proclaimed the beginning of a guerrilla war of national liberation, they posed a deep psychological challenge to Egypt's sense of preeminence and confronted the Egyptian leader with a set of thorny problems. For more than a decade, it had been an article of faith that the hope for doing something for the Palestinians rested on Nasser and his army: That was Egypt's burden and role. Now, in a dramatic reversal of fortunes, Egypt stood paralyzed and ineffective and the Palestinians were raising bright banners and offering a desperately anxious and demoralized Arab world a sign of manliness and courage. The Arabs, in their folklore a martial race fed on tales of courage and sacrifice, had come face to face with a reality that contradicted that image. At that bleak moment, Palestinian defiance and guerrilla incursions provided reassurance that all was not lost. For a while the Palestinians were able to beat Nasser at his own game: Their communiques exaggerated their achievements, and they offered grand solutions and some hope. Whereas Nasser and Egypt seemed resigned to an unhappy status quo, they rejected; while he pleaded before the world, they resorted to force. They were new and he was old; they were the revolution, and he was a missed opportunity.

A master of street politics who knew the political power of images and impressions, Nasser realized that this was a fight he could easily lose and that sooner or later he would have to give substance to his view that the fight with Israel was an interstate matter that required the skills and weight of regular armies. Afraid of the potential for disorder inherent in the politics of his rivals, determined to maintain the initiative in inter-Arab politics and to keep the fragile balance within Egypt itself intact, he threw the war of attrition into the equation. The enemy's fire and punishment were preferable to domestic and Arab disorder. This was to provide an antidote to his rivals' romanticism, proof that the stable, orderly politics he represented were the Arab world's only realistic hope. Surely the guerrillas could help, and Nasser knew their popular appeal and was not about to risk an open attack against them, but the principal role was not theirs. The fight across the Canal was both a fight against Israel – for by then Nasser had begun to state that Israel was bent upon freezing the cease-fire lines and imposing a new status quo in the area – as well as a response to his new rivals in the Arab world. His calculations were largely accurate: The stiff response of Israel to the war of attrition inflicted great damage, but it bought time; it supplied proof of the will to resist. And when Israeli statements began to suggest that the aim of Israel's deep penetration bombing was to topple the Egyptian regime and make the costs of the war intolerable, that was the kind of politics that Nasser could thrive on. Bitter enemies are not particularly good at toppling regimes; the more ruthless an attack against a besieged leader, the more heroic he becomes. So the bombing raids that were intended to topple Nasser wound up making him "the symbol of courageous resistance at a time of national crisis."[19]

Caught between the pressures of those who wanted him to negotiate and normalize a world that had been in constant turmoil and those who were fired up by the need for revenge and restoration of pride, between one superpower committed to his enemy and one that now could take him for granted and synchronize him into its global design, between young revolutionaries who could suddenly see that he had failed to be heretical and rebellious enough and a traditional Arab order that had gained a new lease on life after 1967, there was very little Nasser could do but try to juggle all these pressures. There was no longer a big project under way. Worse yet, he had lost land in a country where ownership of land takes on obsessional overtones. Under him, a country that had been plundered, invaded, occupied, where occupiers came and managed to stay long stretches of time, was to witness yet another occupation.

Nasser's intuition, eloquently expressed to Boumedienne and Mahjub, was correct. Others had to get Egypt off the hook. So he died leaving a mixed legacy, enabling someone like Heikal to say that Nasser's story was not yet finished, enabling a Qaddafi to go on with his own brand of Nasserism, to claim as he does on the cover of his pamphlets and books that Nasser designated him as the trustee – *al-amin* – over the fate of Arab nationalism.

But Qaddafi's version of Nasserism and the Nasserism of the die-hard believers in west Beirut share very little with the late stage of Egyptian-style Nasserism. Qaddafi's is more buoyant, because it is the philosophy of loud, rebellious youth, sheltered from the wounds, the constraints, and the traumas of original Nasserism. Qaddafi's is a desert philosophy engendered by wealth and possibilities. Because his baggage is light – a small population, a high income – Qaddafi could fly as high as his imagination could take him. Nasser's base was a more impoverished, more crowded land, and it set limits to his expectations and possibilities, particularly in the latter part of his career. Whereas Qaddafi's philosophy is bedouin, Nasser's philosophy bore the mark of a crowded, wise – some (including Qaddafi) would say cynical – city that had long been used to applauding winners, forgetting losers, and coming to terms with things it did not like. West Beirut's and Syria's brands of Nasserism are altogether different things. The first was an oppositional doctrine, a protest by Muslim Sunnis against the dominance of Christian Lebanon, a yearning for a Sunni Arab order. It was only natural that the young of West Beirut and the pan-Arabists in Syria would respond to Nasser, for he came to embody both pan-Arabism and (despite his secularism at home) Sunni internationalism.

Qaddafi and his fellow officers neatly illustrate Nasser's predicament: However serious he might have been in his commitment to normalize the Arab system, to reopen channels of communication with powers he had alienated, to sober a generation he himself had fired up with excitement, and to turn his attention to Egypt and her troubles, the hero still had a role to play; the script had long ago been prepared and he could only introduce minor variants. It remained for his successor to play the part. Mr. Sadat had never excited a pan-Arab audience; he had never been a hero, and if he lacked the hero's stature, he also lacked the hero's reputation and was free of the chains that tie heroes to their great deeds.

If anything, Sadat — and this is only human — who had long lived in Nasser's shadow, would find it gratifying to slay the myth that was to a great extent the work of his predecessor — a man he had once known as an equal and who had managed to rise above Sadat and other colleagues to almost mythical and heroic proportions due in some part to the love and devotion of people in distant Arab capitals. This is where the psychology of the leader intrudes: Sadat could hope to compete with his predecessor in Egypt proper, but in the Arab world his predecessor was larger than life. There was perhaps in Sadat's Egyptianness a desire to move from Nasser's shadow into a smaller arena in which his predecessor seemed more real and less glamorized, more subject to errors and to a normal, more tangible assessment. In Egypt, as contrasted with the Arab world in general, Nasser was more likely to be seen realistically, to be criticized.

THE EGYPTIAN SEARCH

While others outside Egypt would hold their memories of Nasser, the real-life people who inhabited Egypt — very much like Mahfuz's characters — would go on debating war and peace, civilization and religion, the Arabs who won and those who lost in 1967, the real intentions of the Soviet Union, and so on. The same debates would repeatedly take place in the higher councils. The new man at the helm, less sure of himself, less entitled to his position, would say, as he did during a meeting with his generals, that there was no other choice but to fight, that it was a matter of survival: To be or not to be. But sooner or later the chatter had to end if the Egyptian state was to remain in command at home, to redeem its standing in the Arab system, to check the appeal to Mu'amar Qaddafi, to challenge the detente of the superpowers and the complacency of Israel. Above all, it had to do something to resolve its own doubts about its own capabilities and integrity, to open a new path. One leader presided, but he seemed paralyzed; he needed his own great act if his Egypt was to come into being. His corrective movement of May 15, 1971, which ended in his victory over the apparatus left by Nasser, was not enough; from the Libyan desert there was a claim that it was the young Libyan – armed with the Quran and with oil wealth – who was more qualified to continue the march. At home there was frustration and skepticism, spilling over every now and then into student riots and clashes between Muslims and Copts; in the Arab system there was a malaise deep enough to prompt a sensitive observer of Arab politics such as Arnold Hottinger to write that Arab radicalism might yet create a social order that resembles "present-day China more than any other society now known to us."[20] Globally, there was a detente between the two superpowers that broke the back of nonalignment that a whole generation of Arab and other Third World nationalists had lived on since the days of Bandung and charismatic leadership such as that of Nehru, Sukarno, Nasser, and Nkrumah.

Politics were now more psychologized than ever: their vocabulary and concerns had nothing to do with concrete policies and issues, but with questions of survival, of *qalaq* (anxiety), of pending storms and confusions. The word that the Egyptian regime and other Arab regimes had used so frequently – the "battle" – had to be made real if these regimes were to survive, and it was in Egypt that the psychological burden of the defeat was heaviest and where the frequency with which the battle was invoked had itself become another political issue. In early January, 1973, a group of the country's most celebrated writers and intellectuals issued a public statement that asked the regime not to further cheapen a word that had "lost its power, effectiveness, as well as credibility." The group said that the references to the battle had confused the young, whose "path was blocked," who worked for their diplomas only to be sent to the front "where they forget what they learned and don't find an enemy to fight." The state had to be honest "if the fog was to be cleared and people were to know what lay ahead."[21]

Recurring like a litany in the statements of officials and critics alike, in works of fiction as well as in more conventional social discourse, was the reference to the path that had to be cleared, the corner that had to be turned. The country's doubts had to be resolved and its fears exorcised, and the leadership was to find in the limited war of October, 1973, a way out of the fog and confusions. It was a gamble; new problems awaited but at least the oppressive stalemate was broken. The war provided Sadat with his great act. The crossing of the Suez Canal became the mandate to create his kind of Egypt ("restore" may be a better word) and to move from his predecessor's shadow. It was a concrete act – a relief and a needed contrast to the volume of words and scenarios – and an answer to the skeptics in Libya, the Fertile Crescent, and the oil states. The crossing was also a metaphor: Men like Mustapha Amin and Ahmad Abu al-Fath, two ancien régime journalists, the first of whom was imprisoned by Nasser and the other exiled to Switzerland, used the crossing to symbolize the break between Nasser's Egypt and Sadat's. In Mustapha Amin's exuberant style, a style that had once served the monarchy, then Abdul Nasser, and finally Sadat, the crossing was a "crossing from defeat to victory, division to unity, shame to dignity, oppression to justice, terror to security."[22] Nasser's Egypt stood for defeat, socialism, Arabism; the new, triumphant Egypt for a "free economy," a more responsible order, an Egyptian Egypt. "June's Egypt" had lost its way; "October's Egypt" regained its soul. The talk of revolution vanished; *Misr* (Egypt) was to become the new symbol. The Egyptian order began its march forward – into the past.

Such was the logic of one important intellectual verdict made by Tawfiq al Hakim, a man rightly described as Egypt's "dean of letters,"[23] in a book that helped launch the phenomenon of de-Nasserization. In Hakim's hindsight – the book was written in 1972 and published after the October War – the entire Nasserist experiment becomes a moment of madness; a leader mesmerizes an entire nation, "expropriates its mind," creates fake victories, and wastes the bread of a poor society in pursuit of a pan-Arabist mirage. Hakim's second thoughts on Nasser and Nasserism have an interesting twist: Four decades earlier, Hakim had written a work of fiction, *Awdat al Ruh* (The Return of the Spirit), which supposedly stirred Nasser's imagination.[24] The work had the standard themes of its time: the West and the East, the yearning for independence, the glory of the bourgeois–nationalist revolution of 1919, the splendor and miracles of ancient Egypt. The passage that must have caught Nasser's attention was an exchange between an austere English administrator who sees things as they are and a mystic Frenchman who sees the deep meaning behind things. This poor, wretched people, said the Frenchman of the Egyptians, still have the spirit of their ancient temples; all Egypt needs is a man to worship, someone who can "embody all its sentiments and wishes." Then the limitations would crumble and the Egyptians would build modern miracles. Nasser's emergence had made him Hakim's hero, but Hakim now saw it all as illusions.

With Nasser's spell broken by defeat, Hakim's nostalgia was now for another period of Egyptian history: the bourgeois, nationalist revolution of 1919. That revolution was the work of Egyptian society "looking for itself, resurrecting its spirit and civilization," whereas Nasser's revolution was made by the state; it was revolution from above, the will of one man whose socialism turned out to be a mere replacement of an old class with a new one, whose deeds were mere sound and fury, and achievements were nowhere to be seen. The "Egyptian revolution" had come full circle: The Nasserist order had imposed a near blackout on the liberal, nationalist phase of Egyptian history. Sadat's post–October 1973 order was to rediscover that phase – in it the archaeologists saw a better, saner, more proper Egypt, a place where the right men made the decisions, where people knew and kept their places, where the state was kept at bay. Its claims were limited, but so too was its reach into the private lives of individuals. "I thought that Egypt's history began on the 23rd of July," observed one of Najib Mahfuz's characters in *Al Karnak*; "it was only after the *al-Naksa* [the June 1967 setback] that I began to look for what preceded it . . . I will not hide from you that I admired that resilience of the opposition and its freedom, the role that the Egyptian judiciary played during that period. The old regime was not totally worthless; it had many intellectual elements that deserved to continue and flourish. The negation of these elements was a factor in our setback."[25]

This kind of political archaeology was primarily domestic. But it had implications for the mix of Egyptian nationalism and Arabism, for the relation between Egypt, where Nasserism governed, and those in the Arab world for whom Nasserism was an exciting change. The urge of Egyptians to look back at the Nasserist period, the natural rage of those who had been victimized by the Nasser regime, or the skepticism of those who had experienced the Nasserist system as it really was clashed with the nostalgia and fidelity of the Arab Nasserists who still saw Nasserism as a grand epic. In Egypt, observed the astute Mohamed Heikal, Nasserism was *hukm* (rule, a regime), but elsewhere in the Arab world it was *hulm* (a dream).[26] The Egyptian urge to undertake an internal audit of the seamy side of the Nasserist system – the tales of torture, the many tales of corruption that provided a radically different picture from the regime's socialist incantations, the pettiness of the men at the helm, the sordid and banal ways in which men larger than life really behave – was in the eyes of the Arab Nasserites sheer blasphemy.

It was suspected that the internal audit was a disguise, merely a dress rehearsal for an attack on Egypt, on Arabism. If a society blessed with such a great heroic figure would still find it within itself to attack his memory and achievements, then there must be something wrong with the society itself, something craven and unprincipled. In contrast to the lofty world of metaphysics and ideology, the private and tangible concerns of Egyptians were petty and irrelevant. If the Egyptians objected to the record of Nasserism, then they could be seen for what they were: petty bourgeois consumers, bureaucrats who play it safe, squeamish men who fail to see a great historical drama at work and who willingly sacrifice their petty concerns at its altar.

This was the first impasse between the Egyptian state and those who came within the orbit of Nasserist experiment, with those in Libya, Syria, the Palestinian community and elsewhere who wanted

Egypt to stay the course, to be, so to speak, larger than it. In large measure, this was the logic of the Nasserist era playing itself out: Revolutions create constituencies, and there are always those who come from afar to believe and to applaud. It takes time to shake off such constituencies, to awaken them rudely to the fact that their expectations are one thing, but difficult realities are another. In some measure this was the predicament of Egypt in the Arab system of states that had been brought about by the defeat in 1967.

A unique blend of pride and weakness seems to have pushed Egypt along in the Arab system since her defeat in 1967; her so-called victory in October, 1973, gave her a margin for maneuver. But the country came up against a new inter-Arab order after October, 1973. This was an order that Egypt helped create. The perception that Egypt did not reap its harvest offers a better guide for understanding the conduct of the Egyptian state than class analysis or the will of the ruler. Behind the Egyptian choices, one can discern more urge and instinct than deliberate policies: a desire to break out, to put the decent past behind, and to turn over a new leaf.

On one level, the Egyptian–Arab disagreements over the diplomatic aftermath of the war – the first disengagement accord, the Sinai accord, the Jerusalem initiative, Camp David – built on top of one another: One step led to the next; the Egyptian leader felt his way through the dark, took a step, raised a storm, then rode it out on his way to the next step. Yet there is a prior explanation that is worth considering. The disagreement can be seen in the different assumptions about the October War itself. The Egyptians fought the war in order to give themselves more maneuverability on the Egyptian–Israeli front, in the Arab system, and between the two superpowers. In their eyes, the October War was a one-shot affair, a way of breaking out of the nightmare of the 1967 defeat. The men who made Egypt's difficult decision in 1973 did not intend that war to be the beginning of a new, sustained war with Israel or of another captivity in inter-Arab politics. Just as Nasser's war of attrition had been a way of regaining initiative in Arab politics, so too was the October War.

Programmatic statements by leaders are not the best way to understand what they do, but Sadat gave a clue as to what lay ahead

113

in his statement, *The October Paper*, published in early 1974. "The world after October 1973," he confidently observed, "was not the same as it had been before." Some homage was paid to pan-Arabism and the brave Syrian "brothers," but the first and primary element in the victory was *al-Wataniyya al-Misriyya* (Egyptian patriotism). The victory, said Mr. Sadat, was the accomplishment of an ancient, homogeneous people that had lived on the same plot of land for seven thousand years. The country had been repeatedly invaded, but it managed to escape the tribal and sectarian divisions that plague other societies. The "seven thousand years" symbol and Egyptian patriotism had been discarded during the Nasserite revolution. Their reappearance in the October Paper was no accident: The Egyptian state was pushing its case for a new deal in the Arab order and reminding others of its advantages – a centralized authority, homogeneous population, an independent nationalism.[27]

We know from the memoirs and revelations of some of Sadat's close associates that there was an urge to prove Egypt's capabilities to other Arabs, a realization that other Arab states were not going to help Egypt so long as the country did not perform its role as the Arab world's principal fighting force. That is why the first shot had to be fired and the crossing accomplished before President Sadat dispatched Sayyed Marei, one of his closest associates and a pillar of the Sadat regime, to Saudi Arabia and the other oil states. There Marei and his delegation were to put before the oil states Egypt's accomplishments and needs. As Marei recalls it, he was under instruction from President Sadat not to ask for any specific sums of money: Other Arabs had to be made to face their obligations.[28] And some poignancies emerge from these meetings: how to calculate the value of Egyptian sacrifices, how to reconcile Egypt's grim and terrifying war with the other Arabs' demand – made by King Faisal – for a "lengthy" and substantial war, how to balance the four hundred million dollars given by Saudi Arabia and Egypt's sacrifices?

These questions were raised as the war itself was being fought on the Egyptian-Israeli front. They acquired greater salience after the guns fell silent and diplomacy began. War, says an Egyptian diplomat versed in inter-Arab affairs, is a "spectator sport."[29] Having helped subsidize the war, the other Arabs wanted it to last longer; they believed that the war was one battle in a sustained military encounter. But the Egyptian elite viewed it as a way of regaining honor, opening up new possibilities and horizons, setting straight the pecking order in the Arab world. What the Egyptian decision makers dreaded most was another stalemate, and that was precisely what the war had produced. A more intractable stalemate still – and probably another war – loomed on the horizon if Egypt were to try for a collective bargain. This was Sadat's reading of the situation; he reasoned that Egypt had enough weight to get its own terms and that was what he opted for.

Sadat could have done other things: He could, for example, have provided the facts about the October War, conceded that the Israelis had crossed to the other side of the canal, and that he needed Kissinger's mediation to save the third army. But he chose not to: Sadat and others in the Egyptian leadership had experienced the trauma and shock of the 1967 defeat. It would have been difficult for them to concede that the battle for which Egypt waited and prepared had ended unfavorably. The national pride of the society, the maneuverability of the state, and Sadat's leadership were at stake. The October War was his war, a source of his own legitimacy, his own great act, a chance to be something more than Abdul Nasser's accidental successor – the meek, inheriting political power. And as the October War took on almost mythical dimensions, Sadat was called upon to make good on the promise of October – his new order of peace and prosperity. This dictated his policies. He had become a captive of his own promises.

THE WAYS OF THE PHARAOH, THE WAYS OF OTHERS

The new order entailed territorial concessions from Israel, help and sympathy from the United States, acquiescence on the part of the oil states, and the cooperation of Jordan and Syria. Sadat reasoned that Syria had no place to go and would be forced to play by his rules; that Saudi Arabia's innate conservatism and its links to the United States would force the Saudis to go along with him. All of this obviously required the cooperation of too many other players.

But if some of Sadat's subsequent troubles were beyond his reach – he could not deliver the Saudis and Kuwait, he could not force Jordan and Syria to see matters his way – many other problems were caused by his style.

Sadat's preference for what he proudly called his "electric-shock diplomacy" faced others in the Arab system with serious dilemmas. Operating from a belief in Egypt's centrality to the Arab world, Sadat tended to underestimate the resources of others; sitting at the helm of a stable polity, he underestimated the troubles of other rulers who presided over countries more difficult to govern. His relations with Syria show how conflicting perceptions over national situations helped erode that alliance. Sadat commanded pliant aides and could take gambles and political risks, because such was the nature of the Egyptian political system. Asad lived in a different world: A member of a minority group governing a volatile country, he had to be more cautious. From Cairo, Sadat could take a relaxed view of Lebanon's troubles, of Palestinian radicalism. Indeed, Lebanon bought Sadat time: It tarnished Syria's appeal; it kept the Syrians and the Palestinians locked in a bloody and costly conflict. But for Asad the stakes in Lebanon were different. Lebanon was his next-door neighbor, and he was caught between the sympathy of Syria's Sunni majority for the Muslim–Palestinian–leftist alliance and his own fear that a victory by that alliance would trigger an Israeli intervention.

Lacking Sadat's base and distance, Asad had to stay in the game and play it with caution. He had to prove, at least to his own population, that he was shackling the Palestinians in order to enhance the Palestinian cause by ridding it of its extremism, and by avoiding the prospects of yet another radical and troublesome regime on the border that might drag Syria into an untimely war with Israel. That is why Asad could not go as far as Sadat and why he disassociated himself from Sadat's journey to Jerusalem. Whoever rules Cairo, observed the astute Lebanese politician Kamal Junblatt in his last political testimony – "his will" – is a pharaoh; whoever rules Damascus is a *wali* (a provincial governor).[30] The pharaoh could go to Jerusalem if he so wished; the *wali* could not. The fight between the pharaoh and the *wali* was not primarily over substance: Both had agreed on the limited nature of the October

War; both had accepted the harsh logic of Israeli military power; both knew what would play and what would not in the world of states. Neither of the two had radical views on the nature of the socioeconomic order. Their alliance faltered over tactics, over their sense of the permissible in their respective political systems. The battle between the two was narrower in scope than it was made out to be after the two had parted company. There were very few takers for the Syrian argument (made in retrospect) that their split with Sadat was ideological in nature, that rival priorities and philosophies had clashed.

Egyptian patriotism Sadat-style was quick to put Syria beyond the pale of civilized humanity. The "brave Syrian brothers" of October 1973 had become dispensable; they were never understood or appreciated by the average Egyptian. Damascus was far away, its politics and ways not easily understood through Egyptian categories. Syria's politics were volatile and unpredictable, her ways entailed risks and violence; Egypt's way was hailed by the civilized world that sets the codes of behavior, that knows the difference between the politics of despair and violence and the politics of responsibility. In the conservative Egyptian sensibility, Syria's politics (not to mention the politics of Libya and Iraq) were a whirlwind of blood and violence. "They are nothing," said the Egyptian daily *Al Akhbar* of Iraq, Syria, and Libya; they are closer to being insane asylums than modern states. Syria is a "Soviet colony" that massacres the Palestinians while talking of Palestinian rights; Iraq's leader, Saddam Hussein, loved the "spilling of blood."[31] For Egypt's stability – the oasis of the area – there is Syria's violence and Iraq's bloodbaths. Some of this is second-hand colonial imagery, some the inevitable difference between a society with a strong, centralized tradition and a culture in which people still take matters into their hands.

The image manipulated above was also Sadat's imagery: we see it at work in a critical speech by him to the Egyptian National Assembly in defense of the Camp David accords. "What is happening," he asks, "in the camp led by the Soviet Union? Syria devastates Lebanon; she comes in and liquidates the Palestinians at Tal al Zaatar and attacks the Muslims . . . then she turns against the Christians." The entire "Soviet camp" becomes a land of "torture, imprisonment, murderers, executions." Egypt is a threat to all those states, for it remains a "democratic oasis" that protects the dignity of man.[32]

Dispensing with Syria and Iraq was a relatively easy matter. The impasse with Saudi Arabia was more problematic, if only because the financial stakes for Egypt were considerable. Sadat had assigned Saudi Arabia the role of financier for his new order; he had assumed that Saudi Arabia would bless the shift of his country away from being the Arab world's military force to becoming its cultural and economic oasis. Saudi Arabia's design was different. The Saudis were not interested in turning Egypt into a viable economic entiry, even if that was within the realm of the possible. States do not charitably build up other states and create problems and competition for themselves. Egypt's demographic weight is awesome; Saudi Arabia is a sparsely populated society that must worry about the ambitions and claims of its neighbors. In Saudi Arabia's scheme of things, the Egyptian decision maker could move on his own, for the Saudis are firm believers in the right of Arab states to sovereignty over matters that lie within their domain, but the Egyptians must stay within the normative and political limits of the group and the overall Arab consensus. The Egyptian urge to break out and do things on their own was precisely what Saudi Arabia did not want.

Saudi Arabia's tribal ways and Sadat's preference for dramatic, solo performances go a long way toward explaining Egyptian–Saudi troubles. Tribes are collective entities that frown on loners; the order of the tribe must be kept intact and involves patterns of consultation, *shura*, ways of doing things through appropriate channels. Mr. Sadat's irreverence toward the accepted ways, his daring to think and do the unthinkable in going to Jerusalem, could only offend the conservative sensibility of a tribal society that sets strict limits on social behavior. Like a tribe, the Saudis' tendency was to wait and hope for the members who had gone astray to return to the fold. Their participation in the Baghdad summit in late 1978 showed that their hope had vanished. The brother was lost for good; his ways had become too eccentric for a world in which *bid'a* (innovation) remains a prohibition.

Then there were the conflicting perceptions between a rising

118

power (Saudi Arabia) and a declining one (Egypt). Each assumed that it would call the shots: the Saudis because they believed that the new world was theirs, that they had become the linchpin of the Arab system; the Egyptians out of habit. The Saudis' weapon was financial; Egypt's was the "one hundred thousand martyrs, the four wars," and Egypt's centrality. Each power chose to see the weak side of the other. To the Saudis, Egypt was a bottomless pit, a lethargic, scarred country, unable to win a war or to stick to a fight. On the Egyptian side there was the pride of the great city, the traditional urban contempt for the people of the desert. For all the talk of rural values and the mystique of the desert, Muslim Arabs are firm believers in the supremacy of the city: The desert appeals to Westerners, but the Arabs' romance is with the city. The hostility of Cambodia's Khmer Rouge to Phnom Penh as a soulless transplant of the West does not find a powerful echo in the Arab–Muslim order. Some of that feeling can be detected in Qaddafi's sermons on Cairo's nightclubs, her unveiled, liberated women, but Islam has traditionally been a religion of the city and Cairo was built by Islam. It was a monument to Islam's conversion of Egypt to the true religion of Allah.

This has given Cairenes the notion that they can reconcile the outside world and the world of Islam. During the heyday of liberal Egypt's experiment, Saudi Arabia and the Arabian peninsula could be looked at with condescension. Taha Husayn's important manifesto of liberal Egypt, *Mustaqbal al Thaqafa fi Misr* [The Future of Education in Egypt], written in 1938, came close to expressing a kind of "Egyptian man's burden" toward the less fortunate areas like "the Hijaz and the provinces of the Saudi Arabian state."[33] Egypt's financial resources may be limited, he observed, but Egypt should help educate those states if Egyptians were to live up to their "leadership and dignity." Nasser's Egypt had the same low opinion of the Saudi state. Under Nasser the contempt took a radical tone: a progressive, socialist state patronizing a decadent, feudal one. But the result was the same.

The world had changed since Taha Husayn's time, and it was no longer what it was at the height of the Nasserist experiment. But societies do not easily surrender their illusions; they do not adjust to their decline as easily as others would like them to. Social scientists removed from the scene may be able to play with indexes and measurements of power and to determine the ebb and flow in national resources and capabilities, but nations persist in their memories. And the Egyptians remain persuaded that Cairo is the capital of the Arab–Muslim order.

Another Egyptian advantage derived from a fact that non-Egyptian Arabs have rarely appreciated: By classical geopolitical definition, Egypt is the only nation-state in the Arab world. Egypt's rivals in the Arab systems were two kinds of states: either minority-based sectarian societies (Syria and Iraq) or dynastic entities (Saudi Arabia and Kuwait). The daring with which Sadat (and before him, Nasser) conducted matters of state reflected the security that came from an established political tradition. Sadat's repeated violations of Arab sensibilities left his Arab critics baffled, lamely insisting that the next violation would prove to be his undoing. Throughout the great turmoil triggered by the Iranian upheaval and at a time when other regimes were running for cover, Anwar el-Sadat was swimming against the current: openly hosting Begin, offering America military bases, offering asylum to the Shah of Iran, inviting others to stand up and be counted. Some of that was vintage Sadat style, some the security that comes from ruling a relatively stable national entity in which nationalism derives from millennial continuity and from the logic of modern nationalism, which played itself out in recent Egyptian history. Both the personal style and the security of statehood can be seen in one of Sadat's many contemptuous statements: "As for the leaders of the other Arab states, it is enough to look at their problems and the problems of their regimes. Hafez Asad now faces the revolt of his people and Saddam Hussein (of Iraq) faces popular upheaval in addition to his troubles with Iran. Even Saudi Arabia now faces internal difficulties despite its prosperity. There are now leaflets in Saudi Arabia that say that there is no ruler in Egypt with a salary of $8 million, no ruler who gambles with the wealth of his people. As for the states of the Gulf, they are threatened by Khomeini . . ."[34]

Old Egyptian cultural and political claims and political advantages helped justify Sadat's separate diplomatic path in defiance of the Arab rich, and so did new grievances. The simplicity of the image with which President Sadat and those in the intellectual establishment who saw things his way worked had its potency: On one side of the divide (Egypt) there was the blood of the October, 1973, dead and the tears of the survivors; on the other (Saudi Arabia and the Gulf states) there were both wealth and self-righteousness.

Two popular concerns that went beyond the confines of diplomacy and politics gave Egypt's diplomatic defection and battle with the oil states personal meaning and drama. In a country in which land is scarce and valuable, there was concern over land and real-estate acquisitions by rich Arabs, a feeling that Arab wealth was making Egyptians strangers in their own land. In a country in which notions of *ird* (honor of one's women folk) still move, imprison, and demean humans, there was concern that Cairo – to quote one influential editor – had become the Bangkok of the Arab world, that Arab wealth was violating Egypt's honor and integrity. Both the land acquisitions and the question of sexual liberties might have been exaggerated, but they were deadly serious and sensitive matters. The leadership did not have to dwell on these themes, but they were there in the country's popular films and magazines, part of Egypt's endless chatter. Arab wealth challenged Egypt's sense of self: Possessed by *arriviste* bedouins, it underlined the cruelty of a world that had gone awry. The imagined prosperity of yesterday had vanished; the change was not the fault of the Egyptian state; the reasons had to do with the costly wars waged by Egypt on behalf of the Arab states.

Sadat was to ride these sentiments all the way to Jerusalem and to exploit them in the aftermath of his deed. His initiative administered a psychohistorical shock to other Arabs. In its wake they would ask questions about him as an individual, but there were questions about Egypt as well. Was his trip an act of surrender, an expression of his and his country's despair? Or was it, as he himself claimed, an initiation of the Arabs into the modern world of states? Was his act the whim of an isolated sultan or was it an expression of Egypt's will? Was not his embrace of the West proof of his own alienation from the Arab world and by implication of his country's as well? There were doubts about Egypt's integrity, doubts that Egyptians are sensitive to and had heard often enough

Qaddafi's description of Egypt as an empty house with two doors, one from which the country "flirts" – notice the sexual metaphor – with the enemy and one with political reaction. The metaphor evokes the moral weakness of a country that changes its ways and where people easily surrender.

Other Arabs have never quite understood Egyptian crowds. The same crowds that once had hailed Abdul Nasser's Arabism were out in full force to greet Sadat's break with it; the same crowds that once had chanted against American imperialism gave Richard Nixon an unprecedented reception in the summer of 1974; the people who once had acclaimed Palestinian and Algerian revolutionaries embraced visiting Israeli negotiators with equal warmth. The malleability and fickleness of crowds trouble those who wish to think that there are durable loyalties that transcend and defy manipulations of rulers and sudden shifts of opinion. How were other Arabs to come to terms with Egypt's mind? Did Egypt speak through Abdul Nasser and Mohamed Heikal? Or was Anwar el-Sadat its authentic voice? The political gap that separated the Sadat regime from the Arab world had cultural and psychological foundations. Whatever his faults and shortcomings as a political operator, Sadat fully grasped this and exploited it: The weak country, its compromised capital, and patient, obedient peasantry would no longer fight and bleed for others. They had other options. Such, at any rate, was the president's gamble and choice.

What was the relationship between Sadat's own transgressions and Egypt's will? The other Arabs could go through the motion of distinguishing between their denunciation of Sadat and their professed respect for the Egyptian people. But the separation was difficult to make in practice. The tight control of the Egyptian media, which filter events and opinions, posed one logistical problem. But there were doubts about Egypt that the Arab professions of goodwill could not cover over, a suspicion that Sadat was not a solitary individual, that he did truly represent Egypt's inner self and her willingness to set aside the sacred struggle and accept a separate peace. Thus the Arab attempt to distinguish between Sadat as a solitary man and Egypt's will made at the Baghdad summit in November, 1978, and afterward, though understandable, is not particularly persuasive. The notion that the Egyptian problem was somehow a personal idiosyncrasy of Sadat, that a different leader would have acted in a radically different way, is one of those imponderables of history. But whatever the correct interpretations, it is wishful thinking to attribute it all to the will and style of the man at the helm. Leaders may read and exploit national wounds and grievances in a particular way, but we cannot fully comprehend why they get away with what they do if we only focus on the leader. The leader may be – as Mr. Sadat put it – a "solo performer on stage,"[35] but a meaningful evaluation of the theater must also take into account the audience's state of mind. It is there that gifted actors succeed or fail; the audience must appreciate and must applaud if the act is to last. To be sure, there were detractors in Egypt who doubted the wisdom of Sadat's path, and more substantial numbers who would have wanted him to do things in a different way – who were opposed to the style and extremism of Sadat's method rather than to the final goal – but overall, Tolstoy's verdict on kings may explain why Sadat was able to move all the way from the first disengagement agreement in early 1974, to the Sinai Accord in September of 1975, to his journey to Jerusalem, then to the exchange of embassies with Israel in early 1979. Sadat was simply an instrument of Egyptian history. The characters in Najib Mahfuz's sensitive fiction with whom this chapter opened wanted it this way, and it is worth restating that Mahfuz's work was written even before the October War. Some wanted to carry on as before, more were weary or dubious about the will and intentions of other Arabs, determined to find another way, to turn a corner.

Other Arabs may not agree, but there are grounds for arguing that Sadat may have been – albeit a bit too extremely and dramatically – an instrument of Arab history as well. Sadat's diplomacy dragged the Arabs, with most of them screaming and feeling defiled, into an honest encounter with the problem of Israel. He made them ask questions they had tried to avoid, face the reality of a state whose name they had previously refused to utter. The unspeakable, demonic entity was there, and a full-blown nuclear power at that, but the illusion persisted that some day the problem would vanish. As Abdallah Laroui poignantly said, it was known that "on a certain day everything would be obliterated and instanta-

123

neously reconstructed and the new inhabitants would leave, as if by magic, the land they had despoiled; in this way will justice be dispensed to the victims, on that day when the presence of God shall again make itself felt."[36] The failure of magic to do it meant that somehow that other entity had to be accepted and mentally dealt with. The "Egyptian mission," claims Sadat's minister of state for foreign affairs, Boutros Boutros-Ghali, was to get both the Arabs and the Israelis to accept, in Sartre's terms, the existence of the other – "faire admettre *l'Autre* – l'état juif – par le monde arabe; d'autre part, faire admettre l'Autre – le peuple Palestinian – par les Israéliens."[37] For the Arab world Sadat may have been codifying, making de jure, making public, a reality felt deep in the psyche of the wider Arab audience: that the Arabs somehow had to find a political and existential way out of the fight, that part of them was no longer there, so to speak, that wealth had changed the ways of many of them, that the fight with Israel no longer figured in their universe as prominently, as intensely as it had before. Egypt possessed the maturity to admit these harsh facts. Bruised and battered by the world, it could admit things that more sheltered purists – in the peninsula, in Libya – could run away from. Egypt, says the perceptive Egyptian scholar-diplomat Tahseen Basheer, had lost its virginity long ago: situated at the crossroads of continents, she had been plundered and invaded and had learned the ways of the world.[38] It was her mission now to teach others that the world will not allow total schemes, that purity is other worldly. Impoverished, crowded, close to the fire, Egypt could state and do things that other Arabs were too stubborn, too provincial, and too sheltered to accept.

THE PUSH OF THE DESERT, THE PULL OF THE MEDITERRANEAN

On his way to his first meeting with King Faisal of Saudi Arabia, Secretary of State Kissinger is reported to have asked President Sadat what to expect. "Well, Dr. Henry, he'll probably preach to you about communism and the Jews."[39] The statement says something about Faisal's obsessions, but it tells a lot more about Sadat. In a way it is the cultural pretension (and reality) of a relatively occidentalized country and leadership. Sadat's statement embraces Kissinger as a fellow modern man and puts Faisal at a distance. The first two speak the language of the age; they are both rational men, players in the modern game of nations. Faisal, however, is depicted as a tribal man, a bedouin with bedouin passions and biases.

Two themes have battled one another in recent Egyptian history: the push of the desert – the reality of a poor Muslim country – and the pull of the Mediterranean. The first suggests shared destiny with other Muslim Arabs and provides the raw material with which recent pan-Arab ambitions have worked. The second theme is th product of Egypt's relatively early initiation into the modern world system, dragged as she was into the modern world economy in the mid-nineteenth century. The first was Nasser's universe; the second came to be Anwar el-Sadat's. The first path was the one that Muhammad Ali opted for early in the nineteenth century; the second was the path of his grandson, Ismael (ruled 1863 to 1879) the modernizer, the cosmopolitan man.

The yearning for the West on the part of Sadat's Egypt is a complex psychological and historical phenomenon. It could be located in the personality of the ruler, but it had a history as well. So too did the resistance to it. The issue of a separate peace was bound to become a civilizational and cultural question, but Sadat's style and choices aggravated the crisis. Isolated from his locale, he slipped into greater dependency upon his American partner. This gave new life to cultural pretensions that had once been vanquished; it revived old fears and doubts about the powerful aliens and their ways, about the integrity of the culture and its wholeness. At the heart of the crisis lay the thorny and explosive problem of cultural dualism between an Oriental self and a modern wrapping, between a traditional culture below and more modern layers on top. Whether he meant it or not, President Sadat was to become heir to a particular legacy, lured by its temptations. Likewise with his critics at home: In brandishing what they thought to be new weapons, they discovered that the issues and the weapons were old indeed.

The roots of Egypt's cultural dualism can be found in the actions of its modernizing rulers and in the accident of its geography, situated as the country is in the path of giants. E. W. Lane's *Manners and Customs of the Modern Egyptians* (1835) gave an outsider's portrait of a traditional society and its equilibrium. A quarter century later, Lane's nephew would write in a preface to a new edition that the book could not be rewritten becuse the Egyptians are "yearly straying from old paths into the new ways of European civilization."[40] People had broken away from the ways of the ancestors and were being drawn into the network of an expanding European-based world economy and culture.

Egypt's rulers were confronted with a challenge and a temptation: the West as model, the West as threat. What under Muhammad Ali began as a legitimate attempt to copy the ways of the West yet keep it at bay turned into total surrender under Ismael. And it is Ismael who has lately been appearing in allegorial Egyptian criticisms of Sadat. Ismael's aspirations went beyond the desire to modernize. His aspiration was, as Nadav Safran writes, "no less than the transformation of Egypt into a part of Europe." To that end, he built "operas, palaces and promenades"; he thought of himself as having a "mission civilisatrice," a drive that led him in his pursuit of an African empire.[41] Ismael forgot where he was, forgot his cultural base, the poor plot of land that had to finance his ambitions:

> His ambition and imagination startled his listeners. In this hot straitened summer of 1864 he was thinking not only of canals and railroads, but of Paris-on-the-Nile and of Ismail, Emperor of Africa. Cairo would have its *grands boulevards*, Bourse, theatres, opéra. Egypt would have its large army, a powerful fleet. Why? asked the French consul. He might also have asked, How?[42]

The dream of turning Cairo into Paris ended in Egypt's financial ruin and her occupation by Britain. But Ismael's dream managed to live on. British colonialism had served its own kind of harsh notice as to the difference between pretensions and the real thing, but some held on to the European myth. Exactly half a century after the landing of British troops in Egypt, Taha Husayn, the influential Egyptian author, educator, and minister of education in the last Wafd government (1950–1952) published a manifesto of liberal Egypt's Western identity. The book expressed the yearning of a defeated people to be accepted by a world that had dominated them, the desire to give cultural mimicry the legitimacy of authen-, ticity by erasing the boundary between Egypt and her occupiers and asserting Egypt's oneness with the West.[43] Kipling's sharp division between East and West was no problem, Husayn assured his readers: Egypt's mind was not an Oriental mind; it was closer to Europe than it was to "China, Japan, India and the countries that surrounded them." Egypt was a Mediterranean civilization; its own illusions and backwardness prevented it from living up to its true self. "We must be able," Husayn told Egyptians, to make the European feel that "we see things as he sees them, evaluate them as he does, judge them as he does."

Egypt's Islam posed no problem for Husayn's cultural and mental geography. A secularist who had little regard for religion, a Francophile by culture, Husayn argued that Islam had not really Arabized Egypt. Just as Christianity – another "Oriental" religion – had converted Europe without orientalizing it, so too had Islam with Egypt: Islam gave Egypt its religion, but it left its Occidental core untouched.

Taha Husayn is a transitional figure between Ismael and Sadat. It is a supreme irony of recent Egyptian history that Anwar el-Sadat, who was part of traditional Egypt's revolt against the heritage of Ismael and the pretensions of the polished layers of Egyptian society, would live to be equated with Ismael, to reenact Ismael's wish and fate. Sadat's conversion is a riddle: Was his Westernism there all along? Had he acquired it through his second marriage to the urbane Jihan el-Sadat? Was it part of his own psychological settling of the score with Nasser, a search for a theater wherein he could outdo and go beyond Abdul Nasser, whom he came to recall as a traditional man? Was it the despair of a leader anxious for help – any help – to keep a crowded, poor society afloat? Or was he stuck with the United States and the West when he found himself cut off from other Arabs?

There is no doubt that Sadat underwent an immense psychological transformation: The man who in the early 1950s had complained to an American journalist that "the West hates the Arabs because they think that we are negroes"[44] became one of America's most popular figures; the man who once hated the West moved all the way to a full partnership with the United States, offering his

127

society as sentry to a barbarian region in turmoil. Anwar el-Sadat, a self-defined peasant from the dusty small village Mit Abu al-Qom, had exceeded his own expectations and travelled far beyond the bounds of his world; he had become more comfortable with American television reporters and French visitors than with former colleagues and friends.

To see his poor, dusty village – as I did out of curiosity, having read his autobiography and wishing to see the cult object that his village came to be – is to come to terms with the drama and ultimtely with the limits and tragedy of Sadat's epic. The personal dimension is undeniably grand: from Mit Abu al-Qom to the Nobel Peace Prize; from a lower-middle-class agrarian base in the Nile delta to the world as his theater. This seduced and propelled Sadat. He himself spoke of it with genuine astonishment at times. In setting aside for his village the royalties of his autobiography and the stipend of the Nobel award – an estimated million dollars – he marvelled about Allah's will and the hand of fate. With disarming candor, he would recall that a hundred pounds were considered a fortune in his village.[45] He would be what every Egyptian boy playing on the banks of the Nile would dream of being. He would go places for those boys; Everyman would become king.

But there is a public tragedy in all this: the escape from one's world, the theater as substitute for action. The dream of turning his impoverished village into something like the English countryside – he insisted that the houses to be built with his contribution should be painted white, for he recalled the quaint charm of the English countryside – was an escape from Egypt's troubles. That the small miracle was to be accomplished by Egypt's biggest tycoon, Uthman Ahmad Uthman, a relative of Sadat and a man whose financial dealings have become a symbol for corruption and inequality, conveys the futility of the act, an incapacity to see and solve problems. Sadat's concept of the self – all a man has to do is find his identity, the autobiography implies – and his idea of the simple village where honest men wait out history, where they accept their lot without *hiqd* (resentment) becomes a smokescreen for failure, a way of looking at troubles and pain without seeing them. That is why Cairo, with its noise and its troubles, its dissatisfied, "negativistic" intellectuals who fuel *hiqd*, became the target of so many of Sadat's sermons. Cairo is politicized – a Nasserite legacy; goodness is in the village where life goes on as before, where people scratch out a living but do it with dignity.

The myth of the village is connected with Sadat's courtship of the West. One wonders whether the idea of Mit Abu al-Qom was not taken out and dusted off for the sake of the West, so Sadat could present himself as a peasant going beyond his world, reaching out for people and places remote. Mit Abu al-Qom has no mystique for a Saudi or a Kuwaiti or an urban Palestinian or Lebanese. When those people go to Egypt they go for the lights of Cairo, for the civility and climate of Alexandria; the rest of Egypt is unknown to them. The people who go to Mit Abu al-Qom to find Sadat's roots on the banks of the Nile are German, French, and American. Arabs would not be moved or taken in by the myth of the village. They have seen such villages and most of them come from such places – places that hold little interest for them, places that they would rather forget.

The rediscovery of Mit Abu al-Qom was part political archaeology – to find the vision of a good, steady order where politics were the realm of the ruler, land in the hands of the landholder, and goodness and simplicity (and toil) the lot of the peasants. It was also part anthropology, an appeal to the West's romance with the exotic, its love for distant, dusty villages from which ambitious young men are propelled to great power and prominence.

The ideal of the village and the American connection keep problems away; they make it possible to escape from pan-Arab troubles, from economic collapse; they buy time and conceal reality. Both are manageable theaters: Sadat is a hero in his village – the local boy made good who gives some of his wealth and prominence to his village. The American connection provides economic protection; it also provides a sense of psychological mobility. Egypt is a world with strict normative, economic, and ecological limits. Sadat's discovery of America at a late stage in his life was an exciting personal saga. The world's mightiest power – and a civilized one as well – becomes Egypt's full partner. Libya, Syria, Iraq fade into cosmic insignificance. Egypt and her president break out in grand style. "Dr. Henry" was the President's friend; President Carter became a friend and a brother. The rich, civilized power from afar

129

will see to it that the Egyptian economy pulls through. The United States is a power possessing money and civilization – a reassuring contrast to neighbors that have plenty of the former but none of the latter. Sadat's success in courting America becomes Egypt's success; his appeal to the West lends credence to Taha Husayn's contention that Egypt's mind and culture is a piece of the Occident. Ismael played the game and lost; he cost Egypt wealth and independence. Sadat played the same game but would, supposedly, succeed. As for independence, it is a relative thing in today's world anyway. Besides, if Egypt had to choose between the patronage and conditions of the United States and those of the oil states, then surely the former was a better option: It is closer to civilization, less offensive to dignity and pride. Ismael's loans and collapse brought the gunboats of the West but we live in a more civilized world now. The donors have no choice but to continue to give: Egypt's and Sadat's weakness become sources of power; both must be propped up if civility and order in the region are to have a chance. The collapse of the Iranian base made the Egyptian case even more compelling: The oasis of stability had to be floated if the area was not to sink into further barbarism and disorder.

The coveted membership in that glamorous world is partly real, for the bourgeois age did leave many things behind on Egyptian soil, and partly an attempt to conceal and legitimate dependency. In that we see the fundamental dilemma of any liberalism removed from the core of the world system. Weak societies at the periphery of the world desperately flaunt the outward trappings of modernity, because the cosmopolitan layers intuitively feel their own isolation. On some level they realize that bourgeois civilization as process eludes them, that they may end up either with its things – in the form of machines or of "operas, palaces and promenades" – or with its outward pretensions and trappings. It is at that point that a line is crossed and the search for membership and identification with the West turns into paralyzing dependency. There is more than a sketchy historical analogy between the fate of Ismael's Egypt and the Egyptian predicament of today. An interesting account (published in 1897) of the fate of the Ismael's Mediterranean dream makes fascinating reading today:

130

Egypt under his [Ismael's] sway, has, to use his own boastful phrase, entered the family of European nations – very much as a bankrupt enters Basinghall Street; but the factories, boulevards, and palaces are only so many mighty mistakes of an obstinate speculator; and the mainspring of any sympathy which he has created between the East and the West is one of debtor and creditor. He has interested Europe in Egypt, by making the European the man in possession of his country.[46]

Are there some parallels between the way dependency was faced in Ismael's Egypt and the way it was handled in 1979 when President Sadat asked the Tokyo economic summit of the major industrial countries for a foreign aid package of $18 billion? To quote *Egypt under Ismail Pacha* again:

Ismail Pacha's submission to European control was a confession of failure, of bankruptcy, and of wrong-doing. Yet, he performed it with the air of a magnanimous prince who was accomplishing a noble deed of patriotism.[47]

In Egypt, wrote Flaubert to Louis Bouilhet in one of his letters from Cairo (December, 1849), "the European is accorded greater respect than the native, so we won't dress up completely [in native costumes] until we reach Syria." In an earlier letter to his mother from Alexandria, he had written: "One curious thing here is the respect, or rather the terror, that everyone displays in the presence of 'Franks', as they call Europeans."[48]

Others had made and continue to make similar observations: There is an awe of Westerners and things Western in Egypt. What Leonard Binder called Nasser's "protest movement" against the West[49] was on some deep level propelled by the need to defy, to say no, to assert some equality with the "Franks." It is easy to say that he overdid it, to note the absurdity of his theatrics, his compulsive search for autonomy and defiance. But nations do things in mysterious ways; they intuit their needs in ways that elude those who are ready with a judgment. The dependency on the United States in Sadat's Egypt, the mystic faith in the "Carter plan," the appeal to the industrialized countries to come to Egypt's aid, show the persistence of that propensity to depend. In their own way they offer a post facto explanation for some of Nasser's grand thea-

131

trics, for his almost neurotic obsession with independence. Egypt is yet to find that middle ground between dependence on the outside world and rebellion against it. The awe toward outsiders persists. That is why there is a legitimacy to the following query: Could it be that Sadat, the self-professed disciple of Sa'd Zaghlul – the symbol of Egyptian patriotism – managed to slay the pan-Arab myth of Abdul Nasser only to become a modern-day version of Khedive Ismael? Had the dialogue with the West and the fondness for things Western degenerated into the old dependency?

However considerable its drawbacks, the Ismael/Sadat Mediterranean temptation has all along had its adherents. Earlier I noted Taha Husayn's defense of Egypt's oneness with the West. The more recent debate about pan-Arabism triggered by the Sadat diplomacy revived the same genre of opinion.[50] Tawfiq al-Hakim's call for "neutralizing" Egypt assigned the country a role as the region's cultural center; just as Egypt was the museum of the world, she was the Middle East's cultural oasis. Politics was not Egypt's strong suit; pan-Arabism was the narcotic of the intellectuals, a catastrophe that befell Egypt and her population. The Arabs had come of age now: They had sufficient "manpower and wealth" to wage their own wars, and they need no longer burden Egypt with their problems, or set the country on a path that "paralyzes her thought, bleeds her, starves her sons."[51] Egypt had better return to its own roots, for all the sacrifices notwithstanding, leadership in the Arab world in now contested by those countries that possess wealth even though they did not "shed a drop of blood."[52] Hussein Fawzi, another Mediterranean scholar, echoed the same themes: Like Switzerland, Egypt should renounce politics and aim for neutrality – the sole "industry" of Egypt is culture, its principal mission is to serve as a broker for world trends. Egypt has suffered the rule of many outsiders; this "qualifies" it to be the "cultural museum" of the world, the cultural oasis of the region. Fawzi harks back to an earlier period of Egyptian history: the 1930s and 1940s, a period during which Egypt sought to deal "peacefully" with the question of Palestine until a "juvenile monarch" (Faruq) pushed it into a "losing war" and then another leader pushed it into a catastrophic confrontation that ended in the occupation of Egyptian land and the destruction and closure of the Suez Canal.[53]

Both al-Hakim and Fawzi were old men, both were nostalgic for pre-1952 Egypt, and both moved between Egypt and Europe. The Arab world was *terra incognita* to them. Beneath the ivory tower of al-Hakim and Fawzi, a generation of youngsters anxiously dip into the culture and artifacts of the West. Hitherto denied access to that glamorous world, they partake of it with vengeance and at the same time travel rapidly away from the poor, pious, traditional society around them.

But the Mediterranean pull has always generated a cross-current. The language of opposition may have differed from time to time, but there is a common denominator: Islam, Arabism, authenticity. The tragedy of Ismael's world view and later, of liberal nationalism, was its incapacity to stay at home with its own world, to keep a safe and respectable distance from the West. This may have something to do with the poor resource base, but there is a proneness to cultural dependency as well. What begins as a dialogue with the West ends in embrace and surrender. Then the legitimacy vanishes, and the adherents are exposed as collaborators. The need to appear modern to a Western audience erodes the base at home; the voice of authenticity reemerges to redeem self and pride. Ismael's surrender gave rise to the revolt of the soldier/peasant Ahmad Urabi in 1882. The failure of liberal nationalism and the incapacity of the generation of Taha Husayn to build an autonomous liberal path brought about the revolt of 1952 – a local breed hostile to Europe and to the vision of Taha Husayn but still distant enough from the fundamentalism of the Muslim Brotherhood, from the chaos engulfing Egypt. Their revolt came, as Safran writes, in the nick of time to spare Egypt the dire consequences of chaos and to stem the tide of fundamentalism.[54] The men who accomplished the revolution were in their own way heirs to the nationalist movement – less pretentious than the cosmopolitan liberals, more of this world than the Brotherhood.

When Taha Husayn wrote his liberal manifesto, another Egyptian, Sayyid Qutb, a brilliant thinker and activist of the Muslim Brotherhood, gave the answer of authenticity and the native culture to Husayn's pretensions. Taha Husayn's division of the world into East and West struck Sayyid Qutb as a fraudulent and incomplete division. Husayn, he said, had forgotten a whole world that had its own vision and integrity: the world of Islam. It was to that world that Egypt belonged, and all else would end in failure.[55]

Sayyid Qutb is no longer around; his activism cost him his life during the Nasser years. But the view that inspired him remains: It moves scores of pious young men and women at the nation's universities; it provides an answer to the complicated problems of a stalemated society. As always, its message is faith and integrity, its material the failure of the dominant order on the battlefield, in solving the problems of identity, in economic matters. New problems – peace, economic crises, the corruption of public officials – are easily accommodated into its flexible container. Its pamphlets and magazines – some undergound, some tolerated – offer a contrast to the banality and hypocrisy of the official media. Its tracts offer some easy solutions, faith instead of detail, but they also tell the truth about treaties, diplomacy, the corruption of officials.

The fundamentalist call has resonance because it invites men to participate – and here again there is a contrast to an official political culture that reduces citizens to spectators and asks them to leave things to the rulers. At a time when people are confused and lost and the future is uncertain, it connects them to a tradition that reduces their bewilderment.

The fundamentalist stand against President Sadat's diplomacy was part of a larger tapestry. It issued from a deep-rooted tradition. The Muslim Brotherhood's opposition to Camp David was phrased in familiar idiom: the struggle of the Prophet, the integrity of Islam, the need for sacrifice, the clash between the world of Islam and the Jews, who will "never abandon their belief that they are God's chosen people." Sadat's whole design was a false one: It accepts a "Middle Eastern order" – the Middle East is a repugnant term to Muslim sensibilities because it defines the Muslim world in relation to the West – "under Jewish hegemony." One cannot negotiate with the intruder and surrender historical rights; some conflicts cannot be wished away. Egypt was invaded before and it must again resort to resistance. All the rulers have to do is abandon their "fancy palaces," their expensive cars, and their pretensions. Islam taught men to struggle and die for worthwhile causes, and the believers must rediscover the will to persevere, the capacity for patience.[56]

Muslim fundamentalism may never carry the day in Egypt. Perhaps the society has gone beyond the puritanism of the fundamentalists and reached the point of no return. The Egyptians are sophisticated people (a cliché, to be sure, but true nonetheless): They know that the task at hand is to keep their world from falling apart, to keep their society functioning. Besides, they know the history of the Muslim Brotherhood. They saw the frenzy of its early idealism degenerate, as the 1940s came to a close, into terror and nihilism. They recall the fate of the Brotherhood's "Supreme Guide," Hassan al-Banna, living and dying by a code of violence and toward the very end of his life denouncing his own followers – most likely to save his own skin – as "neither brothers, nor Muslims." They recall the Brotherhood's collaboration with the monarchy, its curious mixture of reactionary politics and pious sermons.[57]

Short of the fire of the Brotherhood, even Qaddafi's relatively mild austere utopia would not stick on the bourgeois soil of Egypt. Cairo's professional women have long broken with the norms enforced in other Muslim societies. Egypt has the West under its skin. That is why Sadat – and Mrs. Sadat – could propose and pass legislation favoring women's rights at a time of seemingly fundamentalist reassertion all over the region.

There is an instinctive Egyptian dread of great crusades, a preference for those people and ideas who somehow steer a path amidst rival and extreme utopias. The Egyptian social predicament has been deep enough in this century to encourage millenarians and radicals of all sorts: fascists, Muslim fundamentalists, wild-eyed radicals. They had in common what all such movements possess: their belief in another world, in short, what Crane Brinton would call the "revolutionary ideal."[58] All received a hearing, but caution ultimately prevailed: Fascism found an expression in the Young Egypt party, which was a parody of the fascist movement that swept Europe in the 1930s and 1940s; the Muslim Brotherhood thrived at a time of crisis and continues to survive at the present. The Communists made their appearance on the scene with the establishment of a small group in Alexandria as early as 1921; and their fortunes were subject to the wild changes that such movements have suffered, but they remained "for most of the time a small coterie of squabbling and secretive theoreticians."[59] The dominant instinct was for the center: This is what sustained the more-or-less liberal experiment of bourgeois nationalism (1919–1952) and what inspired the revolution that stepped in to arrest the drift toward breakdown and extreme solutions. And this is the instinct that continues to guide the Egyptian ship on its ever-hazardous journey. The dialectic (if you will) between the radical temptation and the world as it is has generally favored the latter. This phenomenon is perceptively illuminated by the Egyptian intellectual Ghali Shukri in a brilliant set of reflections and essays on Egyptian social and political thought entitled *Mudhakkirat Thaqafa Tahtadir* (Memoirs of a Dying Culture). The Egyptian people, he observes, have always been deeply religious; this gave the Brotherhood room for maneuver and material with which to tap passions and to mobilize, but the Brotherhood failed because its reactionary extreme call "did not answer the need of a people yearning for progress." Likewise, Egyptian patriotism fed the Young Egypt party's fascist tendencies, but this extreme line also failed to mobilize a people who have synthesized "in their blood" many civilizations and religions. Egypt remained most hospitable to those who offered "peaceful, moderate ways."[60] This is not the kind of tale that would grip those who see societies driven by the purity of saints and the fire of revolutionaries, but this has been Egypt's tale.

Thus the importance of Muslim fundamentalism is not measured best in terms of its capacity to capture political power. Its power may lie in its ability to destabilize a regime, to help bring it down by denying it the religious cover that remains an important source of political power. Here the 1952 revolution is instructive. The Muslim Brotherhood helped topple the monarchy, but it became the victim and target of the new regime. Fundamentalism may supply fervor, some of the committed manpower, and the willingness to take the risks of political action. Other types – more capable of making compromises, less likely to frighten modernized young men and women – would inherit the postrevolutionary world.

This is where Muslim fundamentalism intersects with the surviving remnants of Nasserism and Arabism in Egypt. While in power, Abdul Nasser was brutal in his persecution of the active, militant Brotherhood. But Nasser's heirs and the Brotherhood share one thing in common: They are part of the indigenous path. Faced with one another, they discover all the things that separate them; faced with the adherents of the Mediterranean path, they can see what they have in common. The fundamentalists see in the Mediterranean path a betrayal of Islam and the Nasserites object on more secular, nationalist grounds, but both believe that the Mediterranean temptation is a mirage. For all his faults, Abdul Nasser remained at home in Egypt. To be sure, his ambitions exceeded his country's means; he made more than his share of errors, but he was never a mimic. He lived and entertained simply; he kept his wife away from the spotlight. These images have power in a Muslim society. Gaps in power between ruler and ruled are expected and tolerated; gaps in culture have a way of compromising the ruler or suggesting that he left his world behind in search of the lights and the glamor of the West. Ayatollah Khomeini's indictment of the shah was caused not so much by the shah's excessive power; it was his alienness, his distance from popular culture and religion. Heikal's Nasser – a simple man with a taste for simple, modest things – taps the same sentiments: The implication is that Abdul Nasser never strayed from Egypt and that Sadat did.

The Egyptian Nasserites' view – like that of Sadat – proceeds from the centrality and weight of Cairo. But they have a different Cairo in mind. As Heikal puts it in his book-length discourse on the Sadat initiative, the Cairo that decides on matters of war and peace is the one that embodies the "pan-Arab idea, current, historical movement."[61] Cairo, the capital of the Egyptian state, is a diminished entity. This is why Heikal faults Sadat's policy: It diminished Egypt and turned the country into a poor, vulnerable state on the banks of the Nile; amputated, cut off from the Arab world, it stood vulnerable and exposed. The old European dream of isolating Egypt from the rest of the Arab world was accomplished. This left the Arab world confused and without its balance but it left Egypt prey to the schemes and offers of others.

How did this come to pass? In the Nasserite view expressed by Heikal, the Egyptian leadership (presumably Nasser and Heikal themselves) should have explained to the population that Egypt was a party to the Arab–Israeli conflict, that Egypt was not fighting others' wars, and that there were serious geopolitical issues involved. Second, Nasser and Nasserism had taken Egypt's Arabism for granted. That, says Heikal in retrospect, was an error. Where a separate national identity existed, as it did in Egypt, there should have been a more vigorous mass-based Arabization of Egypt. Third, the lack of a fair inter-Arab division of labor created resentment and disillusionment in the confrontation states. Other reasons had to do with the harsh treatment by other Arabs after 1967 and with the continual hammering by other Arabs at the worth of the Egyptian experiment. This helped foster despair in Egypt, and the Sadat diplomacy was the product of such despair. If nothing made sense, if Egypt's revolution had been inauthentic (as the Arab left asserted), if its socialism was a failed state capitalism, then why not seek the safety of peace – any peace, on any terms?

But this too shall pass, the Nasserites maintain. The Mediterranean temptation will blow over, and Egypt will be reclaimed by its authentic habitat. Nasser's three circles – the Arab, the Islamic, the African – will prevail once again. Their hope evokes an image of Egypt larger than the riverbed it inhabits, and in the aftermath of the shah's collapse their view rests on faith in the ability of the culture and geography to assert themselves. Tawfiq al-Hakim and Hussein Fawzi's apolitical utopia – the Switzerland example, the neutralization of Egypt – drew fire from a wide range of thinkers. The critics' answers were long, reasoned, and passionate: All rejected the Mediterranean option, all said that it was not worthy of a self-respecting nation. Bint al-Shati (the pen name of a distinguished woman writer) recalled Lebanon's dream and fate: The Lebanese too wanted to be safe hotelkeepers, a neutral Mediterranean nation. Lebanon's collapse was proof that nations that play with their identities and deviate from their habitats play with fire.[62] Others warned that Egypt could not go it alone and lamented the incapacity of the Egyptian pendulum to stop in the middle – cycles of pan-Arabism alternate with isolationist periods; love affairs with the West are followed by calls to revolt and authenticity. Some threw into the debate harsh geopolitical realities. To them the push into the Arab system was not the whim of a charismatic leader but something decreed by the constants of geography: "The destiny of Egypt," observed one of the participants, "has always been linked to that of Palestine in particular and Syria in general. The defense of Egypt and the Canal begins in Palestine . . . It is clear that whoever occupied one of the two countries [Syria and Egypt] instinctively proceeded in the direction of the other as the Crusaders did in one direction and Napoleon from the other. The most recent examples were the British who proceeded from Egypt in the direction of Palestine and Jordan, matched in the other direction by the contemporary Israeli example."[63] Arabism, said the journalist Ahmad Baha'a al-Din, was not a garb to be donned in 1956 and taken off in 1967, donned in 1973 and taken off in 1977; the battles waged by Egypt were not waged for the sake of others. At stake were Egyptian interests and Egyptian security.[64]

Beyond the debates of scribes, a similar set of concerns were put to President Sadat in an important message submitted by some of the five surviving members of the Revolutionary Command Council – the original leading free officers who accomplished the 1952 coup d'état. The message signed by Hussein al-Shafalai, Zakaria Muheiddein, Abdul Latif al-Baghdadi, and Kamal al-Din Hussein had none of the arguments familiar to the hazier advocates of pan-Arabism. The case it made against President Sadat's diplomacy and his separate peace questioned whether an Egypt cut off from the Arab system would be able to survive; it expressed the historic fear of isolation: "We cannot imagine a bright future for Egypt in isolation from the Arab nations. The isolation of Egypt from the Arab nation had been the dream of European colonialism . . . The security enjoyed by Egypt in the shadow of this agreement [the Camp David Accords] is akin to the security felt by a lamb in the midst of a pack of wolves."[65]

EGYPT AS MIRROR, AS STATE

I want to return to where I began: Egypt's meaning to other Arabs and Egypt's struggle with herself. Egypt is the place where Arab history comes into focus. The way other Arabs turned away from Egypt indicates the depth of the Arab predicament in the modern world. Arabs look at Egypt and they do not like what they see – it is not revolutionary enough, or religious and austere enough, or militant enough. There is in what they say a judgment on things

Egyptian, but there is a wider judgment about the state of Arab civilization as well.

The Arab world has become fragmented, and the Arabs have desperately tried to ignore this fragmentation. It was Egypt that provided the harsh confirmation of Arab disintegration that so many had tried to avoid. Egypt's leader was more daring in his break with pan-Arabism than anyone else, and he did it without due regard to formalities and appearances. Egypt's intellectuals were the ones who were most willing to voice their doubts about Arabism. Others surely entertained such doubts, but they kept them to themselves. Egypt was the biggest piece, and its break – made in full daylight and symbolized by Sadat's short flight to Jerusalem – challenged the dogma of unity. There was bloodshed in Lebanon, poverty and treason in Egypt, wealth in the oil states, and Algeria was far away. The Arabs wanted to persist in their unionist myths. The intellectuals wanted to engage in the same polemics; the leaders – at least some of them – had spoken the language of Arabism long enough that it was difficult for them to speak a new idiom. Egypt forced on all of them an encounter with their own fragmentation.

Mr. Sadat's diplomacy was the most dramatic and objectively the most important illustration of the weakness of pan-Arabism, if only because Egypt had been, as Heikal rightly states, "the mainstay of the Arab system."[66] Throughout the preceding decade, however, there had been other "revolts," other "separatist" attacks against the monolithic pan-Arab doctrine. Those must be recalled for it is only then that the Sadat diplomacy can be correctly placed in Arab politics.

The Palestinians launched the first post-1967 attack against pan-Arabism; given their predicament, their economic and political dependence upon the Arab states, their lack of a territorial base, theirs had to be a different kind of attack. But there was no doubt that those who rallied around Yasser Arafat and George Habash in the aftermath of the Six Day War had given up on pan-Arabism, the first group in the name of Palestinian nationalism, the second in the name of social revolution. The duel that raged between the Palestinians and the Nasserites from early 1968 until Nasser's death in 1970 was in essence a fight about the independent rights of

Palestinian nationalism: If the Arab states could not protect themselves against Israel, let alone do something for the Palestinians, then the latter were to construct their own independent politics. And in the final analysis it was Arafat's brand of nationalism, with its pledge of nonintervention in the internal affairs of Arab countries, that found its way into the organized Arab state system, rather than George Habash's revolution. Arafat's narrow focus on Palestinian nationalism and his avoidance of social and ideological issues were in keeping with the new tenor of Arab politics. That is why Arafat's course found a reasonable measure of support in Riyadh. In Arafat's strict Palestinian nationalism there was an acceptance of reason of state. This is not applicable to the two sanctuaries of Jordan and Lebanon, which explains the two civil wars in which the Palestinians came to be involved.

The embrace on the part of the Palestinians, made public in 1974, of the idea of a national authority over any inch of liberated land confirmed the shift that had taken place in Palestinian and wider Arab thinking since 1967 – the state as a reality had triumphed; the wider metaphysical adherence to pan-Arabism was set aside. An intellectual episode that took place in the aftermath of the Six Day War illustrates the shift. When the Egyptian writer Ahmad Baha'a al'Din floated a suggestion for a Palestinian state in late 1967, his call touched off a fierce intellectual debate. Palestine, said one of his many critics, was not a *watan* (homeland), but a piece of homeland. The suggestion of a Palestinian state, argued another, the Palestinian scholar Walid Khalidi, was premature. Priority should be given to "eradicating the consequences of the June 5 aggression." It was the pan-Arab case that had primacy.[67] A decade later, Khalidi was making a plea for a sovereign Palestinian state on the West Bank Gaza.[68] The Jordanian civil war of September 1970, the Lebanese drama of 1975–1977, and the grim Palestinian encounter with Syrian armor in 1976 that had taken its place in Palestinian folklore and memory had driven home to Palestinians why men need states in the modern world and that their place in the Arab world had repeatedly exposed them to the power of others.

Another crack in the pan-Arab edifice was the virtual end of the Ba'th party. A shell called the Ba'th remains, and it claims power in both Syria and Iraq, but President Asad is probably the first leader in modern Syrian history to make peace with Syria's national situation and to accept the limitations of geography and resources. Since the end of World War I a national concensus of sorts developed in Syria that Syria's mission transcends her boundaries and that within those boundaries she is an amputated state. The French severed one part of Greater Syria in 1920 and appended it to Lebanon. Then came the establishment of Transjordan, and in 1939–1940 Syria lost Alexandretta to Turkey. The establishment of Israel in 1948 was in territory that Syria existentally thought of as southern Syria, and finally in 1967 there was the loss of the Golan.

In the post–World War II years, Syria was home to the Ba'th, the pan-Arab party that took seriously its mission of bringing about the one Arab nation. The Ba'thists had stout lungs and plenty of rhetoric – for them Syria was a base, but the dream was bigger than Syria. Hafez Asad was cut of a different cloth; a cautious member of a minority sect, he harbored no illusions about Arab unity. He put his predecessors' entire tradition behind him, accepted a reconciliation with King Husein, and abandoned the infantile Ba'thist notion of bringing Egypt into the pan-Arab fold and making her do the pan-Arabists' bidding.

In an otherwise across-the-board break with the universalism of pan-Arabism, it was only the young group of officers who came to power in Libya in September, 1969, who would raise the old banner in the decade that followed the 1967 defeat. Libya, which had been insulated from the Arab world, was to go through then the same stage that the Nasserites and Ba'thists had gone through in the preceding decade. Qaddafi and his fellow officers were to repeat the slogans that others had tired of; they too were to see the Arab world as one and earnestly to push the cause of unity. The principal difference between them and earlier unionists was that they combined, perhaps for the first time, two forces that had generally been at odds in recent Arab history: oil and pan-Arabism. Coming from Egypt and Syria, the unionist movement had been a claim by poor states for the collective wealth of the Arab world. In the Libyan there was the exception: an affluent society wanting to unite with its poorer neighbors.

Determined to realize the old dream, Qaddafi sought unity with such an odd ally as Bourguiba's Tunisia, but it was Egypt that was the focus of his aspirations. And for four years, he urged unity upon both Nasser and Sadat, although one suspects that the offers were made in a different spirit: He offered Libya to Nasser, whereas he wanted to steal Egypt from Sadat.

In both the Tunisian and Egyptian cases, Qaddafi was urging unity upon two older men for whom he had little if any regard – much older men than himself whom he thought he could eventually push aside. Qaddafi's attitude toward Bourguiba can be guessed at: Qaddafi is a Muslim Arab soldier through and through. Bourguiba could have only seemed like a compromised francophile, a symbol of a bygone age in which Arabs accepted the supremacy of the West and aped its ways. As for the pre–October 1973 Sadat, Qaddafi could hardly be blamed for the low opinion he held of him. That was a more-or-less universal judgement. During that transitional and difficult period, Sadat lacked legitimacy, and many of Nasser's followers within and outside Egypt came to think of Qaddafi as the spiritual son and true heir of Nasser. As it turned out, the source of Qaddafi's appeal lay more in Sadat's seeming ineptitude than in anything that Qaddafi himself had done. And so, when Sadat finally made good on his promise to break the military stalemate, the Qaddafi appeal came to an end. The October War might not have been the glorious achievement that Sadat made it out to be, but it was nonetheless an achievement. Egypt was once again a country with a leader, and thus Qaddafi's bid for unity could be pushed aside. Reenacting the past had had its day, and it was now time for the new realities to unfold.

Since their seizure of power in 1969, Qaddafi and his fellow officers have gradually come to see the differences among Arabs that had previously eluded them. The contrived boundaries had a reality after all; they ought to know that, for their own rather strict immigration policies contradict their talk of pan-Arabism. In the Arab world as elsewhere, the state is the dominant politicoeconomic reality: It protects the wealth of a people from outside claims; it separates them from others who are claimed, protected, and ruled over by other states.

Neither the fire and passion of the Libyan revolution nor its money could turn history around and revive an exhausted idea. Here and there, a few writers and publicists – not to mention some trouble-makers – prospered on Libyan money, repeating Qaddafi's slogans about his Third Theory or carrying out Qaddafi's wishes in Beirut and Cairo. But this was not to be Qaddafi's era. He was an anachronism: what he said and thought in the 1970s other Arabs had experienced and lived through in the 1950s and 1960s. More neutral judges may not think that he is *"al walad al majnun"* (the crazy boy), as Sadat said he was, but this much can be said: Qaddafi's arena is now Libya; his pan-Arab dreams have aborted. Qaddafi's conviction that the Arabs are one nation is no longer shared by a critical segment of Arabs – the students and the youth – who once gave pan-Arabism power in Arab life.

A social scientist at Kuwait University has supplied us with important evidence that substantiates the demise of pan-Arabism and suggests the shape of things to come. He administered a questionnaire to nearly five hundred undergraduates at Kuwait University with the aim of ascertaining their views on pan-Arabism, family, state, and religion. His sample included students from practically all Arab countries. What he found was a remarkable assertion of Islamic sentiment and an assertion of patriotism associated with particular Arab states. In other words, the vacuum left behind after the demise of pan-Arabism is being filled by religious belief on one level and loyalty to the state on another. As for pan-Arabism, the data led the researcher to conclude that discussion of "one Arab nation" and "Arab brotherhood" are myth and exhausted slogans.[69] There is no longer a collective Arab crisis, and there is no use pretending that it exists. The unevenness in the distribution of wealth – a gap of forty to one in per capita income separates the wealthiest Arab states from the poorest – makes a mockery of the idea of human brotherhood. The horizons open to some men and states in the Arab world exceed the imagination of others. Shall we then insist on still seeing the unity of a people because there are roots in common texts and claims to brotherhood? We know the themes and memories that lent unity to the Arabs' consciousness and history: one language, the classical golden age of Islam, the universalism of the Ottoman Empire, the yearning for independence, the trauma of being initiated into an international system in which they were not full participants but mere stakes, the Palestine defeat, the Six Day War, and finally, October 1973. The memories and the bonds remain, but the unevenness in the distribution of wealth and the realities of the state system – the harsh logic of raison d'etat – have done their deed.

The boundaries of Arab states have been around now for nearly six decades. It is not their existence that is novel but the power of the state (inasmuch as that power exists in today's state system) to keep pan-Arab claims at bay and to claim the loyalty of those within. The boundaries are no longer as "illusory and permeable"[70] as they were once thought to be. The states that lie within them are less shy about asserting their rights, more normal in the claims they make. The Arabs who once seemed whole, both to themselves and to others, suddenly look as diverse as they were all along. Egypt's defection was neither the will of an isolated man nor the weakness of a particularly craven country anxious to welcome the West and bid farewell to a sacred myth. The pan-Arab idea that dominated the political consciousness of modern Arabs has become a hollow claim. In an earlier decade, loyalty to a particular state in the Arab world was, as historian Bernard Lewis reminds us, "tacit [and] even surreptitious," and Arab unity was "the sole publicly acceptable objective of statesmen and ideologues alike."[71] Now political thought is more daring in its defiance of the myth, more willing to acknowledge that the Arab states have gone their separate ways.

How a political doctrine seizes people's imagination is a mysterious thing; in our age we do not quarrel with the phenomenon, for we have seen it over and over again. We may wish it to be otherwise, we may want people to be more discriminating, but we accept it as a fact of life that ideas – logical or not, justified or not – grip people and are in turn gripped by them in their struggles. Greatly as we may quarrel with the rationality or objectivity of political ideas, they defy logic and create their own realities. Then they play themselves out: They either create a world in their image to be later shackled by routine problems not anticipated by those who spun the myth, or they live past their time and cease to be sufficiently gripping and moving. Or they vanish and leave behind them a trail of errors, suffering, and devastation.

Prior to the emergence of Nasser as a pan-Arab savior, the doc-

The Arab Predicament

trine of pan-Arabism had been the realm of publicists, intellectuals, and a few officers – in other words, it had been an elite endeavor. Nasser took the theories and the emotions to the masses, and in so doing, he gave pan-Arabism its moment in the sun and then its tragic end in 1967. It does not matter in retrospect how he stumbled onto the idea: The once-shy officer, uneasy around crowds, might have been a peculiar candidate for leadership of the movement; Cairo might have been a peculiar capital, for there were many in Damascus and Baghdad who felt that Cairo was a latecomer to pan-Arab politics, an illegitimate center. But that was the turn that history took, and the idea held Nasser as much as he tried to hold and direct it; it made him plunge into the explosive, unpredictable terrain of Syrian politics for an unsuccessful union with Syria; it took him to Yemen for a small-scale Vietnam of his own, into a society about which he knew next to nothing and into a war which his impoverished society could not afford. Finally, it dragged him into the tragic event of his life and career in 1967. Along the way, the pan-Arab quest turned him into a hero in Libya and Lebanon, Saudi Arabia and Syria, and pitted him into a sustained struggle with monarchies and fellow radicals as well as with Western powers committed to upholding the territorial division of the Arab world against the pan-Arabists' designs.

The circumstances that produced the ebb of Nasserist charisma and pan-Arabism may be *sui generis:* With defeat in 1967, charisma turned to ashes and the conservative oil states made their financial help contingent upon a new style and kind of politics. But there is a broader phenomenon here, and the end of Nasserism is a piece of a bigger puzzle; it is the end of that stage of Third World history represented by men like Nasser, Nehru, Sukarno, Nkrumah. These men were dreamers who sought what one of them, Nkrumah, described as the "kingdom of politics." They sought in politics answers to questions of identity and self-worth and dabbled in dreams and intangibles. But their kind of politics was bound to come to an end, for the nationalist fervor that they embodied can triumph for a moment but cannot last forever.

The exhaustion of the nationalist fervor generally signals the coming to the fore of economic issues and demands, of problems that do not lend themselves to solo performances, to the magic

146

touch of charisma, to the spectacular and psychologically gratifying performance of a Nasser, a Nkrumah, to the theatrics of a Sukarno, to the flair of a Nehru. Less colorful leaders whose links to
the nationalist struggle are often tenuous are the ones who have
to satisfy the new needs. The romantic phase of nationalism is then
over – words and symbols lose some of their power as societies
begin the infinitely more difficult search for ways of putting a domestic order together.

Egypt's diplomacy served a harsh notice on the pan-Arab myth,
but others had broken with it in their own way; the world had
changed and nationalist ideas as such had become somewhat banal
and insufficient. The storm over Sadat's policy was a fight to keep
the myth alive.

If the Sadat diplomacy was a revolt, an exit by a poor society,
the wealthy Arab states had exited in their own way. Great wealth
had practically northernized some Arab states – in material standards but not in culture, to be sure. Distrustful (as they should be)
of the poor, embittered world around them, their wealth had knit
them into the Western-based international economic system. The
new age expected by those who pinned inflated hopes on Arab
wealth was not to come: Wealth only heightened the need by the
wealthy states to separate themselves, to limit the expectations and
demands of others. Neither the world view nor the mechanisms
existed that could create that public project that had tantalized the
imaginations of those among the Arabs who saw the need for economic integration, who could argue on perfectly defensible economic grounds that separate Arab states were too small to stand
on their own, or to provide for economies of scale. About the same
time that Egypt was breaking with the monolithic Arab camp (the
gladiators of the Arab world abandoning their role), Arab wealth
was asserting its own independence, finding its own way into the
world. Consider the following investment statistics of oil wealth:

> The OPEC countries have behaved like other prudent investors in
> disposing of their financial surpluses; that is, they have invested
> almost exclusively in low risk, high yield assets such as government
> securities in the hard currency countries, in stocks and bonds of-
> fered by Western corporations, and in deposits with the 15 or so
> largest multinational banks. Thus, according to the U.S. Treasury

estimates, of a total of approximately $133 billion in financial assets accumulated by OPEC in the period 1974–76, that can be accounted for, an estimated $48 billion was invested in government paper, portfolio and long term direct investments in the industrial countries; another $9.75 billion was loaned to international organizations; and by far the largest amount, $49 billion, or 37 percent of the total, was deposited with private commercial banks, mostly in New York and London. Only $16 billion, or 12 percent of the total OPEC surpluses, went directly to the developing countries, mostly in the form of grants to Moslem countries.[72]

The average citizen in Cairo, Damascus, or elsewhere in the Arab world may not have been well informed about the investment details, but he or she knew about the ways of the wealthy, knew that they had become a separate breed. Egypt's poverty at the height of Arab wealth epitomized the limits and, for many, the selfishness of Arab wealth. In Egypt's turn to the West, other Arabs could see how evanescent was the idea that the Arab world had become an autonomous center of power. Other Arab capitals – Baghdad and Damascus – were more discreet in their dealings with the West, more inaccessible and remote. The oil states could deal with the West from a position of power and affluence – or so they could think. Egypt lacked the cultural distance, the militant pride of Baghdad and Damascus; it lacked the money of the West. Egypt was all too willing to embrace and surrender. But here too there was an undercurrent of opinion in the Arab world that sensed that Egypt's and Sadat's surrenders were not unique and isolated acts, that other Arab states had thrown in their lot with the West as well, that that impenetrable core of self and authenticity had long been violated, that Sadat's only sin was really a matter of style. Other Arab leaders and states were careful or rich or nervous enough to conceal their dependence upon the West – Sadat was too flamboyant, too poor, and politically secure enough to do things in a different way. But surely, many Arabs reasoned, those living in glass houses should not go about hurling rocks at others. The profound truth of Egypt's defection was not to be found in the utterances and self-righeous denunciations of Arab summits but in a column written by a Saudi journalist on the occasion of the exchange of embassies between Egypt and Israel. The column took the form of an ode to Egypt. The column's writer, Fatna Shaker,

148

writes with a straightforward and refreshing honesty, a seeming desire to get to the core of things. "I look for you, oh Egypt," she wrote, "for your depths, trying to find a mere echo of your wishes, something that tells me what you really feel about what goes on in your land . . . I looked for you during the "wedding celebrations" and wondered how you were . . . I yearn for your water and land but your features have changed on me; they are no longer the ones I knew as a child and a youth . . . The raising of the Israeli flag on your land has inflicted a deep wound . . . But you do not bear the sole responsibility . . . All of us, the other Arabs, cannot feign innocence."[73]

In their disillusionment with Egypt, the Arabs expressed their disillusionment with the present. The notion that the "long winter of the Arabs"[74] had come to a close was illusion. Egypt provided the serious and somber reminder that all was not well, that things were falling apart. This is something for other Arabs to settle: Egypt cannot be the laboratory for others' experiments; it cannot be bigger than itself, for in many ways – Heikal notwithstanding – Egypt remains a hemmed-in riverbed on the banks of the Nile.

This cuts both ways, for knowledge of its limitations brings Egypt into a more honest encounter with its problems and responsibilities. Egypt's revolt against Arabism – its search for itself, the vision of a great imagined past – is in part frustration and scapegoating. It is an escape from what a society has to do, from the serious task of putting together a shattered world, reviving a desperate economy, injecting a sluggish bureaucracy with mission, purpose and skills. The great imagined past is a mirage; it can supply inspiration in moments of doubt, but it can become a narcotic, a way of avoiding coming to terms with the society's troubles, of ignoring its stalemate. The July 23 revolution of 1952 is a faded memory. The story of how the young officers overthrew the monarchy has been told over and over again, embellished, and distorted. Once upon a time it was an exciting tale, but it has become routine. It survives as a tired, overworked piece of symbolism; it has become an incantation that no longer grips and moves.

Sadat's symbols – the community of love, the country as family, himself as the "eldest of the Egyptian family" – served the same narcotic purpose: escape, a fake harmony of interests, a curious avoidance of politics. The myth of the family served to freeze the society. That is why Sadat formed and then dissolved political parties: Opposition was tolerated so long as it did not really oppose. Sadat's language – "my army," "my party," "my sons," "my opposition" (to refer to an opposition party that he himself set up) – revealed Egypt's predicament and stalemate. Sadat could not move the society – the best he could do is to stay on top, more like royalty than an active executive. He was beyond politics, beyond criticisms.

In the midst of disorder and breakdown, he maintained coolness and serenity and peddled dreams of prosperity and visions of a static order: *Misr* (Egypt) as the oasis, *al zaim* (the leader) as the focus. Sycophants who flatter, who play by the rules and conceal reality, enjoy access and power. Those who oppose do so by withholding their cooperation, but they deny the country their energy. The machinery of the state is powerful enough to stifle opposition, but it is too weak to do anything about Egypt's lethargic bureaucracy, to solve the country's crises, to check population growth or the urban nightmare. The stalemated society (Crozier's and Hoffmann's writings on France apply even more poignantly here)[75] is given a high moral status. Nasser tried to move forward and in so doing upset the balance of the country; Sadat would keep that balance intact: no prisons, no great crusades, no ambitious pushy bureaucrats, but no work, either. There were a tacit agreement to ignore troubles and to transcend politics. Troublemakers were expelled from parliament, denied access to the media, disowned by the Egyptian family.[76] Once lively organs became safe and banal. The leftist monthly *Al-Talia* now dealt with matters of science and outer space – fitting subjects for a civilized country. *Ruz al Yussef*, which has a long history of hard-hitting journalism, was pacified. One of its issues carried an astrologer's predictions for 1979: There will be peace and prosperity in the area; the shah of Iran will survive in power; more Arab countries will follow Egypt's leadership; massive oil discoveries will turn Egypt into a wealthy country; more civilized countries will come to Egypt's aid and give her love and recognition. This was a serious item – wishes substituting for analysis, dreams for work.

Meanwhile, some of the more gifted and sensitive of the coun-

150

try's youth had been responding in their way to the politicoeconomic decline by means of emigration, what Albert Hirschmann
would call the phenomenon of exit.[77] In one survey of university
students, nearly 85 percent expressed a desire to leave Egypt upon
graduation.[78] In Egypt as elsewhere, emigration obtains a measure
of stability by removing from the system potential dissidents, but
it also removes those who would have been likely to contribute to
the public interest.

Traditionally Egypt was a society whose inhabitants were reluc-
tant to venture to other lands. It possessed the stability of an agrarian order where people stayed, at home, in their minds and values
as well as their bodies. Writing in 1835, E. W. Lane described the
reluctance of Egyptians to leave their native land:

> Love of their country and more especially of home is a characteristic
> of the modern Egyptians. In general they have a great dread of quit-
> ting their native land. I have heard of several determining to visit a
> foreign country for the sake of considerable advantages in prospect;
> but when the time of their intended departure drew near, their res-
> olution failed them.[79]

More than a century after Lane had made that observation, Jean
and Simone Lacouture confirmed it.[80] But now the "dread" of
quitting the native land has turned into a near exodus. The private
gains are easy to document, the private incentives easy to understand. But surely there is a public price. The stability that rulers
covet has an advantage, but societies can stagnate and die even if
regimes manage to hang on to political power. The Egyptian revolution, observed Lewis Awad in an important assessment of Nasserism, has "aged": It needs a new social contract with the society,
a new vision.[81] It will not do to remind younger men and women
of the evils from which the revolution saved them, of the record of
the ancien régime.

Nor will it do to escape into the realm of foreign policy. Geopol-
itics can be a ruler's escape, all the more so when the ruler has a
poor society to run, when his horizons and ambitions exceed his
society's limits. Something about Egypt has always driven its rulers to entertain ambitions that end up braking the back of their
society. This was true of Muhammad Ali, who laid the foundations
of a modern society and then set out to establish an imperial order

only to be broken by the European powers. It was particularly true of Ismael, who wanted to create in Africa the empire that had eluded Muhammad Ali in Asia – all that at a time when he was losing control of his own realm. It was also true of Faruq, who entertained hegemonic ambitions of his own and whose rivalry with the Hashemites goes a long way toward explaining much of what he did in inter-Arab matters. Then there was Abdul Nasser and his drama. The deep structure of his pan-Arabism might have been a desire to escape from the limits of his country: as Awad puts it, to escape from coming face to face with the "wretched millions." Thus pan-Arabism and Arab socialism were a

> way of avoiding the barefoot peasants and the desperate laborers and the millions who belong to neither countryside nor city, just exactly as the Egyptian teacher escapes from teaching the children of the peasantry and the working class because it is not as lucrative as teaching the children of the Kuwaitis, Saudis, Libyans, Algerians, etc. . . . [82]

Sadat followed the same tradition, and at the root of his policy could be discerned the same desire for escape, that same national situation (perhaps it is the combination of internal stability and external vulnerability) that drives the man at the helm of the Egyptian polity to forget where he is, to entertain dreams that his society cannot sustain. In 1978 Sadat boasted and complained (in that unique Sadat style) that a power vacuum in the region was forcing him to "act like a superpower."[83] By that time, and steadily thereafter, the head of the Egyptian state became committed to keeping order as far away as Zaire and Afghanistan: In the aftermath of the shah's collapse, the role that Sadat had coveted as a regional power was his. Of the two previous pillars of American influence, Iran and Saudi Arabia, one had faltered and one had dropped out, and Sadat could argue that his country offered a more reliable base, that he could stem the chaos and the disorder of a region that seemed to be falling apart all around him. His was a society more obedient to its "leader" than was Iran, more populous and daring, more open to the outside world than was Saudi Arabia.

Once again the dialogue with the outside world had turned to

an embrace, and Egypt had swung from leading the protest movement against the West to being its sentry. The same Egyptian talent, the same eloquence and resourceful media that once condemned foreign pacts and security doctrines, was now hounding
those who failed to stand up to Soviet adventurism, who were too
squeamish to identify themselves with American power and
American interests. The zeal with which Cairo once condemned
the Eisenhower doctrine and the "pactomania" of John Foster Dulles
now went into promoting the Carter doctrine and the legitimacy
of an American military presence. Cairo and Baghdad had, as it
were, reversed roles: In the 1950s it was the former that urged
nonalignment and the latter that wanted to do the West's bidding,
to use the power of allies from afar to crush local rivals. Now it
was Cairo that wanted the presence, the patronage, and the power
of distant allies. America's security predicament gave the Egyptian
leader the latitude and maneuverability he wanted. The United
States was willing to abandon its previous reserve, to offer Sadat
the role and the help he wanted.

> In late 1979, with the attack on Mecca, the seizure of the U.S. em-
> bassy in Tehran, the Soviet invasion of Afghanistan, the Adminis-
> tration's attitude towards the Middle East took on a distinctly more
> militant and military tone. American policy towards Egypt lost most
> of the little reserve it had had earlier in the year. Those Americans
> searching out for friends in the troubled Middle East – as Americans
> are wont to search out "friends" – naturally and sometimes enthu-
> siastically set their eyes upon Sadat's Egypt. Playing to the Ameri-
> can public in his opposition to the Soviets, the Iranian revolution-
> aries, and the Saudi fundamentalists, Sadat put his regime on the
> side of the angels with his invitations to play host to the Shah.[84]

The Shah of Iran had left his country with a handful of soil in
February of 1979. Like a "Flying Dutchman" (the description was
that of Henry Kissinger), Muhammad Reza Pahlavi circled the globe
in search of a place of exile. His first stop was Egypt; then it was
off to the Bahamas, Mexico, the United States, Panama, and finally
back to Egypt. Former allies turned away from him. Jimmy Carter
did not want him on American soil. Margaret Thatcher, the "Iron
Lady" of British politics, had made a promise that she would invite

him to England were she to come to power; she was to renege on it after her election in May of 1979. Austria and Switzerland declined as well. "Faithful Egypt," said Sadat, would do what Western countries would not do; Egypt would honor its obligation to a man who had been helpful to Egypt when he had wealth to dispose of, when he was a power to reckon with. "I have done nothing for you," the Shah told his host. "You are the only one to accept me with dignity. The others whom I have helped have offered me no help in return. I cannot understand."[85] Four months later, in late July of 1980, the Shah died a slow and cruel death. Sadat again did it his way. The Shah was given a grand state funeral.

The episode was vintage Sadat – defiant, imperious in his definition of his prerogatives, dismissive of the Islamic–leftist opposition at home that had wanted nothing to do with the Shah. He had stepped onto a world stage: he had outgrown his country.

For Egypt the threat is at home. The tendency of the Egyptian state to go beyond its society and leave it behind is a trap and a mirage: states can never outgrow the world that anchors them and gives them the power and the material with which to meet other states and other people. Sooner or later the base below makes its demands, imposes its limits, serves its own warrant on the dreams of rulers and the illusions of bureaucracies.

Mediterranean European Egypt is no help either. Lawrence Durrell's Alexandria is gone; even he could not find it on a nostalgic trip which he made in 1978 after an absence of twenty-eight years. Alexandria of the "Grand Tour" – "Alex" to the smart set – was but a memory: the "dust has got into the town," he wrote, and "everything agreeable, Western, rich, capitalist and easygoing had vanished." The "smart shops" had folded up; the Greeks, the Jews, the Italians, the French, the Armenians were gone, he lamented. Apathy and dust and the feeling that nothing worked were what the nostalgist came back to.[86] Without the human energy to accomplish tasks, civilization becomes a fraudulent wrapping, a pathetic act of mimicry. Cut off from its roots, alienated from its locale, civilization turns into a nauseating pretension. Then it awaits its death, as less sophisticated, less polished people – claiming authenticity, more connected to the earth – push it into its grave.

154

Egypt As State, As Arab Mirror

BEYOND THE PHARAOHS:
THE "NORMAL" POLITY, THE BURDENED LAND

Sadat's own journey was to end, on October 6, 1981, when young assassins struck during the anniversary parade commemorating the October War of 1973. October 6, 1973, had been Sadat's day; in many ways his great beginning, for prior to that he had been Nasser's accidental successor. The assassination, eight years later to the day, closed a circle. The journey that had begun in the army was ended by disaffected men from the army. He had been a lucky soldier: his luck had run out.

It was a "fluke conspiracy" of sorts that ended Anwar el Sadat's trapeze act. The principal assassin, a disaffected army officer, Khalid al Istanbuli, twenty-four years of age, had been assigned to the parade only days earlier. During the preceding month matters had been stretched to the breaking point in Egypt. Sadat had organized an aggressive crackdown. In early September, 1536 opponents of the regime had been arrested. It had been a desperate act. Those arrested covered the spectrum of political life – the influential journalist Mohamed Heikal, a leading feminist physician by the name of Nawal al Sa'adawi, the firebrand blind preacher Shaykh Abdul Hamid Kishk, whose sermons and cassettes had become something of a sensation in the country, a former Minister of Education by the name of Muhammad Hilmi Murad, a seventy-year-old ancien régime figure, Fouad Pasha Serag al Din, a former Minister of Planning, Ismael Sabri Abdullah, and six members of the board of the Lawyers' Syndicate. The only kind of political men and women spared by the regime, so it seemed in early September, were the sycophants and the conspirators. Among those hauled off to prison was one Mohammed Istanbuli, the older brother of First Lieutenant Khalid al Istanbuli. To his weeping mother Khalid swore revenge: "There is an end to every tyrant," he said. But more than personal revenge was at stake. Khalid al Istanbuli had been part of a cell of Islamicists which had gotten there through the written word, an elaborate theory of tyrannicide. "I shot the Pharaoh," said Istanbuli during his trial. In a "last will and testament" he had written to his parents, his two sisters, and his brother Mohammed, he asked for their forgiveness for all the troubles his

155

deed would inflict on them. "God has guided us to this deed and to martyrdom in the path of God. The ruler had turned capricious and oppressive, and there is no solution for the country save through his murder. We had decided that the Pharaoh of Egypt had to be killed so that God may rescue Egypt from its confusion, its friendship with Zionists, the ruin of morals caused by Sadat and his wife."[87]

The security apparatus of the state had been derelict in the performance of its duty. Military Intelligence had been on Istanbuli's trail for some time. In January of 1980, State Security, *al mabahith*, had reported to Military Intelligence that Istanbuli was involved in fringe Islamic politics. In May of that year, Istanbuli had been questioned by Military Intelligence; he had submitted an affidavit in which he denied belonging to any extremist organizations. Military Intelligence must not have been convinced of his innocence; he was placed under surveillance. The reports on his activities were not reassuring. His older brother was an Islamic activist. There was ample evidence that the officer was under the influence of his brother: he grew a beard whenever he went home on leave from the military, he took part in the meetings of radical Islamic groups. Moreover, his companions in the military had reported a growing zeal and fanaticism in his conduct toward those who did not pray or who were lax in the performance of other religious observances.

The alarm bells should have gone off in early September after the arrest of Istanbuli's brother. They did not. Curiously, as evidence the state was to gather in the aftermath of Sadat's assassination was to indicate, Istanbuli had not been keen to take part in the military parade of October 6; he had asked for leave to go home and be with his family to console them over the arrest of his brother. The request had been denied. Istanbuli would now brace himself to do "God's will." To a friend who was to join him in the attack on Sadat, Istanbuli was to say that an "inner voice" had come to him and told him that it was time to be rid of the tyrant.[88]

Khalid Istanbuli was a child of the July 23 Revolution of 1952. He was born in 1957, a year after the Suez War, during the Nasserite revolution's moment of political ascendancy. It was not lost on his admirers – and he would go on to become something of a national cult figure – that his first name had been the name of Gamal Abdul Nasser's oldest son. It was by the name of Abu Khalid, Khalid's father, that Nasser was known. Istanbuli's father was a lawyer for a public sector company. All in all this was a child of the Egyptian middle class, a faithful product of the sum of its recent history – the gains it had made over the preceding three decades, the roller-coaster ride it had taken through the bravado of the 1957–1967 years, the trauma of the Six Day War, the uncertain verdict of the October War of 1973, then the sudden remaking of the political order after 1973. Things, political things had been named and renamed with such caprice and frequency in the Egypt of the preceding three decades. America, once demonic, had become a savior; the Arabs, once "brothers," had become lepers; the public sector, once the pride of the country, had become a national joke; the bourgeois era, derided only yesterday, was now recast by memory. There were even suggestions that the green flag of pre-1952 be restored, replacing the flag the military regime had given the country. Few lands could have survived these dizzying changes without great strains, without resort to violence.

For his assault against Sadat, Istanbuli was joined by three companions – a reserve army officer, a sergeant in the army, and a childhood friend of Istanbuli, a junior army officer who had quit the armed forces to run a bookstore that specialized in religious books.[89] It was a fifth conspirator, an electrical engineer by the name of Mohamed Abdul Salem Farag, who had provided the writ for tryannicide in a pamphlet entitled *al Farida al Ghaiba* (The Absent Obligation). The pamphlet had been written by Farag five months prior to Sadat's assassination. The role of Farag was pivotal. It was he, a free-lance preacher, who brought the assassins together, who recruited two of the three conspirators who took part in Istanbuli's assault on Sadat. More important perhaps it was Farag, the pamphleteer, who had provided the justification for the deed. Farag had no official religious education; he was self-taught. The intellectual route he followed led to *takfir al hakim* (declaring the ruler an unbeliever). Once the case was made that the ruler had broken with Islam his blood was forfeit. A deadly idea, *takfir* (denouncing someone as a *kafir*, an unbeliever) had come to the political domain in Egypt in the 1970s. In Farag's discourse this was now attributed to the ruler. And Egypt itself was no longer of *dar al Islam* (the house of Islam).

Mainstream Islam had accepted the simple profession of the faith as an attribute of Islam. Men had understood that questioning the faith of Muslims, declaring others apostates, was a ruinous course. Farag would bid farewell to caution: better a "pure" world than a tranquil one. Sadat was not a believer, he was to argue. Islam was both deed and word. The young electrical engineer busy at work putting together his theory of fire and brimstone found his own ancestor: a Muslim jurist, Ibn Taymiyyah (1263–1328). From this renowned and puritanical scholar of Damascus who had struggled to keep Islam on guard against heretics and sectarian deviations, Farag borrowed a deadly theology. Outward profession of faith no longer sufficed. A modern society like Sadat's Egypt was a *dawlat kufr*, a state of unbelief. Against this kind of state, *jihad*, struggle, was an imperative. It was a travesty, Farag was to argue, that pious Muslims should attend to ritual and leave kings and rulers alone: Anyone who said this, Farag wrote, "either does not understand Islam or is a coward."[90]

The (intellectual) ancestor Farag had chosen for himself, Ibn Taymiyyah, had in his time ruled that the Mongols, who had conquered the heartlands of Islam in the thirteenth century, were not pious Muslims despite their formal conversion to the faith. Farag was to render similar judgment on Sadat and the political–military elite which governed the Egyptian state. Between the ruling elite and their zealous challengers the bonds were severed. Farag was not impressed by Sadat's insistence that he was a "believing president." Nor was he moved by the state prosecutors telling him that today's rulers were pious men when compared to the Mongols, who had been a cruel lot who threw the "books of Islam" into the rivers and had made no distinction between combatants and women and children. Times change, he was to say: "The rulers today fight Islam in their own way."

The "pharaoh" had been eliminated, but the state rode out the storm. The assassins expressed the society's confusions and distress, but the band of conspirators could not topple the ruling order. The regime spoke of a dark conspiracy of a secret *tanzim* (organization) engaged in a general conspiracy against the state. There were worries that the army had been infiltrated by the conspirators. But the secret *tanzim* (the security apparatus listed some three hundred members of the *tanzim*) was, for the most part, a straw man set up by the state. The security apparatus had been embarrassed by the assassination of the head of state; the threat had to be magnified if the honor and the professionalism of the security apparatus were to be redeemed. But even the conspirators themselves knew they were a lonely band of men. Few among them thought the country was ready for a general insurrection. The highest military officer among the conspirators, a thirty-five-year-old colonel by the name of Abbud al-Zomor, had been dubious about the assassination of Sadat to begin with. The country was not ready for a general revolt, he had counseled. He had been bypassed by the determined younger man, Lieutenant Istanbuli, who saw his chance during the military parade and made the most of it. He too, the principal assassin, was without illusions: A lesson could be made of Sadat, his successors would be chastened, and oppression and deviation will have been punished.

There was no general plan for a seizure of the state. No fools, the conspirators knew the harsh balance of forces between them and the larger social order. They were "the just ones," they would pay with their lives, they would strike down "the tyrant." But the redemption of the land, the establishment of a just Islamic order in the land of Egypt, was beyond them. Crusaders (that is the way Colonel al-Zomor referred to Egypt's Coptic minority) were on the loose in Egypt; the land could be lost to the realm of Islam as Al-Andalus had been lost in the final years of the fifteenth century; an impious ruler and his wife were mocking the believers: The case for the assassination was easy to make. But the larger matter of overthrowing the ruling apparatus was beyond the conspirators' grasp.

The three hundred conspirators designated by the state as members of the *tanzim* have been thoroughly analyzed and studied. Not surprisingly they were predominantly young. Nearly nine out of ten were under thirty years of age; the greatest concentration were in the 21- to 30-year-old range. On the whole they hailed from the country's urban centers: They tended to confirm the conventional wisdom that Muslim militancy in Egypt has been an urban phenomenon which has yet to touch the countryside. Two-thirds of the militants came from traditional centers of fundamentalist agitation in upper Egypt – towns and provincial capitals like Asyut and Minya and Sohag. (Upper Egypt, lagging behind the rest of the country in socioeconomic achievements, has been a hotbed of religious agitation.) Those who hailed from Greater Cairo, nearly 25 percent of the total, were drawn from the northern belt of the city – newly urbanized neighborhoods which have served as a magnet for rural migrants. These new neighborhoods, places like Bolaq al-Dakrur and Pyramid Road, had a different kind of social and political temperament than the older and more settled urban neighborhoods of Cairo. Here, among the newly urbanized, the distress was greater; the sense of violation, the grievances toward those with income and liberties, more acutely felt.[91]

The discontents of Egypt had forged the new militants and their politics. Its popular mosques, *ahli* mosques, had brought them together. Beyond the authority of the state and its officially sanctioned *ulama* and prayer leaders, popular religion had expressed the bewilderment and the wrath of those excluded from the new ways of Egypt. But wrath could only go so far. The state was too firmly entrenched, the beneficiaries of the dominant order too powerful, to be swept aside by a band of militants. The man at the helm – too provocative, by then a loner cursing the wind – would go, but the social peace would hold.

No sooner had Sadat been struck down than his opponents in the Arab world celebrated Egypt's break with his way. But the Arabs witnessing that drama were to err in their judgment of matters Egyptian. Sadat's murder was not a verdict on the Egyptian–Israeli diplomacy he had undertaken. It was not because of Camp David and the Israeli–Egyptian treaty that Sadat had been struck down. The incautious ruler had been struck down because he hemmed in his own country with the massive wave of arrests before his death; because he had manipulated forces – Muslim fundamentalism – whose fury he underestimated; because the man who had once appealed to his country's desire for safety and to its instinctive dread of great crusades had lived to become too controversial and erratic; because in his appeal to people and lands beyond Egypt the self-styled *fellah* (peasant) who prided himself on his roots in the land came to lose touch with his own world.

To be sure the separate peace with Israel contributed to Sadat's fate and to his end. His enemies in the Arab world could not topple him. But their vehement denunciations of him led him to seek greater acceptance at home, greater obedience. His impatience with opposition and dissent became nearly neurotic: There were enemies everywhere, he was not appreciated at home, he was loved in foreign lands and questioned at home, the country had to see and appreciate his genius and gifts to her. Egypt had been subjected to mighty and dangerous crosscurrents. Old fidelities were being torn to shreds, and a new vocation beckoned. This new vocation – America's ward in the Arab–Muslim realms, a "strategic partner" of Western interests – would call forth its nemesis: a militant yearning for authenticity, a frightened kind of nativism.

Then, too, the policies of Menachem Begin in the aftermath of the Egyptian–Israeli peace contributed their own share to the undermining of Sadat. Begin had made the needed concessions to Sadat on the Sinai Peninsula, but was uncompromising on other fronts. The Begin government pushed on with settlements on the West Bank and Gaza and the Golan Heights. In June of 1981, Israel was to stage a dramatic raid against an Iraqi nuclear reactor; the raid took place only two days after a meeting between Begin and Sadat. A few weeks later there was another Israeli raid against the Palestine Liberation Organization's headquarters in the heart of Beirut. Sadat would do his best to distance himself from these deeds. But it was to no avail. In the eyes of his critics, he was perceived either "as a fool or as a traitor."[92] Egypt was walking away from all she had paid homage to for more than a quarter-century. Sadat would become the sacrificial lamb. The place would take what he had secured for it – American aid, Israeli territorial concessions, an exit from the ruinous course of pan-Arabism – and then damn him all the same.

A more cautious successor, Hosni Mubarak, stepped forth in the aftermath of Sadat's trapeze act. Mubarak was there on the reviewing stand the day Sadat was struck down. He would heed his predecessor's fate. He would not tempt the elements: It was time to knit the country together. He was only (as an Egyptian source was to put it to me) an employee with the rank of president. Not for him was the grandeur of his two predecessors. But he would, for the most part, stay the course. The peace with Israel would be preserved. But Israel itself would be kept at arm's length. The cautious successor would not journey to Israel or succumb to great displays of intimacy or cooperation with its leaders. As one Egyptian sociologist put it, Mubarak always had "good reasons" to decline Israeli invitations "to go to Israel." Mubarak was "neither proud nor ashamed" of the Camp David accords; they were legal treaties; he would abide by them.[93] Likewise the reliance on America would continue. But the open affection for the distant power and the full identification with her would be set aside. Sadat's successor would not think of America as a theater where he was loved and accepted. There was business to transact with the foreign power and he would do it in a sober way.

Sadat's assassins were put to death on April 15, 1982, a mere ten days before Israel was scheduled to vacate the last strip of the Sinai Peninsula and return it to Egypt. The hundreds arrested by Sadat were released, their leaders brought right out of prison to the presidential palace. It was a gesture of reconciliation. Sadat had done his bit for the country. He had secured it America's aid and sympathy; he had gotten Israeli withdrawal from Sinai. There would be more "normal" work for less flamboyant leaders. Reconciliation with the wider Arab world, too, would be easier for the new man at the helm. But the reconciliation would not require a change in Egypt's course. There was no coherent Arab strategy out there beyond Egypt for the Egyptians to return to as repentant men and women. The Egyptians would take their time. They were lucky, they knew deep down, to be spared the hell of Arab and Muslim politics in the 1980s – the carnage and the breakdown, the sectarian wars in Beirut and Damascus, the killing fields on the Iran–Iraq front, the bravado and the delusions of Qaddafi's Libya.

There were moments of national embarrassment – moments like the summer of 1982, when Israel swept into Lebanon and put an end to the Palestinian sanctuary in that country. There was brave talk then of repudiating the Egyptian–Israeli peace and returning to the old pan-Arab vocation. The relative abandon with which Israel seemed to be operating on other Arab–Israeli fronts was galling to large numbers of Egyptians. Guilt over Beirut's ordeal in the summer of 1982 could be discerned among the Egyptian political class. Mohamed Heikal, Sadat's most prominent critic, gave expression to this sentiment. A balance of sorts had obtained between Israel and the Arab world, Heikal observed; Egypt's defection had shattered that balance. Menachem Begin and his minister of defense, Ariel Sharon, were now free to impose their own order on Arab–Israeli fronts. In Heikal's stark vision: "The fact that Sadat's policies had ensured the total and inevitable isolation of Egypt from the rest of the Arab world did more than anything else to give a clear passage for Sharon's tanks on the road to Beirut." Beyond Beirut and her ordeal, there was a more sweeping lament: Egypt had been the "natural leader" of the Arab order; with her defection, Heikal wrote, the Arab world had become "well and truly Balkanized."[94]

But the peace with Israel held. For Egypt, Arab–Israeli wars were now of the past. The state had its own troubles: a crippling foreign debt burden, heavy reliance on food imports which by now accounted for 75 percent of the country's foodstuffs, a budget deficit that was nearly 17 percent of her gross domestic product, a population explosion which was adding a little more than a million people to a country living beyond its means. Rebellions and flamboyance: these were things that Egypt could no longer afford.

It was a failed, yet stubborn Arab legacy on dealing with Israel that Sadat had shattered. For that legacy there were but few mourners. The wily country may have doubted the terms of Sadat's diplomacy. There were, it is true, some among the political and intellectual class who agreed with Mohamed Heikal that the Sadat diplomacy had given Israel a "one-sided pledge of non-belligerence."[95] But there was a wider verdict that issued out of the country's fatigue and yearnings for a different kind of future: That Arab legacy had to be abandoned if Egypt were to find a new way.

The workings of that Arab legacy on matters Israeli and Palestinian had not really changed until Sadat set out to challenge them in so dramatic a fashion. Those workings had been summed up many years ago by the historian Albert Hourani in words that summed up the conduct of Arab governments before 1948 and foreshadowed what those governments were to do in the years to come. "The Arab governments made no preparation, either for peace with its concessions or war with its sacrifices."[96]

Each path had its attendant dangers. To offer concessions was to risk the charges of treason and defection, to be seen as acquiescing in the dismemberment of one's world and civilization. The threat of opportunists passing themselves off as purists lurked; the best was always the enemy of the good. Yet war was its own hell. Its burden could not be distributed fairly among a multitude of Arab players. Even in a world where Arabism made its claims, the question of Palestine did not figure with equal intensity in the universe of all Arabs. Many resented that they were dragged into a fight on behalf of others. And it was always hard for the men who govern to speak candidly about Israel's military advantage. To concede that was to concede the backwardness of one's own civilization, its vulnerability to the might and organization of others. Sadat's gift to his people was a break, once and for all, with that legacy.

It would be easier hence to open up the political life of the country. The military vocation set aside, Egyptians could turn to the social contract between ruler and ruled, the civil society would have a better chance in its uneven encounter with the state. Sadat had flirted with political liberalization. It was part of his opening onto America and Europe. It was the face he wanted to display. But it was not in him. His successor would come under greater pressure still. Mubarak lacked the imperial pretension; he had not been a historic leader or a "free officer" who had gone out to dismantle the monarchy and inherit the realm. He was anxious for an accord with those who had rallied against Sadat; he was not quite as willing to offend. But he, too, was not particularly eager to give away his powers or to erode the large prerogatives of the state.

Shortly after Mubarak's coming to power, a group of self-styled reformers – journalists, academics – proposed to him that he should form a political party of his own, position it in the middle of the political spectrum of the country. The "Sadatists" in the National Democratic Party would be on the right, the Marxists and the diehard Nasserites would play the role of the leftist opposition. Mubarak's own coalition would be something of a buffer between the

free-wheeling beneficiaries of the "Open Door" economy, the "fat
cats" who had done well by the Sadat policies, and the advocates
of the public sector. The cautious soldier brushed the suggestion
aside.

Mubarak would not indulge in a full-scale assault against what
Sadat had left behind. After all, he himself had been picked by
Sadat, brought out of the air force into the political domain. The
gates would not be flung wide open; the air force man did not
trust that he would survive the whirlwind sure to follow. He was
urged to strike at the widespread corruption that came to be associated with the beneficiaries of the Sadat regime. That too was
ruled out. A public display was made of one notorious case of
corruption: Sadat's younger brother Ismat. Behind the protective
shield of his brother's power, Ismat Sadat had risen from humble
and modest means – he had been a truck driver back in 1970 – to
great wealth and power. He ran protection rackets, accumulated a
fortune that the prosecutors estimated to be close to $150 million.
Ismat Sadat was convicted. But the corruption in the land was
widespread. The state was anxious to let well enough alone.[97]

Some symbolic concessions were made to those offended by the
Sadat regime's excessive displays of "modernity." Jihan Sadat had
become a symbol of just how far her husband had traveled beyond
the old world he had come from: She was everywhere, an eman-
cipated, assertive woman, the country's "First Lady," her opinions
on a wide range of subjects always at the ready. The new leader
would tread carefully. His wife, an educated woman in her own
right, would retreat from center stage. The "traditionalists" would
be appeased, the culture's sense of proper and improper ways shown
some deference.

The place used to "harmonizing contending assertions" would
take the path of least resistance. It would dodge great and decisive
confrontations, shun the prescriptions of wholesale changes. Lines
were drawn by the state for the forces at play in the country – both
in domestic politics and in the state's foreign entanglements. Within
the parameters drawn by the custodians of the state, dissent was
tolerated, the competing forces allowed to vent their grievances in
their own newspapers and publications. Beyond these lines few
dared to venture. The officer now at the helm fell back on a famil-

iar prop: He had a hungry society to feed, a burdened land, he would not permit anyone to play with fire.

Elections to the National Assembly were to be held under Mubarak; but the rules were rigged against the opposition. The elections – general elections were held in 1984 and 1987 – gave large majorities to the ruling National Democratic Party that Sadat had bequeathed Mubarak. At any rate the country was not governed in its legislative assembly; the presidency was still ascendant, and behind it the power of the army as the final arbiter of political life. Some running room was given the professional associations; a newly revived bourgeois party, the neo-Wafd party, gave voice to those in the society with a bent toward economic and political liberalization. The neo-Wafd party worked with a potent mix: nostalgia for a "better" Egypt and a more "dignified" era (the 1920s to the late 1940s) with which the Wafd was associated, the pride of professionals and businessmen who wanted a voice in the political life of the country. In the best of possible worlds, the neo-Wafd saw itself as the sole competitor to the state and its ruling party. It is a tribute to the vibrancy of that historical memory and to the strength of the Egyptian bourgeoisie that the neo-Wafd found ample political space in the Egypt of the 1980s.[98]

"Domesticated" Islamic groups which played by the rules were also given a reprieve. The keepers of the Nasserite flame were given their due. The warfare launched by Sadat against the legacy of Nasser was brought to an end. Mubarak was at some remove from Nasser. The great figure did not cast shadows in Mubarak's path in quite the way he did in Sadat's. Only "the bearded ones" (the Islamic militants) were now hunted down, declared beyond the pale. Democracy did not come to Egypt under Mubarak (the military man continued to warn that it was a "democracy with teeth" that obtained in the country), but the state seemed less exalted, less willing to monopolize the life of the country. Without a great sense of an Arab mission beyond her borders Egypt was, increasingly, a more settled and "normal" polity.

A great subtle change was to take place after the passing of the two "kings," Nasser and Sadat: Arabs would now read less and less of themselves into Egypt. The era of Egyptian primacy in Arab politics is of the past. In Beirut and then in the lands of the Gulf and in other Arab lands, a younger generation had its own world and concerns. The young men and women forged by Beirut's long ordeal could not recognize themselves in the order of Cairo. For the generation of the oil boom in the Gulf states the concerns of radical nationalism that Cairo had made her own in the past were ones that bore no relation to their experience and priorities. When a foreign culture beckoned that generation it was the culture of the West, more precisely the seductive culture of America. Egypt's themes were now her own. Her teachers and ideologues, her intellectuals, would journey to other Arab lands to spread the word that the old fidelities remained. But it was idle. The conviction was missing. The men and women of Egypt were not quite "strangers" to other Arabs. But they were now people of a land that had its own dilemmas and had gone its separate way. The questions Egypt asked now seem to be the questions of a burdened land in search of its own balance and its own path.

3

Fractured Tradition:
The Claims of Authenticity,
the Realities of Dependence

Out of the past we make a future.

Thomas Hobbes, *Behemoth*, VI

The destructive distortions of the tradition were all caused by men who had experienced something new which they tried almost instantaneously to overcome and resolve into something old.

Hannah Arendt, *Between Past and Future*
(New York: Viking, 1961), p. 29.

Is this a dream?
Is there a voyage called return?

Adonis, *The Blood of Adonis*
(Pittsburgh: University of
Pittsburgh Press, 1971), p. 32.

HISTORY serves many a harsh notice on civilizations and social orders. There is a temptation to reenact the past, to go back to things one knows and feels comfortable with. But the past is of course punctured; it cannot be regained. There is a profound difference between the real thing that once existed and had its own logic and legitimacy and a conscious, contrived insistence on the wisdom of the past, on its capacity to contain people's lives and explain their needs.

The Chinese revolutionaries, observes Joseph Levenson, accomplished a revolution "against the world to join the world, against the past to keep it theirs, but past."[1] China's success contrasts with the failure of the Arab order. There has been an incapacity to rebel thoroughly against the outside world, and thus to join it, or against the past, and thus to see it for what it is and keep it at bay. To be sure, there is plenty of resentment against a world that has been largely seen as unfair and treacherous, but there is also a great deal of buying into the modern international system. But there is a world of difference between resentment and rebellion, between buying into the ideas and labor of others and actively participating in the world. There has also been a mountain of words about slaying the past. Such was the promise of Abdul Nasser's generation, and surely it was the claim of post-1967 radicals who had vowed to succeed where their predecessors had failed.

But a decade after the new revolutionaries had their chance, and after a major so-called victory over the West in October, 1973, there was overwhelming evidence that the Arab world had come full circle. The vocabulary and concern of Arab politics and the drums to which people were marching showed the remarkable tenacity of the past. Both the Arabs themselves and those who interpreted them were suddenly saying that the Arab world was after all the Arab world — moved by its ancient passion, entangled in its old snares, afflicted with the old doubts and predicaments. Underneath it all, the Sunnis and Shi'ites in Iraq were after all Sunnis and Shi'ites; no ideological pretension of any kind would bridge that gap. Indeed, things were regressing. The most authoritative study of modern Iraq depicts a pattern of retreat. The ruling Ba'th party, which until 1963 had the characteristic "of a genuine partnership between Sunni and Shia 'poor-Arab' youth," had by

1968 become the almost exclusive preserve of the ruling Sunni stratum.[2] Ideological pretensions were equally irrelevant to the Syrian case. The base of Syrian politics was still communal, and the most important hard fact about Syrian politics was the political ascendancy of young countryside Alawites who went into the army and then managed to grab the power of the state. Likewise, the Lebanese civil war that started out with all kinds of ideological claims finally degenerated into a ghastly communal fight. The identification card, which designated not only one's religion but also one's sect, was the final arbiter, the pretensions of ideology were set aside and people presumably were seen for what they really were. Finally, in inter-Arab politics as a whole, it was not the radical nationalists of a decade before who seemed to be setting the tone of Arab politics, but the rulers of Saudi Arabia. Mohamed Heikal, once the propagator of Nasserite ideology, now told his readers that the Arab world had entered the "Saudi era" and that power had passed from the "charismatic revolutionary" state of Abdul Nasser to the "traditional" Saudi state. Radical nationalism was the pillar of the Nasserite order; Islam is the presumed pillar of the Saudi one.

The idea that ideology revolutionizes the world and blows away ancient feuds and weaknesses may or may not be empirically valid, but it has become a dictum of our age. When it is subscribed to, it can magnify the futility that societies experience as they discover those stubborn traits that simply refuse to go away. Then men begin to think that they have labored in vain, that their deeds are like footprints in the sand. Is not the resurgence of Islam that is said to be sweeping the region proof that generations of nationalists, liberal and Marxist ideologues alike, have failed to leave any real sign of their presence?

In the aftermath of Iran's upheaval, the resurgence of Islam has become a grande idée of sorts that explains all. Yesterday's grande idée was the withering away of tradition, the triumph of that great universal solvent, modernization. In yesterday's imagery, societies were to leap, as if by magic, historical stages; they would move instantaneously from traditional society to the rational-bureaucratic stage. In today's evocative imagery, the return of Islam is akin to a desert wind sweeping progress in its way, forcing people

171

back into the world of their ancestors. But today's grande idée may fail us as completely as yesterday's did. The hopes of those among the faithful who sense that a civilization broken and defeated several centuries ago is on the verge of resurrection and the fears of those who see in Islam's reassertion some great revolt against modernity are both mistaken. We must know the real struggles and concerns that people and societies are engaged in if we are to understand why they brandish the weapons they do and why they turn to a particular set of symbols.

What is behind the resurgence of Islam? How much is genuinely felt and how much is mere pretension by people and societies in desperate need of ideological cover to divert attention (their own and others') from excessive wealth or from acute dependency on the very infidels they denounce? What does this "desert wind" consist in besides the closing of beauty parlors, the banning of music, the enforcing of strict dress codes, and the usual incantations against atheistic Marxists? What is the prospect for the *turath* (heritage)? If the *turath* is to win by default (as I will contend here), what is to be the fate of competing options and how did they play themselves out in the aftermath of the June 1967 defeat?

Let us consider an essential distinction made in Joseph Levenson's study of China between *tradition* as a primary, genuine commitment and *traditionalism* as a conscious system of defense. What Levenson said of Confucianism applies to Islam's reassertion and runs through this analysis:

> When Confucian traditionalism comes to be accepted not from a confidence in its universal validity but from a *traditionalistic* compulsion to profess that confidence, Confucianism is transformed from a primary philosophical commitment to a secondary romantic one, and traditionalism from a philosophical principle to a psychological device.[3]

The "withering away" and "return" of traditions are simple images that glide past troubles and realities and miss the way by which and the reasons for which people turn to particular symbols at given moments. The apparent victories of traditions are more often a sign of their decay than their flowering. Traditions are most insistent and loud at the time when they rupture, when patience wears thin, when people no longer really believe, when the webs of meaning and significance have blown away, leaving a society a mere parody of itself:

> The end of tradition does not necessarily mean that traditional concepts have lost their power over the minds of men. On the contrary, it sometimes seems that this power of well-worn notions and categories becomes more tyrannical as the tradition loses its living force and as the memory of its beginning recedes; it may even reveal its full coercive force only after its end has come and men no longer even rebel against it.[4]

Thus the seeming contradiction between the reassertion of Islamic fundamentalism – all the tradition mongering of the Saudi era, all the insistent talk about authenticity – and the unprecedented integration of the Arab world into the world economy and the extensive political and cultural advances of the United States into the region is no contradiction at all. The two phenomena are twins. There comes a time in the life of nations when the outside world intrudes, when it appears with all its threats and temptations. People either respond to it coherently and competently or they lose their bearings. And if they do the latter, they need all kinds of psychological devices: They stress their uniqueness and the great achievements of their ancestors all the more as they surrender to others more powerful and more glamorous than themselves. Reassertion and chauvinism alternate with self-doubt and mimicry. This creates its own vicious circle. The failure of claims and movements, the troubles of a reigning order trying to have it both ways – to insist on its autonomy at the same time that it trades it for what the outside world has to offer – send everyone scurrying for cover. The rulers create fake victories, the citizenry tend to their private matters, and the intelligentsia and politically sensitive either give up or escape into metaphysics and absolutism. Imagined revolutions and breakthroughs follow one another. Salvation is proclaimed, then there is a feeling of disappointment after the dust settles and people discover that the whole rotten thing starts all over again. Authenticity becomes a refuge when practical politics fails to deliver concrete solutions to foreign weakness, to domestic breakdown, to cultural seduction. The connection between the Arab *thawra* (revolution) of the post-1967 years to the Saudi era of a decade later, from the Marxist–Leninist tracts to the fundamentalist exhortations, is not as tenuous as it at first seems. One leads to the other. Both are made of the same material: the desire for a quick fix, that brief moment of elation when all appears resolved before things come tumbling down. Thus "return" and "restoration" must both be situated in their proper context: first in terms of the failure of what passed for revolution, and then in the troubles of the dominant Arab order that waged the October War and then went on, after vanquishing old foes and exorcising old ghosts, to confront different and more deadly dilemmas.

THE "REVOLUTION" CONTAINED

The outcome of the Six Day War was a textbook case of a revolutionary situation, with all its standard ingredients: military defeat, internal exhaustion, the disaffection of intellectuals, a generation gap that was rapidly turning into an abyss, scathing critiques of the most sacred facets of a culture's life. That, at any rate, was the view of those who pinned their hopes on the new revolution – the Palestinian movement – and who broke with Nasserism and the Ba'th. George Habash's own transformation from the pan-Arabism of the Nasser years reflected the new drift. Historically, Arab nationalism had been confined to the political realm; it had not been particularly concerned with socioeconomic questions. Albert Hourani's survey of the "liberal age" in the Arab world had noted the "indifference" of liberal nationalism to social reform and economic justice. This he attributed partly to the "liberal atmosphere of the time," which stressed national independence over all other matters and partly to the fact that "most of the leaders and spokesmen of the nationalist movement either belonged to families of standing and wealth or had raised themselves into that class by their own efforts."[5] Both Nasserism and the Ba'th had presumably tried to do just that. Both had insisted that nationalism without social improvement was reactionary and insensitive; both had pledged their allegiance to a brand of nationalism that incorporated radical reform and socialism. In the light of the June defeat, a younger generation was to dig deeper into the political tradition and the social structure. It was to see in the ideas and deeds of the heroes of the 1950s and 1960s the dead hand of the past. A flood of

new writings – some indigenous, some of the standard revolutionary tracts of Debray, Fanon, Mao, Guevara – opened up new horizons. They gave a revolutionary tone to political discourse; they
underscored the gap between the young and the dominant order.

But revolutions cannot hover in the air. They require concrete
channels, and the channel for the Arab revolution was to be the
Palestinian movement. Where it had once been believed that the
Arab states would liberate Palestine, it was now expected that
the Palestinian struggle would topple the Arab order. Thus, when
a group of young intellectuals was invited to reassess the Egyptian
revolution on its seventeenth anniversary, they performed an autopsy. With the exception of Nadim Bitar, a faithful Nasserite who
insisted that Abdul Nasser still represented the best of alternatives,
all were convinced that Nasser's great deeds were behind him and
that his revolution had been shackled by bureaucracy and tarnished by defeat. For the young philosopher and activist Sadeq al-
Azm, the Palestinian revolution promised a new theory and practice. For the writer Adonis, the new "revolutionary moment" was
the moment of the Palestinians. Other "Arab revolutions" – and
the quotation marks are Adonis's – were real and living revolutions to the extent that they followed the lead of the Palestinians.
A publicist for the Palestinian movement saw the whole Arab order at the mercy of the Palestinians.[6] Three months before the carnage of Amman culminated in the victory of King Husein's army
and of so-called tradition, the radical intelligentsia were convinced
that the Palestinian movement was well on its way to becoming a
total Arab revolution.

This revolutionary moment lasted for three years. Looking back
with the benefit of hindsight, one can see the overwhelming odds
against its success; one can dismiss George Habash's designation
of the four enemies of the revolution – Zionism, imperialism, "Arab
reaction" (Jordan and Saudi Arabia), and "Arab bourgeois regimes" (Cairo and Damascus) – as the kind of messianic stuff from
which revolutionary bubbles and aspirations are made. But to do
so would be to overlook the vulnerability of the Arab order at the
time. There were deep domestic troubles in Egypt; the lines were
drawn in Jordan, and to a lesser extent in Lebanon, between the
regimes and growing Palestinian activism that intersected with lo-

cal grievances; there was despair throughout the Arab world, and people were vulnerable to any remedy, any banner. Moreover, two regimes (Egypt and Jordan) were trying to negotiate a diplomatic settlement and at the same time to cover their tracks, for they had little to bargain with and their ineffectual diplomacy lacked the appeal and the fire of Palestinian deeds.

The outside world intruded into this fight. This was a time when the belief in Third World revolutions, in guns and pamphlets, had a vast radical constituency in the West. Distant lands seething with contradictions and unrest were, after all, part of the revolt against the banality and imperialism of the Western radicals' countries. The future of the world, Western radicals were convinced, would be decided in remote Third World countries. As a French former Maoist recalls it, "Everything seemed possible, beginning with a return to the pure sources of the revolutionary ideal, at the wellsprings of the Third World, with a great strategic detour through countries whose outcasts rose up with empty bellies, guns flowering from their hands. Thus, we invented our own Third World . . . One need only recall our passionate discussions to realize that each epoch nourishes its own hopes of imaginary lands."[7] And because the world is what it is, images and convictions spun in the West (including those about the non-West) filter down to other lands and people begin to see themselves and their own situation in the images of others. This the radical left has always noted as part of its indictment of the asymmetry of the world system. It neglects to note, however, that the same thing happens in radical circles. There, too, there are centers and peripheries. The images about "revolutions in the revolutions" and "decadent feudal orders" filter down to poorer societies and are consumed by others. But the West's Third World was more revolutionary than the real Third World. In the Arab world, as in other regions, there was always the propensity (revealed in the 1967–1973 interlude) for people to forget where they were and to see themselves and their situation through the print and footage of the Western media.

The decisive duel between the dominant Arab order and the Palestinians was fought in Jordan. In Jordan (and later in Lebanon with the Syrian intervention against the Palestinians) the dominant order would demonstrate not only the superiority of its firepower but also the weakness of theory disconnected from the hard facts of political life. No revolutionary tract had an analysis of the bedouins who comprised the base of King Husein's army. The disembodied "revolutionary masses" discussed in the pamphlets were one thing, Jordan's realities were another.

Some time after Jordan's civil war ended, a leading member of the Palestinian movement conceded that many in the leadership did not really know Jordanian society, the hold of the king on his army, or the political and cultural significance of his Sharifian descent. The theorists were convinced that Husein's army would refuse to fight the Palestinians. But the men who fought for the king were mostly illiterates or barely able to read. They were beyond the reach of the radicals' pamphlets. For them the fight was between the king – their chieftain, their financial provider, a man who claims descent from the Prophet – and atheistic troublemakers, townsmen with alien and offensive ways.[8] Belief was pitted against unbelief. Islam was once again a pillar of political authority.

The capacity of the sultan to have God on his side is a recurring Islamic phenomenon. In the confrontation between Habash's Marxism and King Husein's army, the weight of tradition was on the king's side. Consider the following examples. In an issue of *Al Aqsa*, the magazine of the Jordanian armed forces, a soldier asks God to grant Husein victory "over Zionism and the unbelievers." When the headquarters of a radical Palestinian magazine were destroyed in the fighting, Radio Amman told its listeners that a "vindictive hired voice" had been silenced: "One that had tried to poison many thoughts and tried to disconnect you from your past, your traditions and religion." In yet another statement, the Palestinian movement was said to have "surrendered to Satan"; the soldiers were assigned to kill the Palestinians and pray for them at the same time. This was powerful local idiom that would stick, not metaphysical argument. More poignant still was the following short story disseminated to the Jordanian army. Its main characters were a "tough" bedouin soldier and an elegant "effeminate" young man from the Palestinian movement. The latter interrupts the soldier's prayer to talk with him about "revolutionary matters." This is their exchange:

The soldier praying, "Praise be to Allah, lord of the world, the merciful and the compassionate."

The young man interrupts: "Haven't you heard Marx saying . . ."

The voice of the soldier (now rising): "Thee we worship, Thee we ask for help . . ."

The young man again: "But Engels said . . ."

The soldier still reciting: "Say I seek refuge in the Lord of mankind . . ."

The young man: "Forget about such things; religion is the opiate of the people . . ."

The soldier, continuing his prayer " – from the evils of the sneaking whisperer . . ."

The young man; "Counter-revolution is the one . . ."

This time, the soldier turns around and threatens the urban youth, who of course runs away. The soldier returns to his prayer, raises his hands toward heaven and pleads: "Oh Lord, give victory to Husein and his soldiers . . . the soldiers of Muhammad against Zionism, Zionists, and the unbelievers."[9]

Husein's soldiers were the soldiers of Islam; their enemies were revolutionary outsiders, men who had gone beyond the bounds of the community and its ways. The king had prepared for his fight. Once the carnage began, he was in no hurry to stop it. The fight was on and it was a fight for Jordan. Prior to the eruption of the fighting, Husein had said that when the Hashemites came to Amman it was only a small village, and if the time came when he had to leave, he would leave Amman the way it was when his forefathers arrived. Slogans like "all authority to the Resistance" had had their day; Husein was to be the final victor. But some men do not easily change or learn from history. One of the more extreme of the Palestinian movements, the Popular Democratic Front for the Liberation of Palestine led by Nayef Hawatmeh, attributed the defeat to the absence of revolutionary theory. No revolution could be accomplished, it profoundly proclaimed, without revolutionary theory. More sophisticated analyses came from another group. The devastation of the Arab regimes after 1967 had given the Palestinian movement some room for maneuver, but the regimes were now reasserting their control. The Arab states needed heroic deeds after 1967 and the Palestinians were able and willing to provide these deeds. Sooner or later, however, the Arab state system had

178

to strip the Palestinians of their delusions. This they did in Jordan in September, 1970. Six years later, the Syrian army would administer the same lesson in Lebanon.[10]

In the heat of the Lebanese civil war as well there was a feeling that the dominant order could be overthrown, that there were new possibilities. "We feel," said George Habash in mid-1976, "that the reactionary, bourgeois, confessional regime has collapsed and that the Lebanese national movement would make a big mistake if it allowed this regime to be resurrected and reconstructed on a reformist basis. The Lebanese National Movement has a chance to insist on a new Lebanon – a democratic, nationalist, secular Lebanon."[11] But the old Lebanon, although transformed, survived the civil war. The old men who ran things – be they on the right, such as former presidents Camille Chamoun and Suleiman Franjieh and the leader of the Phalangists, Pierre Gemayyel, or on the left, such as Kamal Junblatt – had sons, and to their sons passed their power and the old ways of doing things. Aptly enough, as though to forecast the turn of events in Iran, the fight in Shi'a Southern Lebanon between the old feudal boss Kamel Assad and the left ended in victory for neither. Power passed to Imam Musa al-Sadr, a young Shi'a Mujtahid of the Khomeini variety. In Lebanon, the dominant order remained. The Syrians upheld it and made the Saudis finance their "stabilization" effort. The fight in Lebanon was less dangerous, less loaded with socioeconomic meaning than the radicals assumed.

The real struggle between the old order and the radicals had dominated the 1967–1973 interlude. The old order had prevailed both in Jordan and of course in October, 1973. Whatever the military judgment on the October War, there can be no doubt that the war bought time and helped defuse the frustrations and the radicalism. Writing in early 1973, Arnold Hottinger, a careful analyst of Arab politics, caught the radical mood of the time when he stated that the Arab society that might emerge from the turmoil "might well resemble present day China more than any society known to us."[12] The Chinese analogy was far fetched, but the mood was bleak enough to suggest the comparison. Thanks to the October War, however, Arab politics took a new turn, and the order put together by the Egyptians, the Syrians, and the Saudis was able to contain and outflank the radicals. The fact that the Arabs were unable to maintain a united political front was a problem for the future. It was to be a quarrel about tactics rather than over fundamental socioeconomic issues. By the time this problem arose, "the revolution" had been aborted and the order given a breathing spell.

One need not engage in excessive psychologizing of politics to note that nothing less than patricide was at stake in the early fight between the dominant order and the radicals. Nasser and the Ba'th had flirted with some new ideas, but there existed then a basic continuity with the past when compared to what the young were doing and saying after 1967. The shift from the notorious Ahmad al-Shuqairi to George Habash was a qualitative one. Al-Shuqairi, a sycophant and a braggart, was part of an old culture of defeat and compromise. He spoke the old language and was too much a creature of Arab courts, having served the Saudis and the Syrians as an ambassador to the UN, later shifting his allegiance to Abdul Nasser, who rewarded him with chairmanship of the PLO. Habash represented a discontinuity. He was a public man, ideologically committed, whose path to power came through the cell and the street. By the logic of the old world around him, Habash, a physician, could have gone on to mind his own business (all the more so because he was a Christian), tend to his private matters, and, like other members of his profession, accumulate a fortune. His choice was a break with the ways of the elders: To go beyond personal safety and success and opt for the risks of public politics was to inject into that world a sense of new possibilities.

Then there was the impact of a political and intellectual renaissance of sorts. The young radicals dragged the Arab world out of its provincialism, out of its obsessive concern with the tired themes of its own history into the full light of world events and currents. They connected the Arab world's dilemmas with the dilemmas and successes of others. That it was all done in too mechanistic and imitative a fashion was not seen at that moment. That realization began to sink in after Jordan, when even the most die-hard believers had to concede that the battle with the culture's ways had been lost, that the world of the elders had eluded and outwaited them and bounced back with seemingly new vitality.

As though to convey the parallels between the defeat of the Palestinians in 1970 and the Arab defeat of 1967, it fell to the young radical scholar Sadeq al-Azm to do the same kind of autopsy on the Palestinians as he had earlier performed on Nasserism in his book *Self-Criticism After the Defeat*. September, 1970, in Jordan, wrote al-Azm in a new wave of revisionism, was to the Palestinian movement what June, 1967, was to the pan-Arabist movement. The Palestinian movement had been but a natural extension of the earlier movement, a branch of it. The characteristics that crippled the earlier movement found their way to its offshoot.[13] Palestinian leaders too were more anxious to "strut on the world stage," to give press conferences, to flaunt their weaponry, to put forth easy arguments, than to undertake the patient work of reconstituting a Palestinian nation in exile, doing the steady and painful work that social revolutions entail. If the leaders of the Palestinian movement were giving an average of one-and-one-half press interviews a day — as was reported in a detailed and unpretentious analysis by a member of the Executive Committee of the Palestine Liberation Organization between 1969 and 1971 — was this not proof that people had remained braggarts, that the old world had survived?[14]

Of course the expectation that a brief and spectacular push against a dominant political and cultural tradition would sweep away the past was sheer illusion; like all illusion, it had disappointment written into it. But such was the expectation after 1967, and the disappointment was quick to follow. The same young men and women who had embraced the Palestinian movement became its relentless critics, and Azm's revisionism was but a manifestation of the general disillusionment. The new revolution, like the old Nasserite one, he observed, had exaggerated its achievements; it too had peddled its myths and made the Arab masses live on illusions. Indeed its moment of success was due to the fact that it "renewed and nurtured the old illusions that the masses had been used to and had survived on for a long time." Was not Arafat's statement that he did not expect King Husein to hit with all his might akin to Nasser's statement after the June defeat that he had expected Israel's attack to come from the east and the north but that instead it came from the west? Was not the growth of bureaucratization and profiteering a reaffirmation of an old cultural theme

– the gun serving as a way of exorcising self-doubts and hoarding resources? In drowning the Palestinian movement in words, was the culture doing what came most naturally to it: spinning its wheels, turning everything into a forum for oratory, making and remaking the world with phrases but leaving the substance unchanged?[15]

To the extent that the Palestinian movement represented and embodied the post-1967 Arab revolution, its troubles burst the revolutionary bubble of the post-1967 years. There would be no easy way out; the panacea of a people's war of national liberation was but a brief illusion. It thrived so long as the Arab regimes seemed castrated and so long as the youthful energy tapped by a new wave of thought and practice had the daring and energy to push for a new world. By the time the Arab armies went into action in October, 1973, and the reactionary oil states deployed the oil weapon, the old world had made a stand of its own; it promised its own dawn of a new age.

THE DOMINANT ORDER'S
BRIEF TRIUMPH

The revolution, then, eluded the Arab order, and people were left searching for an explanation of its failure. Nostalgia would have it that the battle was almost won. The political climate of a particular period and the real – as opposed to the perceived – balance of power among contending forces is difficult, if not impossible, to determine. Perhaps the Arab order was as weak as its challengers believed. On the other hand, the power of the challengers may have been ephemeral, their momentum more of a mood than a concrete reality. A greater number of obstacles stood in the way of the Arab radicals than was generally believed at the time.

For one, the Arab–Israeli conflict itself, on which the radicals depended as a catalyst of revolutionary upheaval, was in reality a conservatizing force. Hard as the radicals tried to turn that war into a war of national liberation, hard as they tried to draw parallels with Algeria's anticolonial war or China's revolution, the Arab–Israeli conflict was an interstate duel – and all the more so because the power of the Palestinians was located outside the occupied territories. The two Arab–Israeli wars of the post-1967 years –

Nasser's war of attrition and the October War – served effectively
as sponges: They absorbed frustrations and they demonstrated that
the initiative still lay with the dominant order. The October War,
in particular, satisfied the popular need for revenge against Israel
for the wounds and humiliations of June, 1967. If the Arabs wanted
a new world, a new place in the sun, it was offered to them by
President Sadat and King Faisal. The victory of October, 1973, posed
a difficult dilemma for the Arab radicals. It was risky to question
the achievements of October (and that goes a long way toward
explaining Qaddafi's eclipse in inter-Arab politics, for he dismissed
the October War as a "comic affair") and self-defeating to pay
homage to those who pulled it off.

Inasmuch as the October War became a great historical event in
Arab history – it symbolized, wrote an Egyptian, the return of the
Arab to his proper place in history, the first Arab military victory
after centuries of defeat – there was very little to be gained from
belittling what the dominant regimes had accomplished.[16] When
all appeared lost it was the dominant order that supplied the answers: crossed the Suez Canal when it was believed that it would
be unable to do so; brought about one of the most massive shifts
of wealth known in the history of the modern world system;
promised and for a while seemed to succeed in delivering a brighter
world. Under these circumstances, it was natural enough to dismiss the talk about social revolution. Given a choice, and the dominant order did supply one, people simply chose, as Edmund Burke
would have put it, to be "good patriots," and "a good patriot and
true politician considers how he shall make most of the existing
materials of his country . . . Everything else is vague in conception,
perilous in the execution."[17]

The "perilous" schemes of the revolutionaries and their "vague"
conceptions were shunned in favor of the known world, and the
choice was made that much easier because of prosperity that the
new order promised. In the Palestinian movement itself, the final
word belonged not to George Habash and the Marxists but to Yasser Arafat and the believers in Palestinian nationalism. The latter
were part of the old world, they read the old texts, they were at
home with the dominant tradition. Their demand was a limited
one – statehood – and it was a demand that the Arab system of

states could pay homage to. Thus the Palestinian movement was absorbed into the dominant order – taken into summit conferences, subsidized by the oil states, lent the prestige of Arab diplomatic power. In return, the Palestinian movement had to tame its own radicals, keep *al mabadi? al mustwarda* (the imported doctrines) at bay, accept the rules of the game, abide by the dominant tradition.

The institutionalization of the Palestinian movement had been the consistent demand of the Arab states. Early in the post-1967 years, it was repeatedly made by Nasser and his spokesman Mohamed Heikal; it was even endorsed (at least as long as Nasser lived) by Qaddafi, who asked in early 1970 that the Palestinian movement be transformed into a Palestinian government. This all along was the demand of the oil states that wanted a responsible Palestinian movement. The Rabat Resolution of 1974, which designated the PLO as the "sole, legitimate representative" of the Palestinian people, consummated the deal between the Arab order of states and the Palestinian movement. It was a deal concluded at the height of the dominant order's power. The Arab states had an embarrassment of material and diplomatic riches, or so it seemed at the time. It was time to be benevolent, so they conferred upon the Palestinians what one observer described as a "metaphysical" right to the West Bank and Gaza.[18]

Remaking the social order and settling the local grievances of the Arab world were no longer proper Palestinian concerns. The Syrian intervention in Lebanon in June, 1976, drove home this point. Hafez Asad was bent on decoupling the Palestinian movement from the Lebanese National Movement and the aims of its leader, Kamal Junblatt. In justifying his intervention in Lebanon, Asad would claim that the Palestinian movement had strayed from its proper objectives. In this statement can be seen the difficulty of sneaking radical politics through the back door of Palestinian nationalism.

Vulnerable on its flanks since 1967, the Arab order would not be brought down either by George Habash and Nayef Hawatmeh from the left or Qaddafi from the right. Restoration was as much a possibility as was revolution. The young radicals were convinced that the old order was bankrupt, that its leadership was discredited, that its symbols were battered. In all that they were probably right; but they drew the wrong conclusions about the inevitability of the dominant order's collapse. An exhausted world can still hang on long after it loses its vitality; it can cover up its weaknesses and pull off semivictories; it can rely on the built-in human preference for normalcy, play for time, and then reassert itself. That is what the men in power did with and after October, 1973.

This time it was the dominant order's turn to strut on the world stage. The Arab world had turned the tables on the West. After a long period of decline, there was talk of renewal in the air. Anwar el-Sadat's boastful statement that the Arab world had become the world's sixth power appealed to the historic desire for revenge against the West. To the politically conscious among the Arabs, it appeared that the Arab world had finally managed to find its place in the sun. For a culture that had sustained itself through a long stretch of frustrations and setbacks by dreams of sudden resurrection, it all seemed to make sense and to conform to a cyclical vision of history. This vision witnesses individual careers and whole social orders rise and fall in a way that mysteriously humbles the mighty and redresses the grievances of the weak. In this confrontation, the West, which had always seemed threatening and resolute, was full of its own squabbles, unsure of its power and purpose. The arrogance of the West had clearly come up against all sorts of limits – its own self-doubts and the resistance of others – and it was increasingly obvious to those who had traditionally stood in awe of Western power that there were cracks in the edifice.

The so-called decline of the West may or may not have been an objective reality, but for people and societies long at the receiving end of Western power, October 1973 was a turning point. The wounds inflicted by the West had left deep scars everywhere, and non-Westerners were quick to see the dawn of a new age. The weapons, ideas, and diplomatic skill with which one segment of the world had erected a world system in its own image were now available to hitherto dispossessed groups and nations. In the Arabs' petropower, in India's nuclear explosion, and in the power of the new majority at the UN non-Westerners saw the beginning of a new world.

Even the friends and clients of the West were now compelled to assert their defiance and autonomy. Marcos of the Philippines became openly contemptuous of Western democracy; his "New Society" became more bluntly authoritarian. In the shah of Iran's interview with the Italian journalist Oriana Fallaci, the West was portrayed as a row of vulnerable dominoes. Power and the future belonged to the shah's quest to marry the power of Western technology to the ways of Persian kingship.[19] Yet another client of the West, Mobutu, of Zaire, said he was seeking a future based on the ways of the ancestors, on the wisdom of the bush. He offered his society a philosophy of authenticity, Mobutuism, as an answer to both Western democracy and Marxism. In the shedding of his Christian name for a native one, the local culture of Zaire was presumably reasserting its worth.

But the stage on which the protagonists – the Third World and the West – met and the circumstances of their new encounter were prone to distort the results. This would be seen a few years later when the challenge of the Third World seemed to lose much of its initiative. By then the Arab world, which had led the rebellion, was itself in deep trouble; the shah of Iran's dreams were dashed at home, where all battles and claims begin and end; and Mobutuism could be seen for what it was all along: a cover for collaboration, a bit of glamor and theater sprinkled on top of a world of mismanagement and corruption that culminated in International Monetary Fund (IMF) advisors in virtual control of Zaire's economy. There is, when all is said and done, a difference between pretension to power and the real thing. The underlying weaknesses of the Arab and Third World states eventually came to the surface. But in the immediate aftermath of October, 1973, the impression was one of dazzling success.

In the Arab world, power in the post–October 1973 period belonged to a new group:

> For a generation the men who directed the course of events in the Arab world had been ideologists or officers from the armed forces – or sometimes officers who turned into ideologists or ideologists who tried to behave as if they were officers. Such were Sadat, Assad, Ghadaffi, Boumedienne, Michel Aflaq, Sadam Hussein and many others. Many of these were still there, but they were now being joined by the first instalment of a new breed of power brokers, the

middlemen, the arms dealers, the wealthy merchants who flitted between East and West, between royal palaces and the offices of oil companies – men like Kamal Adham, Mahdi Tajjir, Adnan Khashoggi and others – and by royalty itself, for who in the Arab world now exercised more power than Prince Fahd or Prince Sultan of Saudi Arabia? Could not individuals such as these, it was argued, achieve more for the Arabs than mass movements and radical revolutions?

It is not surprising if in this changed atmosphere men and women in Egypt and Syria felt that the time had come for them too, to see some improvement in their material circumstances. They had known hardship; now they looked for their reward – for more to eat and for better houses to live in. Of course money would have to be found to pay for this, but who would dare to suggest that the Arabs were short of money? It was being said that the Arabs possessed the power to bring the rest of the world to starvation; surely they must have the power to feed themselves? So eyes turned to the oil-producing countries. Oilfields began to loom far bigger in the public mind than battlefields; *tharwa* (riches), it was said, had begun to take over from *Thawra* (revolution).[20]

But the new leaders really represented a variation on an old theme. In a crossroads civilization the triumph of the merchant is hardly surprising. The defeat of the officer-ideologues who dominated Arab politics in the 1950s and 1960s left a political vacuum that the new men, and, behind them, petropower, were now aiming to fill. The new men could draw comfort from the defeat of their adversaries in Cairo and Damascus. The "open-door economy" of Egypt, proclaimed with great fanfare in 1974, and the much less trumpeted but no less real and similar shift in the Syrian economy, could be taken as proof of the supremacy of conservative ways. Those who managed state enterprises during the more-or-less radical interlude of Nasserism and the Ba'th were anxious to make the shift to the private sector, to pay homage to the sanctity of property, to accept time-honored traditions and class arrangements. Furthermore, many of the younger radicals who had been even more audacious, more indifferent to the ways of the culture, were turning up, as one Syrian scholar puts it, "in the Gulf area and the Arabian Peninsula in business suits taking advantage of the 'Black Gold Rush.' "[21]

The deep structure of all this was a reaffirmation of the old order. People may rebel, but they ultimately make their peace. In a conservative world where people are not likely to risk rebellion, where parents and extended families put up all sorts of barriers to rebellion, this was a verdict that the old ways were still the only possible ones. The world of the fathers, so to speak, had won out.

Authenticity, or what passed for it, had triumphed. The victory of the people of the desert was a victory for those who seemingly had remained themselves. The bourgeois, cosmopolitan capitals that had defiled themselves (such as Beirut), and those that had surrendered to imported doctrines (such as Cairo and Damascus), had lost out. In the ruin of Beirut, the Saudis would see the failure of societies that allowed individuals to do what they wished; in the troubles of Nasser and the Ba'th there was an indictment of those who dared turn things upside down. This was a vindication of the cultural and political superiority of some imagined pure tradition.

Several centuries ago, the great North African historian Ibn Khaldun depicted the struggle between the bedouins and the cities as the key to the rise and fall of dynasties and empires. In a new variation on Khaldun's theme, the Arab cities were in decline while the bedouins (both the radicals like Qaddafi and the conservatives in the peninsula) were on the ascendancy. Although no deliberate effort had brought about this remarkable historical shift, the military effort of Egypt and Syria had paved the way for the new order. Oil prices were raised under the cover of the October War; the decision had taken place under peculiar global circumstances, and the shah of Iran was as responsible as anyone for the dramatic increase in prices.

All that was easy enough to ignore and in a way was academic and irrelevant. The shift had taken place and the new success were all the more startling when compared to the failure of what had passed for radicalism and socialism. There was not yet sufficient distance from Nasserism to see its mixed legacy, to judge whether there was some method, some legitimate achievements, behind its sound and fury. The bases of Nasserism − import substitution, a brand of secular nationalism that was neither collaborationist nor excessively xenophobic, the expansion of educational opportunities − had been mixed. Eventually, those who had been through the whirlwind of Nasserism were destined to take stock of its legacy, to decide whether what was done constituted progress or was merely illusions and theatrics or, more likely, a combination of both. But the time to do so was not yet at hand in the mid-1970s. All that stood out then was the success of the new men and the disaster of the June 1967 defeat. A statement made by a Saudi in 1975 to a visiting American journalist was typical of the mood:

> I was educated in Egypt during the time of Nasser, and when I came back I went into the army, because I thought it was the instrument of progress. But then I saw what was happening in Egypt and in Syria and Iraq. I realized that we were left alone to fight the battle of liberty and free enterprise in the Arab world . . . Now ideology has been stabilized. We have proven to the world that we were right. The proof is in the reception of this country's leadership in an Arab world. Saudi Arabia has become an economic and political model.[22]

In other words, it was not so much the achievements of conservative fundamentalism that won out; the outcome was determined by the failure and exhaustion of the adversaries.

For more than a generation, radicals in Egypt and the Fertile Crescent had been saying that the past must be shed if the Arab–Islamic order was to stand up to the outside world. Secular radical nationalism had insisted on its capacity to secure national glory and prestige. But the record told a different story:

> Nowhere has this type of nationalism resulted in an escape from economic dependence and underdevelopment. The only achievements of the great Arab nation in the field of power politics and national prestige have been the work of the oil potentates – the most fundamentalist and conservative of Muslims – in selling their oil with the haggling of skilled businessmen and technocrats (but whose *keffias, agals,* and *abayas* enable them to be associated with bedouin tradition). As for the ideal of the united Arab nation, it has grown ever harder in the face of the evident development of regional nationalisms (Egyptian, Algerian, Moroccan, and so on) to maintain that its realization is hampered only by the "plots" of Israel and "imperialism."[23]

Thus the movement from the era of nationalism and ideology to the era of commissions and the middlemen. In the former, the Arabs had subsisted on Nasser's grandeur; some (unfortunately for them) were taken in by the metaphysics of Michel Aflaq, the theorist of the Ba'th Party, and his abstractions about Arab unity, love, and the primacy of the nation. A decade later, they were being treated to the theatrics of the middlemen, to the great achievements of Adnan Khashoggi; they were told about the "regional packages" – large deals involving Saudi capital, Egyptian labor, and Sudanese land that would achieve, without political struggles and disagreements, the unity that had eluded the pan-Arabists. In the world view of the middlemen and of the technocrats, if ideology were stabilized and passions expunged, the new order would prosper and men would telescope history, buy technological progress off the rack, and leap into the industrial world without disrupting the social mores. There was in this an obvious desire to sublimate politics, to run away from conflicts. In Albert Hirschman's imagery, there was a desire to substitute the logic of "interest" – money making, pragmatic politics, the seemingly benign endeavors of wealth seeking and consumption – for the capriciousness of "passions."[24] It was reasoned that the Arab world had suffered enough from total schemes and romantic visions, that there was plenty of wealth to go around, that the area could do with a bit of normalcy. On the face of it, this was a simple and understandable desire. It seemed benign and safe enough, a Middle Eastern variation upon Europe's story after World War II. Exhausted and ruined by its passions, tired from attempts at domination, Europe would see in economic recovery and the benign pursuit of economic growth a way of extricating itself from historical grievances and conflicts. But success and normalcy produce their own troubles. In an era of intense competition, fatigue points the way out and people are ready to compromise; in a benign world, there are always those who stand for principles, who wish to inject into what they see as a compromised world their own higher ideals and own lofty motivations.

Just as fatigue places a high premium on normalcy, crass success is vulnerable to the contempt and passion of those who believe that they have higher public projects in mind, things more noble, more historically justifiable than personal success and material aggrandizement. Two such public projects exploded the benign order: the Palestinian quest and the fight of Maronite Lebanon for its version of order and civilization. Both projects revealed that the supposedly rational, restrained order was in an inhospitable habitat. There was something ominous and odd about the mixture of outward pragmatism and rationality and the various political and cultural troubles of the Arab order. The massive technology purchases, the acquisition of new skills, the determination born out of success to engage the outside world without the old resentments and inadequacies, and then the political and cultural troubles undermined the new rationality. The troubles of Lebanon offered a pointed commentary on the outward rationality. By the logic of interest, the Lebanese stood to reap substantial benefits from the new order. Traditionally brokers and middlemen, there was plenty for them to do in the post-October 1973 order. But passions won out and the traditional capacity for bargaining broke down. For the young who manned the barricades on both sides, all considerations of finance were degraded. As the Christians' apocalyptic language put it, their fight was for a civilization in retreat: It was a fight not only for Lebanon but for the West as a whole. The West was lost unless Lebanon (their version of Lebanon, of course) was saved. That the West was unable to see it as such was the result of cowardice and greed. Blackmailed by Arab oil, the West had relinquished its moral duty, betrayed itself. In the words of Amin Gemayyel, the son of the Phalangist leader Pierre Gemayyel, "Lebanon's war was the war of a failed civilization [Islam, the Arab world] that wanted to destroy a successful cultural experiment . . . for the Lebanese the scale of destruction does not matter; what matters is the quality of reconstruction."[25] In other words, if Lebanon needs to be destroyed to be re-created, then men must have the nerves for a task of this kind. As for the Western world, says Amin Gemayyel's brother, Bashir Gemayyel: "Its great sin is to leave a small population, that is the Lebanese population, fighting alone for liberty, democracy, for the dignity of man against peoples and groups that deny these values and try to destroy it and to eradicate this country that still adheres to such values."[26] How is the seemingly banal pursuit of economic interests to accommodate such views and historic fears? In this kind of rule-or-die mentality, all calculations of interests are naive or treasonous. That interest alone governs the world was once rebutted in a different context

191

and at a different time by a man who maintained that "passion, humor, caprice, zeal, faction, and a thousand other springs, which are counter to self-interest, have as considerable part in the movement of this machine."[27] Lebanon supplied a confirmation of that view: Individuals are not always neutral umpires or middlemen. Their moral calculus is complex. They do not merely note and philosophically accept large historical and cultural shifts; they become frightened or assertive; they fight for what they know, and they do so all the more ferociously against what they perceive to be banal or smug orders to sweep things under the rug.

Lebanon's traditional role was thought of in apolitical terms: It was assumed that so long as the pan-Arabists accepted Lebanon's unique identity and situation, Lebanon could find its place in the Arab family as a link between the Arabs and the West; as a place for those who played and lost the game of politics and who then needed somewhere to go to write their memoirs or plot their return to power; as a playground for Saudis and Kuwaitis who wished to flee from the climate and puritanism of their own countries; as a banking haven for Syrians who wanted to flee from the politics and intrigues of the military and economic irresponsibility of would-be socialists.

In the view of the "Lebanonists," however, the country had a special mission: to interpret the Arab world to the West, to act as an agent for Western civilization. So long as Arabism was not pushed beyond tolerable limits, Lebanon could have it both ways: live off the Arab world yet think of itself as part of the Occident. The so-called National Pact worked out in 1943 was a compromise: The Christians would accept nominal membership in the Arab world and the Muslims would give up the notion of Arab unity. The two leaders who concluded the agreement, the Maronite President Bishara al-Khuri and his Muslim Sunni Prime Minister Riad al-Sulh, were both reasonable men who made the best of the material at hand. The philosopher behind the idea was a Catholic banker and writer, Michel Chiha, who believed that Lebanon could maintain a Mediterranean civilization if ideology, fanaticism, and politics were kept at bay. The Christian elite at the time understood Lebanese economic dependence upon the Arab world and sought to reconcile this with the cultural affinity with the West. It believed that it could juggle both worlds: Arabism was far away; one could pay homage to it and still go about one's business of trading, publishing, smuggling, or banking.

The alliance between the Maronite militias and the state of Israel that had become public in 1976 was the final nail in the coffin of Michel Chiha's and Bishara al-Khuri's Lebanon. The passing of power in the Christian community from men like these to the Phalangists – who were once thought of by the Christian community as rednecks and lower-middle-class ruffians – symbolizes the triumph of passion in Christian Lebanon over the reasonable logic of interest.

During the struggle for Palestine, the Lebanese Christian bourgeoisie had seen the Israelis as a threat: Both wanted to appeal to the West, both thought of themselves as enclave societies in a culturally alien world, and the Lebanese business community feared that a dynamic Israel would outstrip it economically and be more successful in its appeal to the West. After the establishment of Israel, the Lebanese argued for a division of labor in the Arab world. Other Arab states could pursue a military struggle if they wished, but the Lebanese would appeal to Western opinion and try to awaken the West to the plight of the Palestinians and to the justice of the Arab case.

This worked while the Arab–Israeli conflict was removed from Lebanon's soil – a situation that changed after 1970 when the Palestinians, expelled from Jordan, made their political home in Lebanon. It was then that the glib, superficial Arabism of Lebanon met a test it was destined to fail. The leaders in the Christian community who had known the Arab system and made their peace with it lost to those to whom Arabism and Islam were synonymous and who believed in their own cultural supremacy and in the backwardness of the Arabs. The Maronites, convinced that they were being abandoned by the West (they too heard of the so-called decline of the West), resentful of the post-October 1973 wealth and prominence of the Muslim Arab states, losing control over a country that had become too Palestinianized and radicalized for their taste, and aware that the demographic facts were shattering the myth of Christian majority, did what was previously unthinkable. After a brief reliance on a Syrian connection, they opted for a full break with the Arab system – an alliance with Israel and a full commitment to partition.

Through it all, the advocates of partition would be helped by the obvious culpability of the Arab states that had exported the "sacred Arab cause" – the Palestinian issue – onto Lebanese soil. In other words, the least Arab of countries and the weakest militarily was to bear the brunt of full Israeli retaliation and to accept a parallel and competing system of authority. The Palestinian slogan of nonintervention in the internal affairs of Arab countries was harder to practice than to preach. With Israel willing and able to retaliate for raids into her territory, the Lebanese formula unravelled. The gift of an enlarged Lebanon bequeathed by the French turned into a nightmare, and the Maronite militias took up arms first to defeat the Palestinian-leftist-Muslim alliance and then, a little later, to try to carve out their own state, bidding farewell to the idea of Arab brotherhood. They were now willing to state what had been their conviction for quite some time: that they thought of themselves as a different breed; that they were set apart from the Arab world, in which they were geographically included but culturally separate. Arabism, said a spokesman for the Guardians of the Cedars (one of the Maronite militias) in a tone that reflects the deep-seated fears of a mountainous people, is a backward movement that has nothing to offer Lebanon or the world. "They" (meaning the others, the Muslims, the Arabs, the savages) "would push us into the ocean . . . If they push us we'll take refuge in the mountains and fight to the last man."[28]

The other strand of Lebanese thinking, the case for moderation, was still alive, but the world had grown too grim for it. The son of Bishara al-Khuri reiterated the old case for an apolitical Lebanon all the more urgently when there was so much Arab wealth to share: "In no case should the Christians ignite the antagonism of the Arab hinterlands, where our *interests* are tremendous. The time has passed when the foreign powers protected us. One barrel of oil outweighs all the Christians of the Orient."[29]

But it was no longer Khalil al-Khuri's era or the era of men like him. It was the time of those who thrive on that mixture of fear and "purity" engendered by massive breakdowns and crises. The rise, in the 1970s, of men like Major Saad Haddad, a renegade

officer from the Lebanese army, the chieftain of "Free Lebanon" –
a strip of land in southern Lebanon on Israel's northern border –
was of a piece with the new world around him, a bleaker, more
biased world. A reporter came back from "Free Lebanon" with
Major Haddad's themes: the betrayal of the West and his and his
own men's defense of a decaying, materialist civilization:

> I think all of the Christian world knows what is going on. But it is
> too involved in its own materialist problems. No more human val-
> ues. Religion, it is only by name now. We have been born a Chris-
> tian, so we say we are Christian. Even my Pope doesn't help. He is
> supposed to tell all the Christians of the world to wake up, their
> brothers in Christianity are in danger of being exterminated and
> they have to help. By saying a few words he can change the picture.
> I wrote to the Pope and never got an answer. He is supposed to be
> our spiritual father on the ground, and each father is supposed to
> protect his son, even if he is wrong. How come we are right and he
> is not supporting us? The terrorists are getting volunteers from Iran,
> Libya, Iraq, Saudi Arabia, from all the Communist countries, to fight
> for them. What prevents the Christians from sending funds or com-
> ing as volunteers to help us? We feel left out from all the world
> except by Israel. We are fortunate that we found Israel on our bor-
> der to help us. Israel understood our problem, that we are a minor-
> ity threatened with extermination, and extended its hand to us. They
> ask for nothing, and for whatever they give, I am thankful. I have
> no right telling them I need this and this. But I have a right to ask
> my brother in Christianity.[30]

The Lebanonists once hid behind the notion of majority rule:
Lebanon was said to be more Christian than Muslim, so the Christians governed. Implicitly and explicitly they felt that the West would
continue to dominate and that those who spoke its language and
shared its religious heritage would be partners. The world changed.
The demographic realities were no longer the same. The previously inaccessible Muslim Arabs to the east of Lebanon were now,
in their own way, joining the world; besides, the outside world
had come anxiously courting the Arabs of the peninsula. This was
a nightmare and a challenge to Lebanon's raison d'être and to the
mental geography of the Lebanese, secure as they were in their
belief that they played an indispensable role. Now the ideological
position had to harden: The claim to power would no longer rest
on demography and majority rule but on the supposed superiority

of the minority civilization. To counter the Muslim demographic edge there was the excellence of the Christian minority. This was openly stated: People would no longer hide behind arguments borrowed from Western parliamentary systems – they would simply state that their existential predicament made their political dominance a necessity for survival. "The problem of Lebanon," we are told by a pamphlet of the Phalanges published in 1977, "is the old problem of minorities in the Middle East; it is the old Oriental Question. The Muslim majority, first by virtue of it being a majority and second by virtue of it being a Muslim majority, is tyrannical whether it wishes it to be so or it did not. Because it is in the nature of such a majority to dominate, Christian Lebanon must look for a way of resisting the encroachment of the majority, and the answer lies in "superior man," in militias, in guarantees to Christians.[31] A country that had juggled different worlds was up against the wall, growing more incoherent and frightened, more irrational. To its own troubles were added the ambition and schemes of others – the burden of the Arab–Israeli conflicts, the ambitions of young Libyan officers, the schemes of Iraq, the fears and ambitions of Syria. The Lebanese, who had prided themselves on their modernity, were to treat the world to a ghastly nightmare. "Right" and "left" alike, Christian and Muslim, were dwarfed by forces more powerful than they were.

Lebanon was one problem, the question of Palestine another. Here too there was a matter of principle and passions, one that provided an embarrassing contrast of its own to the smugness of the new era. Nothing so visibly demonstrated the peculiar nature of Arab wealth – its inconvertibility to real power, that frustrating difference between power as resources and power as the ability to affect outcomes – as the incapacity of the dominant order to resolve the Palestinian question. Having exaggerated the achievements of the October War, the leaders themselves fed the unrealistic expectations of the masses as to how quickly things could happen. In the popular mood that prevailed in 1974 and 1975, the recovery of the West Bank and Gaza was just around the corner. After all, the Arab armies had defeated Israel, and Arab oil had cornered America, the power that holds the cards. It was the claim of Arab pragmatism that, once total visions were shed, once the old language and assumptions were transcended, once America was won over, the Palestinian question would be settled in an honorable way: either in the "Jordanian solution" to the West Bank problem – probably the real commitment of the Arab order – or in a Palestinian state, the public commitment stated in the Raba summit conference of 1974. Meanwhile, the Arabs could find their way into the modern world (into the Western international system, of course) without old complexes and resentments. They could invest their new wealth and assume their newly acquired status in the world system.

Having been repeatedly told that the world after October 1973 was a different world, the guardians of the Arab order – the new men – were hard pressed to reconcile their own optimism about a more moderate world with the persistence of that old historic claim against Israel. The fight with Israel stood out as a large unfinished item from yesterday's world: It seemed to defy the outward displays of rationality, the steady insistence that the Arabs were no longer the victims of history. In the short run, the new men's bet was on the possible benefits of the Arab world's "reversal of alliances" (Kissinger's term) away from the USSR and toward the United States. If the world was shaped by America's will, if Israel's policies were a mere echo of American wishes, then the Arab turn from the USSR would be rewarded with a comprehensive settlement that would make it easy for the established Arab order to claim that it led a historic fight to an honorable solution: halfway between the utopia of eliminating Israel from the region and the hell of the post-1967 status quo.

As Kissinger wanted it and phrased it, the Arab elites came to "realize that it is the U.S. and not the USSR that holds the key to what they want."[32] In the post-October 1973 configuration of power, the principal Arab advocates of the American connection justified their power by their ability to deliver the superpower that could deliver Israel. Such was the Saudi claim, which made the deradicalization of Arab domestic and foreign policies part and parcel of a reorientation of U.S. attitudes toward the Middle East. And that too was the position of Sadat, who maintained immediately after the October War that "that man [Kissinger] is the only person who can order that woman [Golda Meir] to get out and be obeyed"[33] and who would claim in April, 1977, that he had successfully "convinced" President Carter of the "necessity of establishing an independent Palestinian state."[34]

Mr. Sadat's dramatic deed – his journey to Jerusalem a few months later – showed his impatience with his own dictum. By then Israel had successfully withstood American pressure, it had mocked the Ford–Kissinger threat to reassess American Middle Eastern policy and dashed the expectations that the Carter Administration could effect a comprehensive settlement. Sadat's deed was to face America with a fait accompli: direct diplomacy between the region's two most formidable military entities. It was not to America's liking, but the Egyptian–Israeli relation had to be underwritten; that was the meaning of the Camp David meeting and then by the Egyptian–Israeli treaty of March, 1979. It was initiated by the two parties and blessed by a cornered America. President Sadat provided his own clarity to the Middle Eastern situation. For him the question was not Palestine but Egypt. The American connection was not inspired by the Palestinian dilemma; it was a politicoeconomic and cultural choice.

The Palestinian question was not felt with equal intensity in the Arab monolith. Frustrated by the incapacity of the superpower to get them off the hook, the Arab states went their separate ways: The Arab center – the moderate camp of Syria, Saudi Arabia, and Egypt – fragmented. The dominant order rode high in the glow of the October War; it made too many promises and it had to pay for them. Egypt was pushed farther down the road of isolation than its president realized; the Syrians hurried to solidify their position and to claim their place as the "principal confrontation state," to "pacify" Lebanon, and to take on the Palestinians in 1976. This was not exactly what the Saudis had in mind when they set out to deradicalize Arab politics in the aftermath of 1973. Egyptian and Syrian policies taught them that allies – even financially dependent ones – can be unwieldy and troublesome. The turn that Islamic fundamentalism took and the attack on the Grand Mosque in Mecca in November, 1979, showed them that the weapons and ideas one brandishes take on a life of their own and are often subject to hostile interpretations, that the forces people unleash and pay homage to can be turned against them and that one can die at the gallows one sets up for others.

THE QUESTION OF AUTHENTICITY
AND COLLABORATION

Would-be modernizers are toppled by the changes they seek; would-be reformers (witness post-Maoist China) push for a moderate critique of a particular order, but they throw open the floodgates of criticism and are outflanked by young dissidents who carry the critique of authoritarianism to its logical conclusion. We are free to choose the symbols we wish to fight others with, but the symbols we use make their own demands.

In doing battle with the polished, compromised liberals and atheistic Marxists, the Saudis found it natural to raise the banner of Islam. Their power and wealth, like all power and wealth, required a cover of some kind, a system of legitimization. The Saudis were still fighting yesterday's battle, and under those circumstances their choice seemed safe and sensible. Having made the choice, they had to live with it. It dictated certain things and precluded others. But the choice turned out to be a problematic one. This would be made clear to the Saudis by the Iranian upheaval.

All along, the so-called Saudi era was less stable than was assumed from afar. In the post–pax American view, Saudi Arabia was a regional power – "regional influential" in Zbigniew Brzezinski's facile language – one of those handful of Third World countries chosen for deputizing by an America traumatized by Vietnam and too weary to go it alone. From the perspective of poor Muslim states, Saudi Arabia was another foreign aid donor in a world of scarcity and constraints. But the same kinds of troubles identified earlier in our discussion of the Third World challenge to the West foreshadow the troubles of the Saudi-organized Arab order that emerged out of the October War. There were weaknesses that victories on the world stage could not correct.

For all its wealth, Saudi Arabia was still an underpopulated, weak country in a region seething with unrest. In its post–October 1973 exuberance, Saudi Arabia could entertain all sorts of possibilities

– it even became fairly convinced that it must combat Euro-communism and try to do something about the left in France and Italy.[35] But all the principal weapons in the Saudis' arsenal turned out, upon investigation, to be double edged. Acquiring arms risked exposing the Saudis to external attack and spawning a military apparatus that has ended the reigns and taken the lives of other dynasts. Industrialization meant the introduction of foreign workers who would "pollute" the moral universe of this once insular kingdom. Aid was a bottomless pit. Gratitude is an elusive thing; most aid recipients are hopelessly uncontrollable. You can't give enough to keep them afloat or to guarantee that they will do what you want them to do. The American connection too was a mixed thing. The great ally was busy on too many fronts, and besides, the Saudis knew their own history: in their defeat of the Hash-emites a century before, they emphasized the foreign collaboration – the British connection – of the Hashemites and stressed their own fidelity to tradition, their own independence. That is why the Saudis seemed to alternate between a Kissingerian kind of gloom about the decline of American power and a reluctance to associate themselves with the United States whenever the United States sought to project its power in the region, to set up military bases or the like.

There was another weakness. Saudi Arabia was not a particu-larly articulate society, and in a political culture like the Arab world, that operated to its detriment. Saudi Arabia produced few if any books and had very little cultural allure. In the battle of ideas, the Saudis were no match for the traditionally eloquent Egyptians or for the intelligentsia based in Beirut. When Saudi Arabia produced books, they tended to be editions of the works of Sayyid Qutb, the prolific activist of the Muslim Brotherhood. But Sayyid Qutb was an Egyptian, and besides, his brand of social discourse preached the virtues of austerity and had a radical socioeconomic thrust, an embarrassing contrast to the luxury and corruption engendered by the new wealth.

All these were limits to the power of those in Saudi Arabia who pondered a restorationist course for the region. But there was an-other dilemma, which had to do with the claims of authenticity and the realities of dependence. Islam and the American connection were a rough juggling act. Tradition mongering was the Saudis' choice, but once resorted to, it made its own claims. The combination of foreign collaboration and conservative religion is a trauma in a region where that combination has been attempted and exposed over and over again. The special relationship between Saudi Arabia and the United States could be defended, perhaps even proudly displayed, so long as the power from afar promised or was said to have promised a comprehensive Middle Eastern settlement. If the same superpower could deliver the technology of war, a settlement on Jerusalem and the West Bank, and a tantalizing array of gadgets and development projects, then surely the American connection made sense. The Russian connection of yesterday's radicals came with atheistic communism; it defiled and challenged the ways of religion. Presumably the American connection came culture free and could be safely contained in the realms of technology transfers, arms sales, and diplomatic deals. Of course it could not, but the separation between power and culture was made for the United States and denied to the Soviet Union.

This could work so long as the American presence was reasonably discreet and modest and so long as diplomacy delivered tangible gains. But the American push into the region was of a far greater magnitude than had been hitherto known, and the frustrations of diplomacy were infinitely greater than expected. The beneficiaries of the post–October 1973 order had a difficult time squaring their own claims of a new world with the pervasive American presence that the new wealth had invited. It was "strange," writes John C. Campbell in a perceptive essay, that "the moment of crisis [the October War] for the United States, which revealed this vulnerability to the new economic power of OPEC, also left it in a stronger position than ever before, as it gained new influence in the Arab world without losing its special relationship with Israel, and as it stepped forward as the principal partner in the security and economic development of the oil producing states of the Gulf."[36] And for a while the post–October 1973 American structure in the Middle East looked awesome indeed. Based on an alliance with the regimes in Riyadh, Teheran, Cairo, and Jerusalem and the acquiescence of the one in Damascus, it suggested the possibility of taming the region's conflicts, containing the Soviet Union, and keeping "castrated" Europe dependent on the United States.

There were tangible American interests at stake, but there was also the challenge of a new frontier. The Middle East was to be what Southeast Asia turned out, after the outpouring of so much blood and money, not to be: a place where America makes a difference, where resources are committed for good reasons. At a time when technology was under fire in the West, a time of debates about limits to growth, the American model was being vindicated in the Middle East. There was an old civilization turning on a large scale to the technology and wares of the United States. The material incentive to recycle petrodollars, to restructure the international system — as the jargon then had it — and to bring the Middle East into it, was propelled, as all such endeavors are, by a cultural drive. Technology, it was believed, could perhaps tame the romanticism of the area, make the Arabs more like others, bring them into the world. This required massive American presence, at a time when the ruling elites in the Arab lands and in Iran had claimed that they had entered a new era and secured a new place in the sun. Thus began what a wise old Saudi jurist described as the "secular pilgrimage" to the peninsula. And the outside world came in bearing its cultural messages and its wares, raising questions of identity, generating an even greater need to conceal, to play up fidelity to tradition. The drama required a brilliant and restrained effort at cultural and technological traffic control, but such an effort, even if it were possible, was aborted by the magnitude of the wealth and the dreams that were entertained by people who had historically lived on the margins of things and by the huge commissions that were there to be made. The Western world had lost the battle of oil pricing; it had to recoup its losses. An erosion of the power of the dominant organizer of the world economy made it possible for the hitherto "insignificant"[37] to raise oil prices, to claim a new place for themselves. The so-called winners of October 1973 could now have the world, or so they believed. The serious questions about their willingness and ability to handle that world, about their capacity to withstand its assaults and temptations were not even raised, let alone answered. Here and there, there must have been some doubts, some fears, but they proved no match for the new ambitions and possibilities. Hard as the regimes would try to wrap themselves in the garb of authenticity, people were witnessing the surrender of their own elites to models and temptations from afar. For a while the contradiction could be wished away by sermons about the supremacy of Islam or the supremacy of Persian kingship over American and Western institutions. But this was a difficult dilemma: the dilemma of any society trying to borrow alien things without falling apart. The seductive machines that produce power for others come with foreign technicians who must work them, and the latter became living reminders of dependency and weakness.

Beyond the issue of a diplomatic settlement, Israel's presumed susceptibility to American influence helped those who opted for an American connection – Sadat, Saudi Arabia, the more cautious regime in Syria – justify and legitimate their broader politicoeconomic identification with the United States. Deep down, there was a psychological vulnerability to America and things American. With or without America's diplomatic power with Israel, the critical and dominant interests in Saudi Arabia and the Gulf states, in Egypt, and to a lesser extent in Syria, were overwhelmingly attracted to the United States. They were convinced that an American-organized regional system was their best choice. It is commonplace that this was the case in Egypt and Saudi Arabia. But Syria too was in this group, less hostile than its rhetoric would suggest. In this regard the memoirs of both Kissinger and Nixon are instructive. In Kissinger's memoirs – in which a Manichean distinction is maintained between "radicals" and "moderates" – President Asad is given positive marks. After praising Sadat as a great statesman (forgotten are the days when he considered him a clown), Kissinger writes of Asad: "Another less significant result of the autumn of crises [1970] was the accession of Hafez Asad to power in Syria in November of 1970. Less visionary than Sadat, he nevertheless gave Syria unprecedented stability and, against the background of the turbulent history of his people, emerged as a leader of courage and relative moderation."[38] Nixon, desperately battling to save his political life in 1974, was still lucid and insightful enough to note the Syrian attitude during his Middle Eastern trip, and, as the following passage makes clear, to foresee the troubles of the expectations pinned on American power:

> In the Syrian capital of Damascus, the oldest continuously inhabited city in the world, American flags were flying for the first time in seven years. Everywhere we went large and friendly crowds turned out to welcome us, despite the fact that our movements and itineraries were given no publicity by the Syrian authorities. I viewed this as a measure of the people's strong desire for friendship with America, for an alternative to the Soviets, and for peace. I noted in my diary, "These people want to be friendly with the U.S. and it runs right down to the rank and file and it goes to the fact that they know the Russians. The Americans, of course, may be in that category soon if we are unable to produce on the peace initiatives that we have begun."[39]

What America's (ascribed) diplomatic prowess did was enable those in the Arab world who were psychologically, culturally, and politically inclined toward the United States to conceal (partly from themselves, partly from others) the deeper motivations of their post–October 1973 embrace of the United States to claim that the American connection was a price that had to be paid for a solution of the Palestinian question. If the road to Palestine went through Washington, then America's friends could be forgiven their enthusiasm for things American. This was one way of dealing with what the Egyptian scholar Lewis Awad has described as the "schizophrenia" of the Arab elite's love for America – "Israel's protector" – and their rejection of Israel.[40] But what if the hopes about America's omnipotence were largely the product of wishful thinking on the part of the Arab advocates of the American connection? Then the fundamental ambivalence about the American presence would have to be faced.

The Arab world had long ceased to be culturally autonomous. No political-cultural movement had given it the distance from the outside world that political orders need if they are not to break down and lose their autonomy. The aloofness from the world system given China by a relatively self-contained order and then by the Chinese revolutionaries from 1949 until the early 1970s had no equivalent in Arab history. India's capacity to somehow remain itself while outsiders came and went differed from the situation of the Middle East – an area that had been situated in the path of giants, that had been courted by outsiders, and whose internal defenses faltered in the face of outside temptations.

The Arab world had long seen itself in Western mirrors, judged itself by Western standards. It did so while systematically denying this. America's eruption on the Middle Eastern scene after World War II was initially approved, for, after all, this was a new power: Here was one way one could have the West without the colonialism, the arrogance, the historical baggage associated with the European powers. Historian Bernard Lewis's statement that Arabs refuse to recognize "America as something generically different from Europe, and untainted with the European past"[41] needs to be qualified. Such may have become the outcome in the 1960s and 1970s, for by then the new power had clashed with a growing nationalism and was seen by the end of the 1970s as a rival to the work of Islam. But this was not the case at the end of World War II and in the early 1950s. This is vividly recalled by Mohamed Heikal in a discussion of early phases of the encounter between the United States and the new regime of the Free Officers: "The whole picture of the United States at that time was a glamorous one. Britain and France were fading, hated empires. The Soviet Union was five thousand miles away and the ideology of communism was anathema to the Moslem religion. But America had emerged from World War II richer, more powerful and more appealing than ever . . . Refrigerators, television and all the instruments of the new life seemed to be coming from America. So the United States wore an aura of success and glamour, shining out above the tarnished failure of the old imperialists, and people were receptive to the idea of the Americans playing a major role in the Middle East."[42]

History, however, took a different turn, and Nasserism clashed with America's designs: Political differences provided a cultural buffer of sorts, kept the United States at bay. The bitterness of the 1967 defeat pushed the Arab world still further from the United States – further than the Arab elite may have wanted. This would be borne out by the turn of events after October, 1973. The success of October enabled the Arab elite to indulge their tastes in alliances, in technology, in models of development – and the American advantage was there for all to see. Americanization and anti-

The Arab Predicament

Americanism are two sides of the same coin. The political anti-Americanism displayed in the Arab states and in Iran as the 1970s came to an end was in great measure an expression of the region's rage at itself; it was a display of agony over cultural surrender. The American push into the region had succeeded all too well. The secular modernized elites, the more cosmopolitan wing of the middle classes and a substantial number of young men and women, had dismantled the defenses of that culture. Its boundaries had become dangerously and uncomfortably permeable. Muslim fundamentalism – or reassertion, call it what you will – was then summoned, as Joseph Levenson's sensitive analysis of China reminds us, as a psychological device, a self-defense, and a way of bridging the paralyzing split between the Westernized culture of the elite and the popular culture of the masses. The memoirs of the Russian populist Alexander Herzen, in describing the cultural dualism of the Europe of his time, depict the Arab–Muslim order today as well:

> In the fundamental fact of its everyday life [Western Europe] that its culture is two-fold, lies the organic obstacle to consistent development. To live in two civilizations, on two levels, in two worlds, at two stages of development, to live not as a whole organism but as one part, while using the other for food and fuel, and to be always talking about liberty and equality is becoming more and more difficult.[43]

To live in two worlds, always talking about self and authenticity (the Arab substitutes for Europe's "liberty and equality"), is becoming more and more difficult. The two worlds in the Arab world were there prior to the October War, as they are in every society. What the new wealth did was encourage and enable the more modern sector in the Arab world to forget the ground on which it stood; it would borrow the language and the trappings of the old world but dispense with its sensibilities and webs of meaning. Fundamentalism symbolized the revolt of the civilization they left behind; it was a desire to close the glaring gap between the claims of authenticity and the realities of everyday life.

In societies of acute cultural dualism, the relatively modernized sectors lay claim to modernity and feel embarrassed about their more backward brethren.[44] Meanwhile, the claim of the more traditional culture is that of orthodoxy and authenticity. Its predom-

206

inant attitude is hatred toward those who have ceased to be themselves, who gamble, whose women mix freely with men, who feel more comfortable with aliens than they do with their own people. Now the balance of power between these two is the real life-and-death political question. When state power is in the hands of the modernized group, as has traditionally been the case in the modern Middle Eastern state system, war is waged against tradition, belief is steadily undermined, and the so-called backward people internalize the embarrassment about their traditions felt by those who continually trumpet their own modernity and capacity to take on the outside world. But what if the claims of the modern sector become increasingly hollow, their modern management skills are visibly defective and inept, and their dialogue with the outside world turns into an abandonment of national culture? This is where traditions reassert themselves and where the comparative advantage of Islam lies: to be able to assert itself and its uniqueness at a time when technology is seemingly blurring the distinctions between cultures, when models of development tantalize people with promises that in the end they fail to deliver.

We have been witnessing the simultaneous advance of the civilization that technology promised and the determined resistance to it. This has left those engaged and those watching wondering which of the two is more real, more authentic. Wherein lies the truth: Is the process of homogenization winning out over cultural idiosyncrasies and differences, or is the world being suddenly claimed by the past because faith in a successful civilizational model is breaking down and once-defensive cultural outlooks are making a comeback? The easy answer would be to assert one line of reasoning, one reading of history. According to the modern reading, a rational order marches on – as it has since the rise of the European world system – obliterating differences, taming the instinctive and the idiosyncratic in favor of greater predictability and uniformity. A variant of this reading was central to the modernization-of-societies world view that dominated social science and the claims of non-Western rulers a decade ago. According to the theories prevalent then, modernization would act as a universal solvent: The forces of uniformity would prevail, hostile and alien worlds would be understood – in familiar categories, terms, and ways.

207

This, one should note, was common to both liberal and Marxist views of change.

The other reading of history would be to see cultures as far more obstinate than they are depicted by the first view. According to this interpretation, cultures ignore universal messages. They assert themselves by showing people what happens if they cease being themselves in order to enjoin them to remain loyal to who and what they are. To say that either reading of history wins out is to underestimate humanity's capacity for what Clifford Geertz calls "moral double-bookkeeping."[45] People try to juggle the past and the present: there is around us as much intoxication with machines and gadgets as there is cultural archaeology – people busy trying to revalidate once-discredited traditions and revive once-forgotten symbols. There is both a submission to a dominant culture and a revolt against it. Sometimes the same people do both: They embrace the dominant model for fear of being left behind and denounce it to affirm their uniqueness at the moment that they feel swept by the current.

Fundamentalism and particularism are, then, not riddles at all: They are a response to the triumph and dynamism of that ascendant civilizational model that began in Europe and of which the United States is today the standard-bearer. The process is illuminated by Immanuel Wallerstein, whose discussion throws light upon the fundamentalism of Muslims, the anguish of that so-called arc of crisis:

> When Western civilization sought to transform itself into civilization pure and simple . . . it was sure that not only God and history were on its side but that all rational men (by which was meant the elites throughout the system, including its periphery) would be on its side as well, at least eventually. Instead what has happened is that everywhere, and more and more, nationalist particularism has been asserting itself. Indeed, if there is any linear equation at all, it is the collaboration of the expansion of capital, the uneven development of the world system, and the claims to differentiation by groups even more integrated into the system – in a dialectical vortex of centripetal and centrifugal forces.[46]

At one point the particularism was expressed in secular nationalist terms. Then fundamentalism took over where pan-Arabism and secular nationalism had failed. Fundamentalism may be too incoherent to govern, but it can topple the world of the elites, shatter their illusions, demonstrate that they have surrendered to the ways of the aliens. Khomeini's appeal – no matter how transient – to mass opinion throughout the Arab world, across the deep divide between the Sunni Islam of the majority of Arabs and Iran's Shi'a Islam, across the historical split between Arabs and Persians, underscored the vulnerability of the Arab order. Reduced to its essence, Khomeini's ideology was pure wrath, directed less against dictatorship than against cultural surrender. That is why the expectation of a democratic path in the ayatollah's Islamic republic was an act of reading into Iran Western liberal sensibilities and categories. The new wealth in the region had ruptured its normative order, and greater numbers of men and women were taking to the ways of the outside world.

As the gifted observer Ali Mazrui has stated, the "barrel of oil" and the "crescent of Islam" were linked and October 1973 represented a resurrection of Islam.[47] But at home, in the Arab states and in Iran, it was clear that the fabric of the civilization was under stress. Extreme Islamic piety and rampant corruption were an unlikely combination; so was the claim to self and authenticity combined with widespread cultural seduction. Having seen the wrath of fundamentalism play itself out in Iran, those people who had only the day before engaged in tradition mongering pulled back. In their own scheme, flouting tradition worked so long as the adversaries were Michel Aflaq and George Habash (both Christians, after all) or the openly secular regime of Abdul Nasser. The new fundamentalism was a more dangerous adversary; it easily pointed out the transgressions of those who had professed their adherence to Islam. The rupture between the traditional ways of the Islamic world and the world of the elite had resulted in acute cultural dualism. The liberal, capitalist West may not openly demand the ideological conversion that Marxism demanded, but technology, cultural wares, long and frequent stays in London, Paris, and New York, and the appealing pop culture disseminated by the United States had done their deed. Home was no longer home, so to speak. It is true that Ibn Khaldun had expounded on the virtues of the bedouins: they were "closer to being good than sedentary people,"

209

he said, but he had also postulated a condition that the bedouin had to possess: self-sufficiency. Once self-sufficiency is lost, all is lost, and the "Bedouin submits himself to the yoke of the city."[48] Traditions, too, demand their kind of discipline and that was clearly lacking in the new order.

Could it be that these expounders of the virtues of the *turath* were so vulnerable on their own terrain because they were not really traditional at all? Could it be that tradition mongering was carried on so loudly because people had deep down broken with tradition and because tradition had ceased to hold them and that they were left "holding it" (Clifford Geertz's important distinction) without real belief and conviction? Knowing that other ways and other valleys tempt them, people try to tell themselves that they are still at home with their own world. Almost every great upheaval that brings a world close to ruin is immediately preceded by a wave of cultural reassertion, by insistent traditionalism. This is not so much opportunism and hypocrisy – although it includes a dash of it – as much as it is a felt desire to reassure oneself that the ground is solid, that the world is intact.

The people who so devoutly professed their adherence to the *turath* were vulnerable because their word was far more deeply penetrated by Western culture than they wished to admit to themselves or to others. We can see the dilemmas of the standard-bearers of the Saudi era in an essay by Arnold Hottinger:

> The members of the Saudi upper crust who are today earning vast sums are not even in a position to form a unified group to help exert a stabilizing influence on their country. They regard the kingdom primarily as a kind of money factory. The "homeland" to which they intend to retire sooner or later is more likely to be Texas or California – places where they are already investing their fortunes, have already built luxurious homes and settled the members of their families. It is there that they look toward future stability, not in Saudi Arabia. Many of these people have studied in Texas or California, their youthful memories are there, and it is there that they plan to flee sooner or later from their desert capitals, which their vast but inappropriate projects have turned into places where money is made and spent but where they consider no genuine style of life is possible any longer.[49]

The vast infusion of wealth enabled men (and some women as well) to exit from their austere societies. The great capitals of the West became close and accessible. It was in London and Paris that the freest Arab press was based and it was to these places that men and women in search of cultural freedom journeyed. The phenomenal flight of capital from the Middle East to the West was but the material expression of a wave of cultural escape plaguing the Arab world in particular and beyond it the Third World as a whole. "All over the world," writes V. S. Naipaul in his haunting novel, *A Bend in the River*, "money is in flight. People have scraped the world clean, as clean as an African scrapes his yard, and now they want to run from the dreadful places where they've made their money and find some nice safe country . . . They are frightened of the fire."[50] In no other great story of civilization have the possibilities of exit been so easily available. One could scarcely imagine a viable Japanese recovery in the nineteenth century if the dominant elite of Japan had had the choice of escape that is available to the Arab elite. The Japanese revolution from above worked, because the samurai who accomplished it made a stand for their own world and posed as effective bearers of national culture. The samurai "were men who had been brought up to believe in discipline and firm government, to cultivate martial virtues, to set duties above rights."[51]

None of this could be said of the guardians of order in the Arab states or in the shah's Iran. And that is why the order in Iran crumbled before the ayatollah's austere example and why the conservative regional order built around Saudi Arabia and Iran had such weak foundations in the Arab world. The danger of emptying that important political space, national culture, is that others – mullahs, radicals, millenarians – will rush to fill it. Where there is a millenarian tendency, as there is in Islam, the failure of practical politics always spawns dreams of resurrection. "Moslems," writes Manfred Halpern, "have been perennially ready for the Mahdi, the messenger of God, who could lead the community in a religio-political leap into immediate fulfillment of all spiritual and material needs."[52] The failure of the dominant order to keep the outside world at bay without falling into the extremes of surrender and xenophobia encourages the latent desire for escape and for totalism.

Thus the resurgence of Islam is a response to the blockage of ideas and the failure of state elites. Nadav Safran's recapitulation of Egyptian political and intellectual history provides an illuminating paradigm that can help explain the drift toward Islamic fundamentalism today. In tracing Egypt's political evolution from the early nineteenth to the mid-twentieth century, Safran identifies liberal and reactionary phases. The strength of the Muslim Brotherhood, which came close to capturing political power, was a response to the failure of liberal nationalism. In the dismal political atmosphere of the 1930s and 1940s, a "romantic, vague, inconsistent, and aggressive" Islamic ideology filled the ideological and political vacuum. During this period, some of the secular nationalists themselves retreated into the fundamentalist fold. Millenarianism spread when the liberal elite failed to live by their own code and when the dominant order seemed blatantly inequitable and compromised.[53]

The noted Egyptian scholar Lewis Awad echoed Safran's conclusions. He observed that from 1800 onward, the dominant order in Egypt was on the side of progress during phases of achievement and retreated into fundamentalism and mythology during periods of crisis. Thus the order favored change during the times of Muhammad Ali (1805–1842), Ismael (1863–1879), bourgeois nationalism (1919–1936), and Abdul Nasser (1952–1967). Millenarianism prevailed whenever the political order failed. It did so during the reign of Abbas I (1848–1854), from 1882 to the bourgeois revolution of 1919, from 1936 to 1952, and, finally, after the Six Day War.[54]

The analyses of both Safran and Awad deal with Egypt, but their theme goes beyond the Egyptian case. The voice of fundamentalism is so insistent today because moderate revolutions from above have failed and because the world outside has been encroaching on the region. That the world outside is invited in by the region's own elite offers no consolation; it only increases the self-doubts and thus the need for some form of rebellion, for an affirmation of self.

The encroachment of the outside world – really its invitation and purchase – posed for the Arabs the prospect of greater *levantinization* – the process of being an intermediate civilization, being, as a thoughtful young Saudi scholar describes it, "every-man and no-man" at the same time.[55] The levant as an idea, as a system, and as a way of life was once restricted to pockets of the Arab world, to a few cities, to small groups of intellectuals and traders. The urge to import and to mimic is now more widely spread. A conscious kind of Islamization provided protection against the prospects and the costs of being a levantine. One need not be unduly committed to the particularism of civilizations to note the costs and to see the scars of levantine identity; these were perceptively illuminated by Albert Hourani:

> To be a Levantine is to live in two worlds or more at once, without belonging to either; to be able to go through the external forms which indicate the possession of a certain nationality, religion or culture, without actually possessing it. It is no longer to have a standard of values of one's own, not to be able to create but only able to imitate; and so not even to imitate correctly since that also needs a certain originality. It is to belong to no community and to possess nothing of one's own. It reveals itself in lostness, pretentiousness, cynicism and despair.[56]

The determined traditionalization of culture was a response to the displayed forms and mimicry. It was inspired, as all revitalization movements are, by fear that assimilation into alien ways has gone far enough and the usual nostalgia that lives in every vanquished civilization with a long memory for a vanished whole world.

THE RULERS' ISLAM, ISLAM OF THE RULED

Phrases like "the resurgence of Islam" are so powerfully evocative that they make us lose sight of the real struggles that men and societies are engaged in. We think of great crusades, of a powerful desert wind devastating the achievements of progress, of societies being dragged back into the middle ages. But things may not be what they seem. People summon the spirits of the past to help them achieve very precise goals. There is a penetrating passage in Marx that helps explain why we hear from the past precisely at a time of such profound crisis in the Muslim order:

> Men make their own history, but they do not make it just as they please; they do not make it under circumstances chosen by themselves, but under circumstances directly found, given and transmitted from the past. The tradition of all the dead generations weighs like a nightmare on the brain of the living. And just when they seem engaged in revolutionising themselves and things, in creating something entirely new, precisely in such epochs of revolutionary crisis they anxiously conjure up the spirits of the past to their service and borrow from them names, battle slogans and costumes in order to present the new scene of world history in this time-honoured disguise and this borrowed language. Thus Luther donned the mask of the Apostle Paul, the Revolution of 1789 to 1814 draped itself alternately as the Roman Republic and the Roman Empire, and the Revolution of 1848 knew nothing better to do than to parody, in turn, 1789 and the revolutionary tradition of 1793 to 1795. In like manner the beginner who has learnt a new language always translates it back into his mother tongue, but he has assimilated the spirit of the new language and can produce freely in it only when he moves in it without remembering the old and forgets in it his ancestral tongue.[57]

In some cases the spirits are summoned simply because people are trying to find something with which to combat remote, smug, or oppressive state elites. The balance between state and society has been fundamentally disrupted in the Arab–Muslim order. The claims of the state have increased, and so have the resources at its disposal. In previous times, men coexisted with political authority – they made their peace with it so long as it left them alone. Today the state elites wish to turn the world upside down, and the popular culture finds no more effective weapon of resistance than Islam. In Syria and Iraq, narrowly based state elites (the Alawis in the former, the Sunnis in the latter) monopolize power, brandish the symbols of national security, and hoard resources for themselves. Devastating, as they do, other channels of opposition, they leave men with that one thing that the elites cannot monopolize: religious devotion doubling as piety and as a political instrument.

The opponents of the Syrian regime have, as it were, discovered religion, for the men in power and their clan (the Alawis account

for ten percent of Syria's population) are of a different breed. To
the normal gulf between ruler and ruled have been added historic
sectarian differences and suspicions. The tendency of power to seek
shelter, to exercise itself in the dark, in small groups, led the Syrian
regime into ever-deeper trouble. The insecurity of the man at the
helm – itself a rational response to the uncertainty of governing in
Syria – led him into greater dependence upon fellow Alawis, a
dependence symbolized in his reliance on his brother, Colonel Ri-
faat al-Asad. Political power presented a traditionally rural, de-
prived minority with the chance to have its day in power and to
hoard wealth. Capricious dictatorship is not a new theme in Syrian
history, but this one took on the quality of a grave moral violation,
because its perpetrators were of a different breed and because there
were so many beneficiaries, so many brothers and cousins anxious
to ride the coattails of the group in power.

In the cycle of terror and counterterror between the security apparatus of the regime and the fringe Muslim Brotherhood waged
with particular intensity in 1979, the tactics and passions of the
true believers in the Brotherhood may have been somewhat extreme, but they served as a vehicle for the resentments of the Sunni
majority. The terror displayed the abyss between society and the
state. The massacre of more than sixty Alawi cadets in June, 1979,
by the duty officer at the Aleppo artillery academy revealed the
depth of the hatred: The cadets were no longer the symbol of national security in a sacred fight with Israel but the beneficiaries of
a regime of privilege and corruption. The Brotherhood eluded the
regime's determination to crush it because it fed off the sympathies
of the majority of the population: Its finances came from traditional Sunni merchants; its sympathizers were more than the
handful of "extremists" they were said to be in official rhetoric.

We can see the Brotherhood's concerns in an underground publication in October, 1979: President Hafez Asad is a "fox" (in the
public imagery the Alawis are devious and conspiratorial), his
community a pack of "wolves" known for a history of treachery
and collaboration. There are also standard bourgeois themes and
moral appeals: the violation of property rights, the sanctity of homes,
the honor of women. "It is decency alone," said the Brotherhood,
"that prevents us from mentioning those enslaved of our sisters

215

and daughters." Political power had broken all limits, had laid its hands on the wealth and honor, the *'ird*, of others, said the Brotherhood to the ruler, "so we rebelled for our dignity, for we are Muslims, oh enemy of Islam, . . for the Muslim does not fear and does not grovel . . . we rebelled for our country that you sold cheaply, for our blood that you spilled so callously, for our brothers whom you eliminated in the dungeons of Unity, Freedom and Socialism"[58] [the slogans of the Ba'th party].

A manifesto of the Brotherhood, made public in September, 1979, asks the ruler some questions about "national unity" in Syria:

> How could national unity be realized when the overwhelming majority is enslaved by the minority?
>
> How could national unity be realized when Rifaat al Asad and his gangsters dominate the army and the regime and monopolize the nation's wealth?
>
> How could national unity be realized when *al sulta* [the ruling authority] persists in the corruption of moral principles, in the subversion of morality and education so as to destroy the spirit of resistance and struggle in future generations? Could national unity be realized by sacrificing the Golan [Heights] and promoting the traitor into a president of the republic?
>
> If this is what is meant by national unity we refuse it and we call upon all others to refuse and combat it.[59]

Thus Sunni Islam thrives in Syria as a mode of protest against those who have used the power of the state to restratify class relations, to accumulate fortunes unimaginable to those who have to work for a living, to obtain sexual liberties and prerogatives that tantalize and outrage those without them.

A Syrian scholar has analyzed the intersection of religious devotion and opposition in a thoughtful unpublished essay. Of the Muslim Brotherhood's tactics and of the functions of the mosque, he observes,

> in its strategy to displace the regime, the MBM [the Brotherhood] has been using the same tactics which were applied by the Muslim guards in Iran to bring down the Shah. The chanting of hymns at dawn and the teaching of religion on the minaret's loudspeakers throughout the day represent an impressive campaign of mass political socialization. For the first time in Islamic history women are

invited to the mosques in special sessions to receive Islamic education. The government has imposed restrictions on the means and
times when the religious instructions can be given, but it has failed
to stop its momentum. Men and women, especially young people,
flock to the mosques in increasing numbers in order to pray or to
receive Islamic education.

The MBM considers the Alawis to be seceders from Islam, and
since it is decreed in the Quran, the Muslim Holy Book, that the
blood of seceders shall be upon them, any Muslim who sacrifices
his life in carrying out God's order will be a martyr whose place
after death is in Heaven.[60]

Likewise the political grievances of Shi'a Islam persist in Iraq (witness the expulsion of Khomeini once the struggle between Khomeini and the Shah was on), because the one continuity between
Iraq under the Hashemites and today's more radical Iraq remains
the unequal access to state power that enables the Sunni minority
to rule either as a partner of foreign interests, as was the case with
the Hashemites, or in the name of revolution, as the military now
claims. The forms change, but the world remains the same. In Egypt
fundamentalism persists because the political order of the Free Officers has yet to allow the citizenry to enter the political arena. No
sooner had the Iranian revolutionaries brought down the Pahlavi
dynasty than President Sadat warned against the rise of ayatollahs
in Egypt: those who wanted to engage in politics, he insisted, should
go to the parliament, those who wanted to engage in religious
matters should go to the mosque. There would be no mixing of
religious and secular matters in Egypt. Putting aside his statement's doctrinal vulnerability, for classical Islam does not easily
accept the separation of politics and religion, Sadat overlooked the
emasculation of parliament in his own political system, which has
made parliament such a poor rival to the mixture of politics and
religion. Were Sadat to have offered a viable parliamentary option,
there would have been a more balanced duel between orderly politics and millenarianism. His failure to do so, part of the broader
failure to solve the question of political participation in Arab society, leaves the fundamentalists with ample room for maneuver.
Politics has been driven into the mosque and the symbols of opposition have been avowedly religious, because the ruling elites

remain bent on monopolizing political power. A young Tunisian – in a relatively modernized, relatively democratic country – put it this way: "There is no other way to hold a meeting except in connection with the mosque, no way to speak out."[61]

For the Arab world, the drama of Iran was the spectacle of men and women in the street making and remaking their own history. Win or lose, they were out there demanding to be counted and heard. All the Arab elite's attempts to say that Iran's troubles were peculiar to that society and to point out the detailed (and legitimate) differences between their own countries and Iran were beside the point. The Arab elite knew, as the guardians of the French ancien régime in 1789 knew that revolutionary ideas spread and that the revolution next door might be a crystal ball in which they could see their own future. Both panacea and plague, the Iranian revolution had to be dealt with psychologically and politically by the neighboring Arab order for reasons long ago spelled out in Burke's masterful statement on the French Revolution:

> Formerly, your affairs were your own concern only. We felt for them as men because we were not citizens of France. But when we see the model held up to ourselves, we must feel as Englishmen, and feeling we must provide as Englishmen: Your affairs, in spite of us, are made a part of our interest, so far at least as to keep at a distance your panacea, or your plague. If it be a panacea, we do not want it. We know the consequences of unnecessary physic. If it be a plague, it is such a plague that the precautions of the most severe quarantine ought to be established against it.[62]

The half-hearted attempts at democratization reported, in the aftermath of the Iranian revolution, in Kuwait, Saudi Arabia, and Iraq were part of a frantic attempt to quarantine the Iranian upheaval, to deny the relevance of Iran to the Arab situation. But these measures could only be cosmetic, for at stake was nothing less than the culture's style of authority. The institutions and the habits of mind needed to allow the citizenry to become more than sheer spectators were nowhere to be seen in the Arab–Muslim order. On that score regimes on both the right and the left were equally assailable. Whether they repressed the name of revolution, in the name of order, or in the name of national security, the results were the same. Nor did the so-called bargain – the denial of political rights in order to obtain some concrete gains – seem to make sense. In the ideology of the hard state, the eggs have to be broken on the deferred promise of the omelet. According to the dogma, men and women get something in return – powerful modern armies that protect them, social welfare, or some other gain. But in the Arab world, Caesar had taken without reciprocating. The brittle states on top had little by way of military victories and socioeconomic achievements to show. To be sure, they had produced a shift in the distribution of world wealth in October, 1973. But this only highlighted the crisis of political authority and gave the struggle over authority a particularly grim dimension.

The crisis of democracy and of authority was no longer the question of political rights granted or denied or of politicians ranting about nationalism or engaged in metaphysical speculations about Arab unity. Access to power now meant phenomenal fortunes – fortunes unimaginable to those located outside the state. The word had always commanded its share of wealth in the Arab–Muslim world as it has and does elsewhere. Control of the means of destruction had always paid off. Some in the public sector had done reasonably well for themselves under the semisocialist orders of Nasser and the Ba'th. But now the stakes were of far greater magnitude. The returns on other economic endeavors seemed insignificant when compared with the staggering fortunes made by the ruling stratum and by the middlemen who provided the state with weapons and large technological projects. It was difficult to tell where public authority ended and personal plunder began. Even in a world where political power is expected to help itself to wealth, there were limits to public patience. Into the tidy, benign world of the middlemen crept a new force: *hiqd*, resentment, hatred of corruption, a feeling of relative deprivation.

Liberalism, Marxism, and other ideologies are constructs, labels, but resentment is all too human and real. At their best, ideologies still fail to capture reality, to stir emotions. But resentment can be a hurricane. Iran's rebellion and the anguish of the Arab world were fed by resentment, a feeling that the winners had taken too much, that their wealth was all the more difficult to live with because it enabled them to violate established pieties, to do things that ordinary people could not do or get away with. Religious faith and a sense of relative deprivation combined against the new economy of speculation, against the way the windfall society distributed its gains and what those who got the lion's share did with those gains. Woe to him who incurs the wrath of the petty bourgeoisie, writes the Lebanese leader Kamal Junblatt in his political will.[63] The traditional middle class – the artisans, the bazaar merchants, the clerks, those with traditional educations, those living on fixed incomes – summoned God and national culture on their side in a battle that involved the always inseparable domains of interests and values.

The fight over culture and values is never carried out over intangibles and sacred things but rather over power and who will wield it and resources and who will command them. The power to define culture, the permissible, the good is political and economic power. The wrath of the traditionalists, of the middle classes was directed against a powerful new (though classical) triangle that moved the post-1973 outcome: (1) foreign entrepreneurs, with their resources and skills – their access to world markets that dwarfed national capitalism; (2) the local middleman who cuts the red tape at home and moves with remarkable ease abroad; (3) the ruling authority that grants contracts, that buys massive technology, that now more than ever could raise men to new heights of power and foster the growth of new classes if it wished – that could make the lifesavings of a local merchant or of generations of bazaars trivial in comparison. Nativism became, as it has classically been and will remain, the rallying cry of those who lost out in the boom.

The appeal to national culture was part of the reclamation of the national economy. If foreigners were getting their way with the help of middlemen, it must be because of the fawning devotion of the ruling stratum to things alien; as for the success of middlemen, it must be the product not only of access to court but also of a willingness and capacity to move in the foreigner's universe: to discourse in a foreign language, to move easily in the foreigner's hotels and boardrooms, to allow one's unveiled wife to mix with infidels. Politics and culture intersect, and the only way to break the hold of that triangle on vast national wealth is to break it where it counts: challenge the ruling authority, reclaim the political system in order to perform the twin functions of cultural purification and economic autonomy.[64] Those who lead such a revolt are never those anonymous masses ritually spoken of in radical polemics. They are comparatively better off, they have resources, they are articulate. Of them could be said what Crane Brinton wrote about "revolutionists" in general: they are not "in general afflicted with anything the psychiatrist could be called in about. They were certainly not rifraff, scoundrels, scum of the earth. They were above all *not* worms turning."[65] The temptation to reduce large rebellions and upheavals into theories of psychological unsettledness misses the drama that moves people to take on the power of seemingly awesome military and administrative machines – machines that have very few qualms about liberal rights, that are capable of responding with great zeal and ruthlessness to protect what they have.

That the order seemed to come apart at the seams during a period of relative success and affluence is no riddle at all. As de Tocqueville said, social orders are more likely to be challenged when things are going rather well and when people sense the possibility of improvement than during periods of decline. The post–October 1973 order was unprepared for the contradictions it had brought about. This was a world with a different agenda, all the more so because the dominant order was trying to tone down what had been the legitimating principle in the preceding era: the Arab–Israeli conflict.

The dream of sublimating politics into finance and wealth was short-lived, as was inevitable. Wealth creates dissatisfaction on the part of those who take it for granted, resentment on the part of those who feel that others have more than they do. The simple notion of a man as worshipper, man as consumer offered to the region in the aftermath of October 1973 was far more dangerous than was thought: It raised the usual questions of equity and justice and (because wealth had come from the outside and was being spent to acquire stakes in a more glamorous world) of authenticity. In the new situation, a populist strand of Islam offered people a way of attacking inequity without being branded with the stigma of communism or atheism. Against the world of the elite came this way of dissenting while holding onto one's tradition and heritage. Was the smashing of casinos, nightclubs, and gambling spots that cater to the Arab rich and to the wealthy Egyptians during Egypt's food riots of January 1977 an act of Islamic piety or an expression of rage against those who could afford the things denied to the majority?

In a world where the overwhelming majority of people is subjected to severe moral prohibitions and to the grinding demands of material survival, the capacity of the few to get their way generates dangerous strains: Are the inherited values and the established pieties still worthwhile or is the class that violates them in error? Even in a patient society like Egypt things reached the boiling point in January, 1977, and the demonstrators (overwhelmingly young) drew the line for the regime. The official explanation, communist agitation, underlined the gap between the old explanations and the new realities, the flights of the guardians of order into old dogmas and reflexes. More realistic analyses found their way into the official press after the riots were suppressed in a stream of blood and the loss of seventy-nine lives. Egyptian society, observed Lutfi Abdul Azim, a respected editor of *Al Ahram al Iqtisadi*, is full of time bombs: The majority of Egyptians have come to feel like "undesirables" in the new "consumer society." There is a dangerous economic split between the poor majority and the fortunate few. The demonstrators who burned and looted were only one side of the story; the more meaningful one was the "silent majority" that stood by and watched. Why should the average person care, Azim asked, when he hears tales about belly dancers on Pyramid Road earning in one night what would take him several years of toil?[66]

In the rhetoric of the dominant order, the *turath*, the tradition, had been burdened with defending inequality and with fending off egalitarian claims and Marxist groups. President Sadat had consistently used Islam and "authenticity" to battle secular radicals. His prime minister, Abdul Aziz Hijazi, when queried in 1974 about the legitimacy of the new wealth, replied with a verse from the Quran: "Some of you We [God] have placed over others in rank."[67] In 1975 the grand shaykh of al-Azhar Abdul Halim Mahmoud joined the political debate on matters of equity by rendering the judgment in favor of the regime usually rendered by shackled religious institutions: Islam was for private property, discussions of equity are heresy, he who dies without his private property is a martyr. The *fatwas* (learned religious opinions) of the shaykh of al-Azhar on property rights and on Marxism, put together in an extremely shallow book,[68] were an important part of the regime's defense of its economic policies. When his conservative views were contested by others – including some who provided "irreverent" details of the wealth and investments of some of al-Azhar's leading personalities – the regime was quick to note that the shaykh was the "living symbol" of all Muslims and the attacks against him go beyond permissible bounds.[69]

The point of this is that Islam is many things. Those in power who rail against radical Muslim fundamentalists forget that they too mix religion and politics. The quoting of scripture back and forth between those who rule and those who challenge was of course not a matter of piety. Scripture was part of a grubby political process entailing the distribution of wealth and power, the desire of some people to accumulate wealth, and the frustration of others who suspect that the game is rigged. In more secular societies, the scripture is different – it may consist of the myth of private enterprise, the essential oneness of capitalism and freedom or public control of the means of production, the socialist imperative. In political cultures in which the debate (including the part of the ruling elite) takes on blatantly moral and religious coloring, those on the fringes of power come to phrase their demands and grievances in time-honored categories and precepts that are easily understood and disseminated. The foreign, learned tracts of Marxism are inaccessible and full and made duller still by those in the Arab world who translate them literally and rigidly, who ritually parrot their verbiage in small circles of alienated, ineffective intellectuals. In contrast, the popular sermons of Shaykh Abdel Hamid Kishk – a spellbinding Cairene orator whose commentaries cover the entire gamut of social and political issues, such as official corruption, the oil money that should go to liberating al-Aqsa Mosque in Jerusalem but instead goes to European vacations and investments, wild rents, and furnished apartments in Cairo where the wealthy violate public morality – are couched in a familiar and moving idiom.

Our urge throughout the years of the Cold War to reduce the

world to a battle between liberalism and liberalism's stepchild, Western Marxism, led us to believe that the world had become more and more uniform. But the entry of broad segments of the population into the political process has shattered these assumptions. For when hitherto marginal and dispossessed people came into the political arena, they brought with them their language, their folk ways, and their old memories as well as their new grievances. The facade put up by the more cosmopolitan rulers and the intellectuals cracked. Faced with the local idiom and sensibilities, all ideological constructions seemed thin and contrived. The popular culture was less changed than the modernists had told themselves and others. The Islamic world is no more Islamic today than it was a decade or a quarter century ago. It only seems more so, because mobilization has succeeded in bringing into the political arena classes and individuals traditionally cowed by political authority and convinced that power is the realm of people other than themselves. The invincible leaders of yesterday, so sure that they had the answers, are no longer sure today. Fewer and fewer people in the Muslim world today are convinced that Mustapha Kemal Ataturk, the prime secularizer who served as an example for the shah in Iran and for Abdul Nasser in Egypt, was the genius he was once perceived to be. The Turkish state led the movement to secularism in the Muslim world. In the eyes of the true believers, the cultural price paid by Turkey for this change was immense; the benefits were not easy to see.

Inflation and other complicated economic matters may seem to be beyond the reach of the local mujtahid and of the average member of the urban petty bourgeoisie, but the sophisticated technocrats and economists who man the bureaucracy do not show that much more skills and talent. If we were to take the modernists at face value, the duel between the state and its fundamentalist challengers is one between reason and faith, sustained modern inquiry and dogma. But such is not the case. The tracts of the Muslim Brotherhood on economic matters may strike a skeptical reader as hopelessly out of date, imprecise, and naive. But so do governmental pronouncements. In a detailed study of the economic liberalization in Egypt we found, for example, that the writings of the Muslim Brotherhood were hopelessly theological and simplistic and their views on the "Muslim economy" they would want to build not particularly illuminating.[70] The open-door economy, they insisted, was doomed, for it was an "un-Islamic" economy. One did not have to borrow alien models; Islam had a "total economic system." True prosperity required self-reliance and persistence: The only hope for Egypt was through increased production, and the root cause of nonproductivity was deviation from Islam. Islam alone was capable of increasing productivity, for "it turns labor and work from a routine task to an act of worship."[71] But we found the arguments of the proponents of the open-door economy – the importers who dismantled the tariff system, the representatives of multinationals who insisted that taxes should be done away with and that legislation protecting workers should be scrapped so as to attract foreign investors – equally shallow and simplistic. At a time of intense economic nationalism the world over, the proponents insisted that government intervention is the root of all evil, that a totally free economy – whatever that means – will provide enough income and employment, that the civilized world will come to Egypt's aid through a Carter plan or a new variation on the Marshall Plan. If the polemics of *al Daʾwa* (the organ of the Muslim Brotherhood) were escapist, so too was the world portrayed in the glossy and glib *October* magazine, which is the regime's mouthpiece. If *al Daʾwa* runs away from reality and toward some imagined pure, just, Islamic economy, *October's* vision of life – its tantalizing advertisements, the high life it depicts, its society pages – is equally removed from Egyptian realities. One dogma battles another; one form of escape matches another.

Beyond this lies another, broader matter: the quality of the political imagery, the style of authority debated between the dominant order and its challengers. The polemics of Khomeini and the literature of the Muslim Brotherhood in Egypt and Syria are full of holes. But what of the censored official press in the Arab world? Does it fare any better, does it offer more penetrating and living inquiries? The lamentable quality of the secular discourse, its embarrassing subservience to the powers that be, and its demeaning of the truth in favor of flattery and hypocrisy leave all but the most naive and trusting skeptical about the claims of the state, dubious about what they read, vulnerable to rumors and messianic calls.

225

Both the dominant order and its challengers ask people to suspend disbelief. The men in power do not offer more open, honest, empirical discussions of social problems than their messianic challengers. They offer the citizenry only faith. If faith is all it takes, then inherited religious dogmas have a chance, for they meet the claims of the state on the religious dogmas' own terrain.

From a distance, some of the guardians of order in the Arab and Muslim states appear modern, secular, rational, reformist, whatever the labels may be. This was the cultivated image of the shah of Iran, of a Sadat or of the Tunisian Habib Bourguiba; this is the impression these men wanted to create in that part of the world whose approval they sought and whose trappings they admired. But are these men really modern men: Are they as different at home from their fundamentalist challengers as it is presumed in the West? Or do these men show a different dimension of themselves at home, a more dictatorial, more superstitious one, with the result that the political culture suffers the ailments and limitations of tradition yet without the webs of meaning that softened it and made it bearable? We know that the Shiᵖa imam in Iran or the Supreme Guide of the Muslim Brotherhood claim that their deeds are inspired by divine revelation, that they carry out God's will, and that disobedience to them amounts to waging war against God's design. But the secular rulers, the men who tell us how modern they are, also put forth claims that amount to divine inspiration. "I am not entirely alone," said the shah to an interviewer, ". . . I am accompanied by a force others can not see. My mystical force. And then I get messages. Religious messages . . . I believe in God, in the fact of having been chosen by God to accomplish a mission. My visions were miracles that saved the country. My reign has saved the country . . ."[72] Sadat too claimed divine inspiration. In his reconstruction of his life's events – all the way from escaping drowning as a child to his "mission" to Jerusalem in November, 1977 – he cultivates a sense of destiny and divine guidance: He is saved from certain death; he survives an era of turmoil and madness (the Nasserist phase) largely through his "faith"; then he sees his way to a "sacred mission" to spread the gospel of love and brotherhood. "This is the story of my life," he writes in the prologue to his autobiography, "which is at the same time the story

of Egypt since 1918 – for so destiny has decreed."[73] And short of
divine inspiration, the presidency-for-life of a "modern" man like
Bourguiba, who monopolized the political life of his country from
its independence in 1956 until he was finally pushed aside in 1987,
was clearly at odds with his claims to being a "new" man: Even
when ailing, he remained the supreme source of authority.

The shackling of society at the behest of the exalted leaders had
confirmed the traditional style of authority; the modern veneer
given that leadership, either through its command of a foreign language or through the steady cultivation of a progressive image was
put on more for export than for home consumption. At home the
leadership continued to relegate the citizenry to a marginal place.
The infallible leader was but an extension into today's world of the
infallible imam (as in Shi'a thought), the official governmental line
an extension of religious orthodoxy (as in Sunni orthodoxy). The
Egyptian scholar Hassan Hanafi has interpreted this phenomenon
in an essay that helps rehabilitate the question of political democracy in the Arab world and restore it to its rightful place. In considering the question of political authority and liberty in the Arab
world – "our thousand years crisis," as he calls it – Hanafi connects the orthodox religious view of the world as a reflection of
God's will with the dominant style of political authority:

> From such a static view of the world issued the idea of the Only
> Leader (al Za'im al awhad), the Grand Saviour, the Faithful Presi-
> dent, the Divinely Inspired One, the Teacher who commands to be
> obeyed, who expresses the interests of all the people, who embodies
> all, who borrowed all the characteristics of God in knowledge and
> ability, who hears and observes everything, who pronounces on
> every occasion either directly or through the channels of censorship
> and communication. As a result, there is no longer any difference
> between Sunni thought which emphasized institutions and Shi'a
> thought which focuses on the Infallible Imam who will fill the earth
> with justice as it had been dominated by oppression.[74]

The equating of opposition and religious unbelief and of the
dominant order and orthodoxy is an old political stratagem. While
it persists, both the rulers and their opponents will tax the *turath*
with their claims: the rulers with demands for total obedience, for
religious vindication of what has been done in this grubby world;

227

their opponents with a vision of a successful order that makes today's necessities and shortcuts look like treason and more compromise. The struggle becomes all the more difficult, for once religious orthodoxy is called upon to sustain political authority there is a natural urge on the part of those pushed out of the world of power to claim that they too wish to re-create God's world and to purify the religious heritage.

The task of what one Arab analyst calls the "dissociation" of religious and political authority remains: It is a task that Arab–Muslim societies are yet to face up to candidly.[75] Because the realm of politics and human affairs is never clear, it is simplistic to say, as Arab radicals are prone to say, that people have to destroy their past and do away with historical forms and inhibitions. The disjunction between what people say and what they do is always present; change is introduced in spurts. The modest, grubby domain of politics must be distinguished, to the extent possible, from God's realm, lest the former become unduly messianic and the latter unduly contaminated. This has more to do with the quality of what political man does than with the inhibitions and injunctions of classical scripture.

So far the attempt has been avoided not only by the conservative dominant interests but also by those who claimed to represent the new politics. Of the latter regimes, the writer just cited observes: "Instead of confronting *al Salafiyya* [the dominant religious orthodoxy] they turned it, whenever in power, into an instrument and a pillar for their power. Thus the ideology of the Religious Institution became the ideology of the rulers – even the revolutionary ones among them."[76] The task of distinguishing the two will leave the dominant order without the crutch of religion, and that is why the men in power have refrained from such an undertaking. But in the long run it will tone down messianic expectations, it will remove from the push and pull of political life the expectation that some perfect utopia can be resurrected, and perhaps it will enable societies made up of Christians, Shi'a, Sunnis, Alawis to arrive at a modicum of national unity. It may be useful in the short run to unleash Islam against Marxism, but what will this do to a society with a substantial Coptic minority? Sadat's war against *al mabadi al mustwarda* (the imported doctrines) backfired, as the strife be-

tween Muslim fundamentalists and Copts that broke out shortly
before his death was to show. In the absence of a more secular
orientation, the prospects for any measure of unity in Syria between the Alawis – who are considered seceders from Islam by
orthodox Muslims – and the Sunnis must be poor at best.

Likewise, Saudi Arabia's Wahhabi heritage, a memory from its
simpler, more pristine past, may enable the Saudis to play up their
fidelity to tradition, their role as bearers of Islam's original simplicity, their homeland as site of its initial triumphs. But this too can
backfire. By the vision of original Wahhabism, much of today's
Saudi Arabia – its wealth, the ways of its young men and women,
its friendship with infidel powers – represents a compromised society. That Islamic zeal that the dynasty pays homage to can be a
double-edged sword. It can shore up the order. But it, too, can
acquire a life of its own, make demands for purity that no political
order could accommodate.

Shrewd men, the custodians of the Saudi state know their own
history. In that history religion was, alternately, a prop to the political order and a force pushing it into its grave. The first Saudi
state (1744–1818) emerged in the heartland of the Peninsula. It
was born of a mix of dynastic ambition and religious zeal: Two
men, one Muhammad Ibn Saud, a tribal chieftain, and the other
Muhammad Ibn Abd-al Wahhab, a religious preacher, came together in a small Arabian hamlet and laid the foundations of a
remarkable partnership. It was, if you will, a coming together of
the Sultan and the Quran. And for a while the partnership proved
a great success. The enterprise expanded in every direction: There
were territorial conquests and considerable booty for the warriors.
But the zealots did not know when to stop. Fresh campaigns always beckoned and godly warfare knew no limits. When the
Wahhabi warriors overran the two holy cities of Mecca and Medina, they ran afoul of imperial Ottoman authority. The Sultan in
Constantinople prided himself on his title as Guardian of the Two
Holy Places. Small desert quarrels now became high imperial politics. An expedition by Egypt's ruler, Muhammad Ali, undertaken
on behalf of the Ottoman court shattered the Saudi realm.

The great desert warrior, Abdul Aziz Ibn Saud, who founded the
modern Saudi state early in this century had understood the fate

of the first Saudi state. (There was a second Saudi realm, 1824–1891, but it fell to intrafamily intrigues and squabbles.) Ibn Saud would take no chances. Islam was unleashed early on in the territorial conquests that knit the vast realm together. The *Ikhwan*, a religious military brotherhood, provided the shock troops with which Ibn Saud had conquered the coveted holy cities in the Hijaz in the 1920s. But no sooner had he prevailed than he was up against the zeal of the *Ikhwan*. The shrewd ruler accepted the hegemony of Pax Britannica in the waters of the Gulf and in bordering realms – Transjordan and Iraq and Kuwait – and was a beneficiary of British subsidies; the *Ikhwan* were still eager to play with fire. For the *Ikhwan* the bordering states were *bilad kufr*, countries of unbelief, and the whole modern concept of fixed national borders a heresy from the infidels. They had accepted Ibn Saud as a leader so long as there were new lands to conquer. But the leader had now come to rest. The conquest of the holy cities of Mecca and Medina had brought the desert warriors into the settled and benign cities of the Hijaz. For Ibn Saud it was time for consolidation of the realm. Powers beyond (the British in the waters of the Gulf, Muslim rulers with a vested interest in the pilgrimage to Mecca) had to be conciliated. Religious passion had to be harnessed if the realm were to survive. Ibn Saud took no chances: The *Ikhwan* were demolished in 1929; the learned professional *ulama* of the realm were enlisted in defense of order and routine.

It would take half a century before a radical religio-political movement was heard from again in Saudi Arabia. A young band of zealots struck in November of 1979. They were led by a militant ideologue, a self-styled Imam (a religio-political leader) by the name of Juhayman al-Utaybi. The rebels pulled off a daring deed. In November of that year (less than a year after Khomeini had triumphantly returned to his country to impose his Islamic state) they seized Islam's holiest shrine, the Grand Mosque in Mecca. The episode was a source of genuine embarrassment to a dynasty that prided itself on its custodianship of the holy cities of Mecca and Medina. Juhayman and his followers were flushed out of the Grand Mosque by a sustained military operation that lasted two weeks.

Juhayman's themes were the themes of a millenarian movement: the "pollution" of the realm, friendship with Christian powers, the abdication on the part of the establishment ulama and their subservience to the holders of political power. The state had made the ulama its partners; Juhayman went after the ulama: They were hired men, he said, who sold their souls to the devil in return for material rewards. The whole social and political order – the monarchy, the vast religious establishment and the educational system it controlled – was written off by Juhayman and his followers as un-Islamic.

Juhayman's rebellion was put down in a welter of blood. The pretender was killed. The ulama indicted the jumbled theology he had let loose; Juhayman was too marginal a figure. The state was firmly entrenched, and the mass of its citizenry was shocked by the violation of the sanctity of the Grand Mosque by the zealots. A complex welfare state had emerged in the Peninsula. The Saudis remembered the history of their land: the hunger, the anarchy, the bedouin raids, the insecurity of life and possession. The Saudis had secured the peace. Everywhere around them the people of the Saudi realm saw in what had been happier lands (Iran, Iraq, Syria, Lebanon, Egypt) either massive disorder or poverty. They had been spared the disorder. Few were willing to answer the trumpet of the pretender.

Religious extremism would make a more limited run in 1990–1991. Foreign (read American) forces had rescued the realm and thwarted Saddam Hussein's bid for domination. Infidels had defiled the realm, preached the religious radicals. The foreigners were here to stay, they were sure. The custodians of the realm enforced a tight social order; "Islamic" education was the norm throughout the land; religion accounted for a third of the curriculum in Saudi schools. The ulama were pampered and given their niche in the social order. The air waves and the printed media turned out a steady diet of Islamic sermons and piety: The liberals groaned under the weight of it all, wanted the power of the *mutawwa* (the religious police who enforce religious ritual and observance) curtailed. Still the purists pushed for more: "Islam" had to rule, the quiescent ulama replaced by a more hardened breed of religious activists. Some of the religious radicals were employed by the state; a handful were academics and religious scholars employed in the kingdom's state-run and subsidized institutions of higher learning.

These men could not be ignored. The sacred symbols and the political language they deployed against the state were the very stuff of which the political order's legitimacy was made. The fundamentalists played with deadly material: the "American connection" of the regime, its more daring foreign policy in the Gulf War and its aftermath.

It had lingered, and was left unresolved, that explosive question of the boundary between religion and politics in the Arab–Islamic tradition. In the mid-1920s, Ali Abdel Raziq, a young Azhar-educated judge, had the daring and insight to publish a book that openly called for the separation of religion and state, that stated that Islam was a spiritual–ethical construct that had nothing to do with political matters. According to Abdel Raziq, the mixing of politics and religion was the deed of the caliphs who governed like any other mortals but hid behind religious justifications. In reality, the caliphate had nothing to do with religion: It was a secular, administrative institution of men who usurped power in the way men normally acquire political power. The sooner Muslims understood this the better: Faith would then become strictly faith, politics would be what politics have always been about – the exercise of power, the governing of people and goods.[77] It is sad – at least for a secularist – that the simple case made by Abdel Raziq is yet to be learned, that people remain tied to old chains, doomed to repeat the old themes and to resort to the old lines of escape.

The Islamic state that tantalizes the true believers and frightens those in the West who worry about the receding of civilization is a memory that makes the present order look hopelessly compromised. No one knows what an Islamic state would or would not do, would or would not look like. Memory may imagine and resurrect – on paper, in sermons, in the tracts of the true believers – a world that was once whole and autonomous. But past orders cannot be resurrected. Ideas and systems – liberal, Marxist, Muslim, whatever – become a cover for power, an apology for decay. Behind the labels lurk the struggle for power and the fears and ambitions of men. Reality devours the scheme, and people are left insisting that it was betrayed or disfigured only by greed or incompetence. Or they are left using the forms of a particular civilization – its methods of punishment, its sacred words, its outward displays of devotion – as a smokescreen behind which they engage in sordid or banal matters. Then the fight begins anew over the symbols themselves. What was presented as a solution becomes a new battleground.

Where is the true Islam – in Khomeini's view of things or in Sadat's, in Saudi Arabia or in Qaddafi's Libya? Radical-fundamentalist Islam is one form; bourgeois Islam is another; reactionary Islam is yet another. Some read socialism into Islam. They insist that their radical economic policies can be found in this or that scripture, in the record of this or that caliph, in this or that *hadith* (saying of the Prophet), but their adversaries find in the same Islam high regard for private property and inequality. The Muslim Brotherhood condemns the Egyptian treaty with Israel, but al-Azhar, Egypt's and the Muslim world's most distinguished institution of Islamic learning, gives its approval to the treaty as the opinion of Islam. "The ulama of al Azhar," we are told in an official opinion, "believe that the Egyptian–Israeli treaty is in harmony with Islamic law. It was concluded from a position of strength after the battle of the *jihad* and the victory realized by Egypt on the tenth of Ramadan of the Year 1393 [October 6, 1973]." And to show how flexible traditions can be, al-Azhar found a precedent for the Egyptian–Israeli accord in the Prophet's diplomacy and conduct of war and peace and the treaty he concluded in 628 – the Hudabiyah Treaty – with the clan that then controlled Mecca.[78] Once again the question arises: Where is the opinion of Islam – in the tracts of the Muslim Brotherhood or the rulings of al-Azhar? There is no happy conclusion to the drama of politics, no shortcut to justice.

THE WAYS OF THE ANCESTORS, THE WAYS OF THE WORLD

The quoting of scripture can lend courage when courage is needed for difficult undertakings; it can connect people and societies to their origins and remind them of the path they have traversed. For as we were long told by Edmund Burke, a society wrenched away from its past and its roots may be a society without a future. Wholesale indictment of a political order and open warfare against

233

a society's history may be polemically elegant but they can turn into a nightmare: "No one generation could link with the other. Men would become little better than the flies of a summer."[79] But here is to be found a warning: Fidelity to the past and a connection with it must be honestly felt. One cannot simultaneously bulldoze the past (as so many of the wealthy oil states have done) and claim honesty to it. The huge construction projects reveal, if anything, a broken connection with the society's world and history, a desire to obliterate and forget, a contempt for the past. In this frenzied world, people have indeed become "summer flies," and some have become vultures. Caught between insistent trumpeting of tradition and heritage on the one hand and open and real violations of the past and the traditional on the other, societies can push the gap between reality and symbols beyond tolerable proportions.

The Iranian revolution burst on the scene with Khomeini claiming that the final victory of Iran's Islamic revolution will be on the day when Islam comes to rule the whole world. That was the promise of the Bolsheviks as well, whose revolution ended only when the world revolution and socialist internationalism won out. There was a case for prudence in Iran's conduct, for doubts as to whether that stubborn Arab world would take to Iran's revolutionary ways. But the doubts were cast to the wind. The Iranians pushed at the Arab world: They came bearing their scripture, their message of redemption and deliverance. They did so for a decade – from the onset of the revolution in 1979 until Ayatollah Ruhollah Khomeini called off his campaign against the Iraqi state in 1988 and acknowledged the limits of his revolution.

Throughout that bloody decade it was not so much Iran's material force that worried the custodians of the Arab world. That kind of force they could balance and deal with. To borrow (again) the terms of Edmund Burke's classic discourse on the French Revolution, there was Iran as "faction" and "sect" and there was Iran as a state, and the sect was more terrifying. Its center was in Iran, but it had tributaries elsewhere in the Muslim world. "The faction is not local or territorial but it is a general evil . . . Where it least appears in action, it is still full of life. In its sleep it recruits its strength and prepares its exertion. The social order which refrains it feeds it. It exists in every country . . . and among all orders of men in every country." For a good part of a terrible decade. Iran was a land in which nothing seemed to matter: not commerce, not industry, not conventions and laws, "a land were nothing rules but the minds of desperate men."[80]

Iran's crusade, though, failed to sweep aside the dominant Arab order of states. The Arab states withstood the buffeting. In very fundamental ways the Iranian revolutionaries did not fully understand the Arab states they sought to change. It was a cynical order of states that the Iranian revolutionaries sought to overturn. Iran's radical nationalist experience represented by the leader Muhammad Musaddiq had aborted in the early 1950s, blocked by American intervention which had brought the ascendancy of Mussaddiq to a quick end. Dressed in clerical garb, Iranian nationalism stormed through with a vengeance under Khomeini a quarter-century later. But the Arabs had been numbed by all they had known. They had had their fling with radical politics. Under Nasser and the Ba'th Party in the 1950s and the 1960s, the Arabs had known the full range of radical nationalism; the initial promise, the rise of new classes, then the world closing up again. They could not summon the passion. The Syrian writer Sadeq al Azm put this matter in accurate historical perspective: The Iranian revolution was in his words a "delayed replay of a powerful trend that had already exhausted itself and served its purpose in the Arab world. Hence, the often inarticulate but inescapable feeling of Arabs that there is something of the *deja vu* in what unfolded in Iran."[81]

The Iranian Revolution's fire and passion targeted the Iraqi state and the dynastic states of the Gulf nearby. If the revolution were to catch on, it was these states that had to be swept along. The Iraqi state seemed particularly vulnerable. This was a jerry-built structure, an artificial realm of Kurds in the north, Sunni Arabs in the valleys of the Tigris and the Euphrates, Shi'a Arabs in the southern hinterland. The Shi'a were the country's majority, shut out of political power. It was not hard to summon up the vision of Iraq's Shi'a population taking to the revolution next door. Iraq had the shrine cities of Shi'a Islam; it was the repository of a good deal of its sacred history. When he was an exile on the run, Ayatollah Khomeini had made his home in the Shi'a city of Najaf, in southern Iraq; he had lived there for more than a dozen years. This was the "eastern flank" of the Arab world. That is Iraq's image of itself, and that is the sort of thing that Arab nationalists had said of Iraq. A virulent form of Arab nationalism took root here: The frontier province where the Islam of the Arabian Peninsula had long mated with Persia was nearly neurotic about its "Arabism." This would be the battleground between an Iranian revolutionary state garbed in Islamic radicalism and the Arab order of states. Beyond Iraq were the sparsely populated dynastic states of the Peninsula and the Gulf.

Hard as the Iranian revolutionaries would try to present their crusade as some Islamic millennium, as the coming together of an oppressed underclass, the Arabs nearby insisted that the campaign was one of Iranian primacy. In Khomeini, Iraq's custodians of power and the rulers of the Arab dynastic states would see a "turbaned Shah" bent on dominating the waters of the Persian Gulf and its commerce. That cruel Iraqi upstart, Saddam Hussein, would be shored up by the wealthy regimes nearby. Oil wealth would see him and his regime through a long campaign of attrition.

The fragility of the Iraqi state had been exaggerated. The Shiʾa of Iraq did not flock to Khomeini's banner. Fear of their brutal ruler was one factor; attachment to home no doubt another. What was once an unwieldy Iraqi realm of sedition and recurrent rebellions had been remade by the Baʾth regime, which had been in power since 1968. The place had been pacified, turned into a republic of coercion and fear. For the tumult of its past there was now the eerie silence of an "oriental despotism." The place had become increasingly urbanized, hence easier to monitor: Four decades earlier its population had been predominantly rural; now some 70 percent of the country lived in the principal cities. Agriculture had stagnated as the officers and ideologues of the Baʾth built a terrifying "national security state" with considerable staying power. The government bureaucracy with its oil income now dominated the economy. The despot ruled, as in the past; this time, though, he was also the one who put bread on the table.

With cunning and ferocity to match, the warden at the helm of the Iraqi state resorted to what he and his apparatus of terror described as a mix of *Tarhib* (terror) and *Targhib* (inducement) to keep the order intact. There was wealth to buy off the disgruntled and to compensate the families of those who perished in the regime's military campaign, and there was unsparing terror unleashed against those who refused to be cowed. The Shiʾa had had their own great clerical figure: Ayatollah Muhammad Baqir al Sadr, a luminary of the Shiʾa world, an intellectual in his own right, a prolific author. Sadr had been dubbed "the Khomeini of Iraq." This had marked him, and the regime put him to death in April of 1980 – shortly before it was to launch its war against Iran. There was a clerical family of high calling, the Hakim family: The senior member of that family, Ayatollah Muhsin al Hakim (died 1969), had been the highest religious authority in the world of Iraqi and Arab Shiʾism. Ayatollah Muhsin al Hakim's sons were natural claimants to leadership among Iraq's Shiʾa. The regime would take no chances; scores of that family were murdered or scattered into exile. Furthermore, the course of battle on the Iran–Iraq frontier provided no deliverance. The divisions of the "armed Imam," Ayatollah Khomeini, would be contained by the Iraqis. Iran was a solitary state now pitted into a hopeless campaign. Zeal and passion could not overcome the Iraqi ruler, and the wealth made available to him by the Saudis and the Kuwaitis, and the free access he had to Soviet and French weapons, to "dual use" American technology. The Iraqi despot posed as the gendarme holding off the challenge of an enraged revolutionary state. The Iranians were the revisionists, the Iraqi presented himself as the defender of order and commerce and borders.

The dynastic states, too, survived the revolution's moment of enthusiasm. These states had substantial and disaffected Shiʾa populations. The small principality of Bahrain had an absolute Shiʾa majority with no political entitlement; the Shiʾa of Saudi Arabia, concentrated in the oil-bearing Eastern Province of the kingdom, were at odds with the country's Wahhabi orthodoxy, a community of outsiders. The Shiʾa of Kuwait constituted perhaps a solid 25 to 30 percent of Kuwait's native-citizen population, with legitimate grievances. Kuwait's Shiʾa were active in its commerce and trade, but political power was denied them. There would be some material for the Iranians to work with in the dynastic states of the Gulf; the limitations on the Shiʾa religious ceremonies and on those annual displays of self-flagellation and sorrow, the severe con-

237

straints on Shiᵓa jurisprudence and legal affairs, a relative sense of deprivation that the oil wealth at the discretion of the rulers had not been equitably shared.

But the Shiᵓa were a minority population. Their activism – what little of it there was – fed a Sunni backlash. The discontent had not been wide or deep enough to begin with. That old unwritten social contract between the dynasties and the Shiᵓa populations – political protection in return for relative quiescence – withstood the storm. The Shiᵓa had too much to lose. In some perfect world, they would have raised the standard of revolt; they would have shed no tears for the rulers had those rulers been struck down. But these communities knew their habitat. The Saudi dynasty was merciful when compared to what that vast "Quran belt" in the Saudi heartland would mete out to the Shiᵓa. The Sabah ruling family in Kuwait may not have been the most enlightened of rulers but they were reasonable men when judged against the fringe elements of Sunni fundamentalism, and what those men would do to the order and prosperity of the city-state. And soon the Shiᵓa activism gave way to a campaign of terror. An assassination attempt was made against the *Emir* of Kuwait in 1985. There were other episodes of subversion. With this resort to terror, Shiᵓa activism had peaked and burned out. "Respectable" Shiᵓism – the privileged merchant families, the professionals who wanted to press for their rights but to stay within the limits of order – was frightened off. By the time Ayatollah Khomeini told his "revolutionary children" in the summer of 1988 that the crusade of virtue and terror had to be written off, the Shiᵓa rebellion in the Gulf had fizzled out.[82]

"Whoever eats the Sultan's bread fights with the Sultan's sword," goes a Bedouin proverb. The rulers of the dynastic states disposed of enormous wealth. They had not asked for sacrifice and vigilance. They had only sought a measure of social peace, and that they would secure as the revolutionary decade played itself out. The Shiᵓa were a people of *taqiyya*, dissimulation. They were the quintessential outsiders. They had lived, as it were, within the catacombs of history. In realms where they had not ruled, like the realms on the Arab side of the Gulf, they had the habits of quiescence: They distrusted political power. A *Mahdi*, a savior, had summoned them to a new undertaking. But he hailed from the other side of that Arab–Persian divide. His message of revenge, of punishing the wicked and the mighty, they no doubt understood. It was in the most natural of ways their outlook, their inherited history. But there was that balance of worldly power. And that the Iranians had not been able to overturn.

For all their labor of a decade, for all their attempts to establish "sister republics" in the Arab world, the Iranian revolutionaries secured a political base only among the Shiʾa of Lebanon. They secured it with scarce treasure; they subsidized the downtrodden, the newly urbanized among the Shiʾa. To Lebanon – through Syria – came some of Iran's resources and revolutionary passion. The Iranian message found some adherents among Lebanon's "hewers of wood and drawers of water." But the ground had been tilled a decade or so earlier. A great organizer, a mullah of awe-inspiring charisma, the Iranian-born Imam Musa al Sadr, had made his home among the Shiʾa of Lebanon. He arrived in the country in 1959, a young man thirty-one years of age. Ten years later he towered over the politicians and clerics of his sect: Long before Ayatollah Khomeini acquired his political kingdom, Musa al Sadr had built some rudimentary political institutions for the Shiʾa, tried to rid them of their political timidity. On the eve of the Iranian Revolution, Sadr "disappeared" while on a visit to Libya, a victim of foul play by Qaddafi. But the work he did would pay off for his inheritors and for the Iranian theocrats.[83]

The Shiʾa of that country had awakened to a sense of power and violation. In Iran's patronage, and in the very prestige of Iran's revolution, the Shiʾa of Lebanon were to find a "revolutionary example." This was an old game in Lebanon – the search for foreign patrons on the part of Lebanon's tribes to tip the scale of power their way. The Maronites had been masters of that game. They had practiced it for centuries. During different stretches of their history, they had drawn on the protection of the Holy See, France, and then on American power. The Sunni bourgeoisie of Lebanon's coastal cities had ridden the coattails of the larger Sunni–Arab world beyond Lebanon. Now it was the turn of the Shiʾa. In the Persian state, and in its transformed symbols of radical Shiʾism, they saw a chance to assert their claim to the country that had always snubbed them and seen them as crude country yokels with little if any culture or polish.

The "armed Imam" in the east had his theocratic state, his *wilayat al faqih*, the governance of the Muslim jurisprudent: Lesser Shi³a mullahs in the towns of Lebanon's Shi³a hinterland, and in the slums of Greater Beirut which had become a magnet for the Shi³a migrants, would attempt a parody of that distant experiment. Israel's invasion of Lebanon in the summer of 1982 was another factor in the rise of the Shi³a: The Israelis shattered the Palestinian sanctuary in West Beirut and in the ancestral lands of the Shi³a in South Lebanon. The Israeli invasion was to prove a curious midwife of a Shi³a awakening. In routing the Palestinians who had become the masters of large chunks of the Muslim part of the country, the Israelis did for the Shi³a what they had not been able to do for themselves. They rid them of a Palestinian dominion. Then Israel's occupation of the Shi³a lands in the south closed the circle. It gave a people emerging from a long slumber, and from a tradition of quiescence, an ennobling myth of resistance. The Shi³a took on the Israeli occupation; suicide drivers struck installations and convoys, a bloody struggle between occupier and occupied raged for a good deal of 1983–85. To an apolitical population came a cult of "martyrdom" and political resistance.

By the end of 1985, the Israelis had pulled out of the bulk of South Lebanon. The small Shi³a world of Lebanon had been thoroughly transformed.

Two Shi³a revolts were to be rolled together in Lebanon of the 1980s: a moderate Shi³a movement which sought for itself and its kinsmen a place of primacy in Lebanon's politics commensurate with the demographic weight of the Shi³a as the country's largest sect, and a radical movement that threw caution to the winds and succumbed to the delirium that an "Islamic republic" in Iran's image was within reach. The first revolt was made of Lebanon's own material: the primacy of the religious sect and the clan, and the will of "big men" leading their communities. This revolt was the work of Imam Musa al Sadr and what he left behind. It worked with the achievements of the Shi³a – and their resentments: with the new money, the new education that the urbanized had bought for their children with money made in faraway places, and the heightened political awareness. The second movement, that of the so-called Party of God, paid little homage to Lebanon's realities, or so it claimed. Its inspiration, and its funds, came from the Iranians. It was led by more marginal men who saw a chance to inherit the ruins of the country and pushed on with an audacious enterprise.

But the Iranians and their Lebanese wards could not remake that stubborn land of minorities. No revolutionary doctrine and no deeds of terror could overcome the primacy of place and of geography. Iran was far away, the city of Beirut was a cynical city of trade and services by the Mediterranean. There was no treasure here (unlike Iran with its oil wealth) with which the faithful could erect a reign of virtue. Lebanon lived in the shadow of two larger powers – Syria and Israel. The utopia of a realm made pure and whole could not go very far in Lebanon.

Western hostages could be held and traded in Lebanon on Iran's behalf; local warlords could claim intense piety – and the power that came with it. But the stubborn geography of Lebanon and its realities would prevail. The more astute among the Shi'a mullahs knew the country, and knew that wild schemes would not flourish there. Sayyid Muhammad Hussein Fadlallah, the most influential of the Shi'a clerical estate, a man that the Party of God claimed as a "spiritual guide," disabused the zealous of their maximalist fantasies. (For his part, Fadlallah always kept a discreet distance from the Party of God.) In early 1984, when the Shi'a movement was at its peak, the cleric who had acquired considerable power and prestige among the Shi'a of Greater Beirut dismissed the idea of an Islamic republic in Lebanon. The "objective conditions" did not exist for an Islamic state in Lebanon, he observed. Such ideas were dismissed by the cleric as "leaps into the void." There was a "larger balance of forces" that had to be considered.[84] That "larger balance" did not take long to make itself felt. In February of 1987, the Syrian state dispatched its army into the strongholds of the Shi'a zealots. A massacre of twenty-two of the Party of God's men at the hands of the Syrian forces underlined the determination of the state to assert its hegemony in Lebanon and to rein in the chaos and the revolutionary passion.

During what passed for the liberal age in the Arab–Muslim world, the liberals searched for the West's success and ended up importing its disembodied forms and pretensions, alienated from their habitat, and, when things really mattered, betraying their own principles. In Marxist movements and groups, sterile molds and the usual phrases about the "proletarian revolution" and the "petty bourgeois" failed to capture the predicament of the world; that is why there was no living Marxism in the Arab world. Now the traditionalists insist that they have the proper remedy: Islam, the *turath*, the ways of the ancestors. They say nothing about what they intend to do with young men and women who have seen other ways and who do not wish to return to some imagined pure tradition. The discourse of the traditionalists is hopelessly simple in its assertion that the tradition lives and that there is an Islamic way of education, of income distribution, of government. It has yet to face up to the change that has swept the Muslim world.

The people who surrender to the ancestors are, strictly speaking, surrendering to strangers. Between those branded as followers of Western models and those insisting on the ways of the ancestors, the fight should be carried out with mirrors. Both want a world with preconceived models; both want to spare men and women the agony of choice and of experience. Authenticity can be as much an escape as dependence and mimicry can be. Joined together, as they often are in the Arab world, they tell us that a civilization has ceased to work. The point is thoughtfully made by the Egyptian Ghali Shukri in an attack against the polemics of authenticity: Despite their seeming opposition, the two views – the one that sees salvation in return to Arab–Islamic or Phoenician or pharaonic roots and the one that sees it in escape to European or American civilization – converge. Both abandon present reality in favor of a deal offered either by the strangers or the ancestors. In this way they forfeit the opportunity to learn from both strangers and ancestors. Both created their own models.[85]

None of the talk about authenticity or ancestors has given the Arab world the self-confidence to sort out its relationship to the West or to choose among the ideas, technologies, and development models tantalizingly held before it and come up with a viable mix. Side by side with the talk of autonomy and authenticity has been a paralyzing vulnerability to the wares of the West that manifests itself in the urge to buy the latest inappropriate technology, the largest kinds of technical projects. An arid technicalism has swept the region – concrete and steel, prefabs, nuclear power, construction projects, financial deals, talks of financial deals, and so forth: the West devoid of the social system that gave rise to it, the West without its ideas, its art, its books, its counterculture.

In the affluent Arab states, as in Iran under the shah, a merger had taken place between the technology of the Occident – its harsh side, its salesmen, its brutal empiricism – and the despotism and tribalism of Near Eastern traditions. There is no place in such a hybrid for books, for artisans, for folk culture, for ideas – no honest encounter with the discontents of civilization. Once upon a time, the Orient – to use that overused artificial distinction between Orient and Occident – prided itself on its spiritualism and divided the world into a spiritual East and a materialist West. Nowhere is the idea of the materialist West as firmly entrenched as it is in the Arab world today. The real West is a mix of ideas and techniques, technologies and social institutions; the other West – the one bought by Arabs and others – is dry and oppressive and ultimately a weak cardboard structure. The "Asian Germany" that the Shah wanted to turn Iran into (as he described it) epitomized the dream and its fate. It was decreed by administrative fiat that traditions be obliterated, that "embarrassing" popular celebrations be banned and forgotten. The dark side of Iran had to be expunged and the gadgets and machines had to be displayed as an alibi for civilization.

No sooner had Iran collapsed than the tired theme was replayed in Iraq with all the talk about a rising regional power, all the statistics about capabilities and achievements. Consider the following report about Iraq's quest for modernization, which highlights the mixture of technology and regressive social structure. The country bent upon entering the nuclear age, we are told in this report of mid-1980, strictly regulates the usage of privately owned typewriters. Only friends of the government are given licenses to acquire them. Typewriters smack of political freedom, of pamphlets and agitation. What is allowed is a wide range of luxury goods from the West: "perfume from France, clothes from Italy, and toys from the U.S." All is stocked in government-owned stores and made available to the new elite:

243

Life for this new educated elite can be sweet indeed, provided mouths are kept shut and fingers don't pound typewriters. In Baghdad, Iraq Stores Co., a downtown department store, looks like Christmas-time as crowds of affluent young Iraqis shop for everything from Chanel No. 5 to basketballs endorsed by Bob Cousy, the Boston Celtics player of the 1950s.

For the children of this elite there is aisle upon aisle of clothes and toys. The store's director explains that a special blue-ribbon committee made up of representatives of all the important ministries meets once a week to decide which clothes and toys should be imported from the West. "The needs of the children come first," he says.[86]

Anything for the children: anything, of course, but typewriters and political freedom. For them the West is to be bought without its anguish, its troubles, its creativity, its cultural freedom. We shall provide the glamor of the world for them, but we shall spare them the path that the West took to get it. We shall not dwell on thought and dissent, but there are plenty of Pierre Cardin fashions – proof that a once-backward world has finally arrived at modernity.

Writing at a time when illusions were easier to entertain, the French scholar Jacques Berque expressed a wish for a marginal civilization to combine advanced technology and its own social structure and come up with something better, not only for itself but also for others:

Whereas in so many more "advanced" countries the machine dissociates man from nature and imprisons him far from the green shade of the tree of life, in the gloomy landscapes of artificiality, the Arab can, through the machine, recover nature and become natural again. Even the very suddenness of his contemporary history may serve him, after having burdened him; it has not left him time to forget his unifying mission. He has overlept our bourgeois centuries. To the modern world, divided and hard pressed, the beneficiary and victim of analysis, he will be a harbinger of freshness through the completeness of his attitude to life.[87]

The statement was pure sentimentalism when it was written; it is more obviously so now. It was one of those illusions that outsiders come to fix onto a region they adopt – that not only will it find its own way but that it will help others as well. We may of course want to enquire why such illusions are entertained and expressed, but that is another tale. What matters is that they are expressed and then imported by the people to whom they refer. Nature imitates art and such illusions become part of national self-delusions. The "overleaping of bourgeois centuries" foreseen by Berque did not and could not happen. The result was the hybrid of cultural and technological mimicry with regressive social institutions, the lack of fit between people's ideas and habits on one side and their machines on the other.

Less than two decades after Berque made his prognosis, he came face to face with a different reality. This time, in an interview in 1980, he lamented the demise of "the Orient," "the East." Orientalism, he observed, was over, because the East was no longer distinctive. The Muslim world had entered "the game," he said; It now plays it just like the others do. Berque was baffled; his East had failed him and become occidentalized.[88]

But just as his early image of overleaping bourgeois centuries was wrong, Berque's latter assessment is mistaken as well. "Normalization" too – his term – is illusory, another easy way out. The problem has to do with the mixture of hyperauthenticity on the one hand and civilizational vulnerability on the other. Underneath the hyperauthenticity there is a vulnerability to outside models that must be candidly faced. Like all prohibitions and denials, this vulnerability grows more powerful and obsessive the more it is denied and covered up with exaggerated cultural rebellions and exaggerated claims to radicalism.

When the liberal generation in the Arab world pondered the great issues facing them, they did it against the background of total confidence – their own and the West's – in the Western model. Likewise, the Marxists who wrote the trenchant tracts were sure that Marxism blew away historical inadequacies, ethnic biases, and created a new man. Today these illusions are denied to those who engage in political struggles and those who interpret them from a safe distance. Arab liberalism turned out to be a fragile plant. The ground under the feet of the self-styled Arab liberals cracked over and over again. There was to be no "liberal age" in Arab politics. As for Marxism in its Arab variety, it was always a parody. Arab reality mocked the contrived categories of Marxism. Long before the truth of Marxism receded in societies which had hoisted its banners (the Soviet Union and its constituent republics, Eastern

Europe, Yugoslavia) and we were treated to the spectacle of malig-
nant nationalisms returning to history from the world of the dead.
Marxism had been a pathetic parody in Arab–Muslim lands.

The secularist impulse took a savage beating in the Arab world
of the 1980s. A circle was closed: Christian Arabs had played a
leading role in the development of Arab nationalism. They had
begun their work in the final years of the nineteenth century, when
liberal nationalism rode triumphant. They were the tribunes and
pamphleteers of Arab nationalism. A century later, the Christian
Arab communities had become marginalized. There was no use
denying it, or retreating, as some Christian Arabs did, into hyperauthenticity. Christian Arabs were on the run. The town of Bethlehem on the West Bank how has a Muslim majority. Palestinian
Christians were abandoning their land in record numbers: 2000
people a year out of a population of 45,000. There were 30,000
Christians in Jerusalem in 1944. Four decades later their number
had dwindled to 11,000. In Lebanon the Maronite Patriarch estimated that half the country's Christians had emigrated since the
onset of the civil war in 1975. In the aftermath of the American-
led campaign against Iraq, there were indications that Iraq's Christians, too, had begun to look for an exit from the country. The
Christian intelligentsia had been "more royalist than the king," a
Lebanese Christian author rightly observed, often more zealously
pan-Arabist than the Muslims.[89] Perhaps that way the demons of
religion could be warded off. Deep down many Christian Arabs no
doubt knew that Arab nationalism was at its core "covert Islam,"
and covert Sunni Islam to be more precise.[90] They had given it
their best effort, but the Arab political order had been transformed
and "culturally Islamized."[91]

A young teacher, a character in *One Thousand and Two Nights*, a
work of fiction by the skilled Syrian writer Hani al Raheb, takes us
close to that deliberate new interest in Islam. This character brings
to Islam the whole bitter disillusionment with his society: the "lack
of freedom and bread," the cynicism of the men in power, the
official truth that beats the drum of foreign threats and leaves men
in the dark about their own land, the crushing mediocrity everywhere. The young teacher explores the early history of Islam: He
reads into that history the conditions of his own society, he searches

246

for historical parallels. Rebellions against oppression become of particular interest to him. His quest troubles his superiors. "Let us be done with these explorations of the past. You know our students and their environment," his supervisor tells him. "We are not done at all," the young schoolteacher answers. "I am going to continue to interpret the revolution of Islam the way I see it. That is the only thing left for me that makes me feel alive. I am under siege, cut off from any choice. I need one thing that leaves me with some self-respect."[92]

At some remove from Hani al Rahib's Syrian homeland, a struggle was to unfurl in Algeria which dramatized the impasse between the authoritarian state and its Islamicist challengers. The fight in 1990–1992 between a ruling *nomenklatura* and an Islamicist opposition illuminated all the great themes of radical Islamic politics. An authoritarian postcolonial apparatus which had been in the saddle since independence had – as the Arabs would put it – eaten the green and the dry. It had devoured competing centers of power. The ruling party, the National Liberation Front, lived off the memory of its anticolonial struggle and exhausted that great legend. Three decades after independence, in 1990–1991, the ruling party sanctioned a pseudo-parliamentary process.

It was a time of "ballot chic" in the world, and the rulers thought they could give the failed state the cover of popular sanction. They miscalculated. A loosely assembled Islamicist opposition beat the ruling party in municipal elections held in 1990. The challengers, the Islamic Salvation Front, swept the municipal elections of 1990, gained control of 32 of the country's 48 provinces, picked up 70 percent of the popular vote, overwhelmed the ruling party in the capital city of Algiers. It was to be a repeat performance in the year which followed. In the first round of general parliamentary elections, in December of 1991, the Islamicists won 188 out of 430 parliamentary seats while the ruling party carried only 15 seats. The defeat of the rulers was to be sealed in the runoff elections scheduled for mid-January of 1992. The army then stepped in and aborted the process. Algeria had seen it all by then: The rulers launching an electoral process whose verdict they could not honor; the Islamicist challengers prevailing in a democratic process of sorts while running down democracy as a Western imposition; the Algerian bourgeoisie, its professional associations and "modernist" women coming out into the streets to hail the armed forces, cheer them on, and plead with them to protect the cultural freedoms of a Mediterranean society caught between an Islamic calling from below and a history of exposure to the fashions and the ways of Europe – principally the ways of France.

There are different ways of reading the defeat handed out to Algeria's ruling party, the National Liberation Front, by its Muslim fundamentalist challengers. By one reckoning, the defeat of the ruling party was a defeat of secularism per se. The lights would have gone out in Algiers. This would have been Qom by the Mediterranean. It would be tough going for the women of the country, for its modernists; it will by harder to get a drink, or see a porno flick, in Algiers. We have been here before: The Islamicists launch a revolt of a thousand discontents. The revolt is first led by academics, by "soft" advocates of "authenticity" (indeed it was a Western-educated philosophy professor who headed the Islamic Salvation Front). Then the true believers prevail, impose a reign of virtue and terror, and large numbers of Algerians will take to the road, particularly to France, providing Jean-Marie Le Pen, the leader of the French Right, with ample proof that he had been right all along in his worries about the "purity" and the future of France.

But we flatter Algeria's autocracy if we fall for this sort of interpretation. Above all Algeria's elections were a verdict on the postcolonial state and its entire baggage – one-party rule, the command economy, the repressive state living off the faded memories of the great anticolonial struggle, and the cynical *nomenklatura* that talks left and lives right. This is not so much the Tale of Qom, as it is a variant of the tale that unfolded in the Soviet Union under Mikhail Gorbachev. Here, too, in the Algerian setting, there was the spectacle of half-hearted reform bringing ruin in its train. And in President Chadli Benjedid there was even a Gorbachev-like figure playing, alternately, the role of cop and would-be emancipator. Benjedid had emerged out of the bureaucratic-military structure of the ruling party and the army. A colorless army colonel, he was thrust on the scene in 1979 by the collective apparatus. There was nothing special about him. There were signs, though, over the course of the preceding decade, that he came to understand just how deep the rot was.

Algeria's and Chadli Benjedid's moment of truth came in the fall of 1988, when riots swept the principal cities of the country. The young took to the streets. Their grievances were bottomless: underemployment, lack of basic consumer goods, food prices, the ruling party's monopoly on power and privilege, and truth. It was a ferocious revolt that targeted government buildings and state-owned property. Several hundred demonstrators were killed by the army: the state acknowledged the death of nearly two hundred demonstrators; other estimates ran as high as five hundred. This had been the Algerian people's army and its link with its revolutionary past. After the riots were put down, Benjedid was repentant; he told his people that he understood the message of the revolt, conceded that large numbers of those picked up in the crackdown were subjected to torture, promised that the state would change its ways, held up the prospects of free elections, political pluralism, market reforms.

Benjedid had difficult material to work with. The Algerian state had fallen on hard times. Its agriculture was in disarray; the country was forced to rely on imports for two-thirds of its food. The strategy of industrialization and import substitution has reached a dead end. Oil income plummeted from a high of $13 billion in 1970 to $5 billion in 1988; the state is heavily in debt, a total of $30 billion in foreign debt, with the bulk of oil revenues earmarked for debt servicing. Moreover, Algeria has changed in very profound ways: 75 percent of the population is under the age of 25. For the young urban poor and the half-educated, the legend of the ruling party and its *combattants* summoning the Algerian nation back from the world of the dead in the struggle against France is like a tale of a Thousand and One Nights. It was not their tale or their world.[93]

Alexis de Tocqueville had bequeathed us a truth that despotic regimes have yet to understand: "It is almost never when a state of things is most detestable that it is smashed, but when, beginning to improve, it permits men to breathe, to reflect, to communicate their thoughts with each other, and to gauge by what they already

249

have the extent of their rights and grievances. The weight, although less heavy, seems then all the more unbearable."[94] Chadli Benjedid had introduced the ballot, and left the door ajar. The secular political parties were too feeble to mount a challenge to the rulers. There was in the wings a man of the past, Ahmad Ben Bella, the country's first president. But Ben Bella was in his seventies. Behind him were sixteen years of imprisonment, and nine years of exile. Thus it came down to the state and the Islamicists. Only Islam and its urban networks – the intellectuals, the freelance preachers and their foot soldiers, the young urban poor – were left with any vitality.

After the years of the anticolonial struggle, and the 1970s when Algeria took the lead in pushing for a "new international economic order," the masks had fallen. It was easy to see now that those trips to all those anti-Western international conferences were only shopping trips for the wife and kids, easy to understand why Chadli Benjedid must have envied the fact that his predecessors ruled at a time when men and women were still held by political magic. Benjedid was pushed aside by the army – a sacrificial lamb. The Islamicists and the army: These were the forces left after the dust had settled.

Islam will of course offer Algeria no way out. In Algeria today there are two forms of escape: to France and to the comfort and the haven of the past. In other words, into the world of the foreigners, or the world of the ancestors. Islam can drape the failure, and cover up the hurt. The army can preserve the rot and awe its challengers. Meanwhile the society drifts. Those middle classes rescued by the army can hold onto the myth that they called on the army because it alone could preserve the reign of light versus the forces of darkness. But it is a deadly bargain that was struck in Algeria, one form of despotism versus another.

The failures of the Arab order have been many, and I have elaborated them (repeatedly and unfairly, it may be said) without a conviction of a finished model that makes things work, of an alchemy that makes people and societies behave justly or rationally.

Caught in the midst of a massive historic crisis, buffeted by powerful outside forces that have made their world pivotal and exposed, the Arabs have fallen back on the symbols and weapons

250

they know best: their religious identity. The skeptic may call this illusion and frustration; those bigoted in favor of Western civilization will dismiss it as a revolt against modernity, a return to the middle ages, as evidence of "barbarism."

But history is not the domain of judgement. It is easy to judge but hard to understand the ghosts with which people and societies battle, the wounds and memories that drive them to do what they do. Even if we disagree with people's choice of allegiance, we must understand the reasons for their choice, the odds they fight against, the range of alternatives open to them. The renaissance of civilizations is used as a weapon because so many in the Muslim world and the Third World as a whole feel that they live in a world constructed and maintained by others They constantly feel judged, scrutinized: Human rights campaigns point out their brutality; successful and sophisticated media put them and their methods of punishment, the way they treat one another, on display. A more energetic Occident plays havoc with their sensibilities, gets more done, even recovers their own history for them. "All that I know of our history and the history of the Indian Ocean," laments Salim, a character in V. S. Naipaul's *A Bend in the River*, "I have got from books written by Europeans. If I say that our Arabs in their time were great adventurers and writers; that our sailors gave the Mediterranean the lateen sail that made the discovery of the Americas possible; that an Indian pilot led Vasco de Gama from East Africa to Calicut; that the very word *cheque* was first used by our Persian Merchants – if I say these things it is because I have got them from European books. They formed no part of our knowledge or pride. Without Europeans, I feel, all our past would have been washed away . . ."[95]

To deal with the predicament of their place in the world, the losers in the world system have alternated between the quest for the Occident's power and success and the desire to retreat to their own universe, to try to find their own values, to rebel and say no to those who judge and penetrate. Entry into that alien, glamorous world has proven as difficult as return; hence the incoherence and breakdown of so many Third World societies.

The renaissance of civilization may be a mode of resistance, but only "up to the point that the detour becomes the journey."[96] The resurrection of Islam puts before Muslims the solution of their own tradition, and if that helps them conquer some of the self-contempt that colonized people feel in the modern world, then it must be seen as a positive development. What people who profess to be Muslims will do with the solution, how they will interpret that tradition, remains to be seen. "The quality of a faith," writes V. S. Naipaul, "is not a constant; it depends on the quality of the men who profess it."[97]

A Japanese critic observed that my usage of the terms "fundamentalist" and "fundamentalism" to describe the kind of Muslim sensibility illuminated above was misleading. Why not, he asked, use the terms "nativist" and "nativism"?

> What is a nativist? He is a man who sticks to the perception of the world lost. To him the whole world should be in the Arab world, instead of the Arab world in the whole world. To him the Arab world must be the self-completed world. It is a great pain to every people who had once lived in a self-completed world to admit that their world is nothing other than a small part of the whole world . . .
>
> The opening of Japan to the outside world was done in 1868. I have never lived in Japan when Japan was the whole world to the Japanese. But still I am sharing this nativist's sorrow. This sorrow was conveyed from father to son, then to grandson.[98]

There is in this statement an invitation to the Arabs to accept that theirs is no longer a self-completed world. To it might be added the consolation that few people, if any, live in "self-completed" worlds any longer, that "we" and "they" alike have been dragged into a world inhabited by others, that we must hear and honor other claims, that our will and our material interests must come up against those of others.

At the root of the nativist view of the world is a utopia — a memory of a world that once was that can be adorned, worked over, and embellished to suit current needs. In the modern world, utopias can serve as correctives, as antidotes to cynicism, as sources of inspiration. But utopias can be pushed too far. Our imagined utopias turn out to be the source of much of our misery: We never quite approximate them, and we feel all the more diminished for failing to replicate the glories of our ancestors or the perfection of our plans.

Notes

~~~~~~

Translations of Arabic titles are my own.

PREFACE

1 Michael Walzer, *The Company of Critics* (New York: Basic Books, 1988), p. 20.
2 Fernand Braudel, *The Mediterranean and the Mediterranean World in the Age of Philip II* (New York: Harper & Row, 1973), p. 901.

INTRODUCTION

1 Clifford Geertz, *The Interpretation of Cultures* (New York: Basic Books, 1973), p. 23.
2 Jihad al-Khazin, in *al Sharq al Awsat,* March 7, 1980.
3 See Bernard Lewis's *History: Remembered, Recovered, Invented* (Princeton: Princeton University Press, 1975), pp. 67–69.
4 T. E. Lawrence, *Seven Pillars of Wisdom* (New York: Penguin, 1962), p. 42.
5 Malcolm Kerr, *The Arab Cold War* (New York: Oxford University Press, 1971), p. v.
6 Jubran al Tueni, in *al-Nahar al Arabi wa al Dawli,* January 13, 1980.
7 Michel al-Hayek, "The Seventies of Lebanon, the Eighties of the Arab," *al Nahar al Arabi wa al Dawli,* January 13, 1980.
8 Bernard Lewis, "The Palestinians and the PLO," *Commentary,* January, 1975, pp. 41–42.
9 Fouad Ajami, "A Malady in the Mideast," *The New York Times,* December 27, 1978, p. 23.
10 Abdallah Laroui, *The Crisis of the Arab Intellectual* (Berkeley: University of California Press, 1976), pp. vii–viii.
11 Dunstan Wai, "Revolution, Rhetoric, and Reality in the Sudan," *Journal of Modern African Studies* 17, 1 (1979): 71.

Notes

12 Claude Lévi-Strauss, *Tristes Tropiques* (New York: Atheneum, 1974), pp. 401, 403–404.

13 Michel Foucault, *The History of Sexuality*, Vol. 1, *An Introduction* (New York, Vintage, 1978), pp. 95–96.

14 Michael Oakeshott, *Experience and Its Modes* (Cambridge: Cambridge University Press, 1966), pp. 107–108.

15 Oriana Fallaci, "An Interview with Col. Muammar el Qaddafi of Libya," *The New York Times Magazine*, December 15, 1979, p. 128.

16 Lévi-Strauss, *Tristes Tropiques*, p. 405.

17 Franz Kafka, in *The Great Wall of China* (New York: Schocken Books, 1946), pp. 160–161.

18 Hafez Jamali, "Notes of Dictatorship and the Romanian Revolution," *Al-Hayat*, February 19, 1990.

19 Mustapha Kamil Al-Sayyid, "Slow Thaw in the Arab World," *World Policy Journal*, Fall 1991, p. 716.

20 Thomas Friedman, *From Beirut to Jerusalem* (New York: Doubleday, 1989), pp. 76–105.

21 Amin Maalouf, *Leo Africanus* (New York: W. W. Norton, 1989), p. 124.

1. ONE'S WORLD AS IT REALLY IS

1 Abdallah Laroui, "The Arab Revolution Between Awareness and Reality," *Mawaqif* 10 (July–August 1970): 138.

2 The Center of Political and Strategic Studies of al-Ahran, *Watha'ig Abdel Nasser* [The Documents of Abdul Nasser], vol. 1 (Cairo, 1973), p. 226.

3 Adonis, "Introduction," in *Mawaqif* 1 (October–November 1968): 4. Adonis is the pen name of the Syrian writer Ali Ahmad Said.

4 Alexis de Tocqueville, *The Old Regime and the French Revolution* (Garden City, N.Y.: Doubleday, 1955), p. 147.

5 In *Sources of Chinese Tradition*, ed. William Theodore de Bary, et al. (Garden City, N.Y.: Doubleday, 1955), pp. 147, 164.

6 Michel Aflaq, *Nuqtat al Bidaya* (Beirut, 1971). This is a collection of Aflaq's post-1967 statements.

7 Halim Barakat, "Alienation and Revolution in Arab Life," *Mawaqif* 5 (July–August 1969): 38–39.

8 Zaki Neguib Mahmud, *Tajdid al Fikr al Arabi* [The Renewal of Arab Thought] (Beirut, 1971). See also his essay in *Mawaqif* 1 (October–November 1968): 5–14.

Notes

9 Marshall Hodgson, *The Venture of Islam*, vol. 2 (Chicago: University of Chicago Press, 1974), pp. 194–195.

10 Bassam Tibbi, "On Contemporary Arab Thought: Descriptive Writing and Revolutionary Writing," *Mawaqif* 3 (March–April 1969): 96.

11 Ibid.

12 Adonis, "The Problems of Literature and the Intelligentsia," *Al Adab* 6 (June 1968): 4–5.

13 Ibid.

14 Adonis, "Introduction," in *Mawaqif* 2 (January–February 1969): 3–4.

15 Sadeq al-Azam, *Al Naqd al Dhati Baʾd al Hazima* [Self-Criticism after the Defeat] (Beirut, 1968).

16 Malcolm Kerr, *The Arab Cold War* (London: Oxford University Press, 1971), p. 135.

17 Azm, *Self-Criticism after the Defeat*, p. 58.

18 Ibid., p. 133.

19 Ibid., p. 112.

20 Ibid., pp. 118–119.

21 Adonis, "Introduction," *Mawaqif* 4 (May–June 1969): 3–4.

22 Abdullah al-Qusaymi, "So that Harun al Rashid Would Not Return," *Mawaqif* 1 (October–November 1968): 24–40.

23 Taha Husayn, *Mustaqbal al thaqafa fi misr* [The Future of Education in Egypt] (Cairo, 1938): pp. 18–19.

24 Sami al-Jundi, *Arab wa Yahud* [Arabs and Jews] (Beirut, 1968); *Sadiqi Ilyas* [My Friend Ilyas] (Beirut, 1969); *Al Baʾth* [The Baʾth] (Beirut, 1969); *Athadda wa Attahim* [I Challenge and I Accuse] (Beirut, 1969).

25 *Al Wathaʾiq al Arabiyah*, 1967, pp. 690-692.

26 Jundi, *Al Baʾth*, p. 10.

27 Clifford Geertz, "After the Revolution: The Fate of Nationalism in the New States," in *The Interpretation of Cultures* (New York: Basic Books, 1973), p. 235.

28 Jundi, *Al Baʾth*, p. 160.

29 Ibid., p. 35.

30 Ibid., pp. 144–145.

31 Ibid., p. 157.

32 Ibid., pp. 17–18.

33 Jundi, *Arab wa Yahud*, pp. 40–47.

34 Ibid., p. 43.

35 Ibid., p. 44.

36 Ibid., p. 55.

37 Albert Camus, *The Rebel* (New York: Vintage Books, 1956), p. 150.

255

Notes

38 Jundi, *Athadda Wa Attahim,* pp. 56–57.

39 Jundi, *Arab Wa Yahud,* p. 181.

40 Ibid., p. 180.

41 Jundi, *Sadiqi Ilyas,* p. 86.

42 Nadim Bitar, *Min al Naksa ila al-Thawra* [From Setback to Revolution] (Beirut, 1968); Sadeq al Azm, *Naqd al Fikr al Dini* [Criticism of Religious Thought] (Beirut, 1969).

43 See Elie Kedourie's essay, "Religion and Secular Nationalism in the Arab World," in A. L. Utovich, ed., *The Middle East: Oil, Conflict, and Hope* (Lexington, Mass.: Lexington Books, 1976), pp. 181–194.

44 Muhammad Jalal Kishk, *Al Naksa wa al Ghazw al Fikri* [The Setback and Cultural Invasion] (Beirut, 1969); and *Al Ghazw a Fikri* [Cultural Invasion] (Kuwait, 1967). See also *Al Marksiyah wa al Ghazw al Fikri* [Marxism and Cultural Invasion] (Cairo, 1965); *Al Qawmiyah Wa al Ghazw al Fikri* [Nationalism and Cultural Invasion], (Beirut, 1970).

45 Kishk, *Al Marksiyah,* p. 42.

46 Ibid., p. 41.

47 Ibid., p. 88.

48 Kishk, *Al Qawmiyah,* p. 67.

49 Ibid., p. 167.

50 Clifford Geertz, *Islam Observed* (New Haven: Yale University Press, 1968), p. 64.

51 For a perceptive interpretation of the role of Islam in "revolutionary" Algeria, see Ernest Gellner, "The Unknown Apollo of Biskra: The Social Base of Algerian Puritanism," in *Government and Opposition* 9, 3 (Summer 1974): 277–310.

52 Kishk, *Al Qawimayah,* p. 233.

53 Daniel Lerner, *The Passing of Traditional Society* (New York: The Free Press, 1958).

54 Islamic fundamentalism, like any other system of beliefs, can lend itself to a variety of interpretations. Imaginative people can read virtually anything they want into a particular tradition. Both the Muslim Brotherhood and King Hassan of Morocco would staunchly defend their adherence to the Quran and the strictures of Islam. Which of the two is more authentically Islamic? The question is the stuff of which bloody struggles are made.

55 Wilfred Cantwell Smith, *Islam in Modern History* (New York: Mentor Books), p. 161.

56 As reproduced in Sa'd Jumah's *Al Mu'amarah Wa Ma'rakat al Masir* [The Conspiracy and the Battle of Destiny] (Beirut, 1968), pp. 239–240.

57 Salah al Din al Munajjid, *Amidat al Nakba* [The Pillars of the Disaster] (Beirut, 1967), p. 40.
58 As quoted in *Munajjid*, pp. 61–63. For an analysis of the episode and its significance, see Bernard Lewis, "The Return of Islam," *Commentary* 61, 1 (January 1976): 47.
59 See Munajjid, *Amidat al Nakba*, pp. 119–120; and Bitar, *Min al Naksa*, p. 155.
60 See Muhammad Izzat Nasr Allah, *Al-Radd ala Sadeq al Azm* [An Answer to Sadeq al Azm] (Beirut, 1970), pp. 207–209; Sadeq al-Azm, *Naqd al Fikr al Dini*, p. 48.
61 Nasr Allah, *Al-Radd ala Sadeq al Azm*, p. 208.
62 Sa'd Jumah, *Al Mu'amarah*, p. 215.
63 Al-Munajjid, *Amidat al Nakba*, p. 95.
64 Ibid., p. 10.
65 Ibid., p. 136.
66 Ibid., p. 49.
67 Ibid., p. 49.
68 Ibid., p. 47.
69 Ahmad Baha' al-Din, *Thalath Sanawat* [Three Years] (Beirut, 1970), p. 163.
70 E. H. Carr, *The Twenty Years' Crisis, 1919–1939* (London: Macmillan, 1956), p. 147.
71 De Tocqueville, p. 146.
72 See the thoughtful analysis of the connection between "situationism" and leadership in Robert C. Tucker's essay, "Personality and Political Leadership," *Political Science Quarterly* 92, 3 (Fall 1977): 383–393.
73 Alexander Herzen, *My Past and Thoughts* (New York: Knopf, 1973), p. 333.

2. EGYPT AS STATE, AS ARAB MIRROR

1 Jean and Simone Lacouture, *Egypt in Transition* (London, Methuen, 1958), p. 33.
2 Jamal Hamdan, *Shakhsiyat Misr* [Egypt's Personality] (Cairo, 1970), pp. 495–499.
3 Muhammad Jalal Kishk, *Kalam Li Misr* (Speaking to Egypt), (Beirut, 1974), pp. 102–103.
4 See Nadav Safran, "Engagement in the Middle East," *Foreign Affairs* 53 (October 1974), pp. 45–63.

5 Quoted in Edward Said's *Orientalism* (New York: Pantheon, 1978), p. 84.

6 Leo Tolstoy, *War and Peace* (New York: New American Library, 1968), p. 732.

7 Anwar el-Sadat, *In Search of Identity* (New York: Harper and Row, 1978), p. 180.

8 Najib Mahfuz, *Al Maraya* (Cairo, 1972), p. 196.

9 Muhammad Ahwad Mahjub, *Al Dimuqratiyah fi al Mizan* [Democracy in the Balance] (Beirut, 1973), p. 162.

10 Malcolm Kerr, *The Arab Cold War* (London: Oxford University Press, 1971).

11 Ahmad al Shuquiri, *Al Hazima al Kubra,* [The Big Defeat] (Beirut, 1972), p. 208.

12 See Mahjub, *Al-Dimuqratiyah fi al Mizan,* p. 162, and the recollections of President Boumedienne, in Lutfi al-Khuli, *An al Thuwara, fi al Thawra, wa bi al Thawra* [About the Revolution, In the Revolution, With the Revolution], (Beirut, 1975), p. 169.

13 For different accounts of the student rebellion, see Muhammad Jalal Kishk, *Madha Yuridu al Talabah al Misryyun?* [What Do the Egyptian Students Want?] (Cairo, 1968); Mahmoud Hussein, *Class Conflict in Egypt,* (New York: Monthly Review Press, 1973); and the excellent memoir by Wa'il Uthman, *Asrar al Haraka al Talabiyya* [The Secrets of the Student Movement] (Cairo, 1976).

14 Uthman, *Asrar al Haraka al Talabiyya,* pp. 28–29.

15 Ibid., p. 16.

16 The statement is reproduced in Kishk, *Madha Yuridu al Talabah al Misryyun?,* pp. 95–98.

17 See *Wathaiq Abdul Nasser* [The Documents of Abdul Nasser], (Cairo, 1973); vol. I, for the proceedings of the Arab Socialist Union of September 14–18, 1968. The proceedings were dominated by a lively exchange of opinions and reflections by students, workers, and others. For the statement cited, see p. 542.

18 See Ibrahim Issawi and Muhammad Nassar, "An Attempt to Estimate the Economic Losses Inflicted on Egypt by the Arab–Israeli Wars Since 1967," Third Conference of Egyptian Economists, Cairo, March 1978 (in Arabic).

19 Avi Shlaim and Raymond Tanter, "Decision Process, Choice, and Consequences: Israel's Deep Penetration Bombing in Egypt, 1970," *World Politics* 30 (July 1978), pp. 498–499.

20 Arnold Hottinger, "The Depth of Arab Radicalism," *Foreign Affairs* 51 (April 1973), p. 504.

21 See Tawfiq al Hakim, *Wathaiq fi Tariq Awdat al Wa'i* [Documents on the Road to Awareness] (Cairo and Beirut, 1975), p. 47.

22 For the view of Mustapha Amin, and others who share his perspective, see *Madha Ba'd Harb Uktubir?* [What After the October War?] (Cairo, 1974), pp. 23–24.

23 See John Waterbury's "The Opening: Part III: De-Nasserization," *American Universities Field Staff* 4, (1975), p. 1; Tawfiq al Hakim, *Awdat al Wai,* [The Return of Awareness] (Beirut, 1974).

24 Tawfiq al-Hakim, *Awdat al Ruh* [The Return of the Spirit] (Cairo, 1933).

25 Najib Mahfuz, *al Karnak* (Cairo, 1974), p. 57. This novel, it should be noted, was written in 1971.

26 See Fuad Mattar's dialogue with Mohamed Heikal, *Bisarah An Abdul Nasser* [Frankly Speaking about Abdul Nasser] (Beirut, 1975).

27 Muhammad Anwar el-Sadat, *Waraqat Uktubir* [The October Paper] (Cairo, 1974).

28 Sayyed Marei, *Awraq Siyyasiah* [Political Papers], Vol. 3 (Cairo, 1978), pp. 738–756. Marei's memoirs provide an extremely useful perspective and an abundance of information on contemporary Egyptian politics. Marei was an ancien régime politician who did well during the revolutionary years and then went on to become one of Sadat's closest advisors.

29 The quote is from a personal discussion with Tahseen Basheer in Cairo in December, 1978.

30 Kamal Junblatt, *Pour le Liban* (Paris: Stock, 1978), p. 171.

31 *Al Akhbar,* December 5, 1978, p. 5.

32 Center for Political and Strategic Studies, *Muatamar Kamp David* [The Camp David Conference] (Cairo, 1979), p. 136.

33 Taha Husayn, *Mustaqbal al Thaqfa fi Misr* [The Future of Education in Egypt] (Cairo, 1944), p. 389.

34 *Al Ahram,* October 11, 1979.

35 Anwar el-Sadat, *In Search of Identity* (New York: Harper & Row, 1978), p. 137.

36 Abdulla Laroui, *The Crisis of the Arab Intellectual* (Berkeley: University of California Press, 1976), pp. 31–32.

37 See the interview with Boutros Boutros Ghali conducted by Jean-Pierre Péroncel-Hugoz, "Quelle Diplomatic Pour d'Egypte En Paix," *Politique Internationale* 5 (Autumn 1979): 11.

38 Lecture delivered at the Johns Hopkins School of Advanced International Studies, Washington, D.C., April 9, 1980.

39 Edward Sheehan, "Step by Step in the Middle East," *Foreign Policy,* 22 (Spring 1976): 18.

40 Quoted in John Marlow, *Spoiling the Egyptians* (London: Andre Deutsch, 1974), p. 105.
41 Nadav Safran, *Egypt in Search of Political Community* (Cambridge, Mass.: Harvard University Press, 1961), p. 34.
42 David Landes, *Bankers and Pashas* (London: Heinemann, 1958), p. 209.
43 Husayn, *Mustaqbal al Thaqafa fi Misr*, pp. 18–19.
44 Sheehan, "Step by Step in the Middle East," p. 7.
45 On this topic see one of Sadat's most revealing interviews, in *Al Ahram*, December 26, 1978.
46 Blanchard Jerrold, *Egypt under Ismail Pacha* (London: Samuel Tinsley & Co., 1879), pp. vi–vii.
47 Ibid., p. vii.
48 *Flaubert in Egypt*, ed. and trans. Francis Steegmuller (Chicago: Academy Chicago Limited, 1979), pp. 42, 29.
49 Leonard Binder, *The Ideological Revolution in the Middle East* (New York, John Wiley, 1964), pp. 198–229.
50 The views of Hakim and Fawzi and their critics are brought together in an extremely useful work edited by the Egyptian scholar Saad Ibrahim, *Urubat Misr* [Egypt's Arabism] (Cairo, 1978).
51 *Urubat Misr*, p. 109.
52 Ibid., p. 112.
53 Ibid., p. 114.
54 Nadav Safran, *Egypt in Search of Political Community*, p. 140.
55 Sayyed Qutb's answer to Taha Husayn carries the same title as Husayn's work, *Mustaqbal al Thaqafa fi Misr*. Jedda, 1969 edition.
56 Fundamentalist views are expressed in the Muslim Brotherhood's monthly magazine *Al-Daʾwa;* the critique of Camp David was in the November, 1978, issue.
57 The story of the Muslim Brotherhood and its Supreme Guide Hassan al-Banna has been masterfully told, with new evidence, by Rifaʾat al-Said in *Hassan al Banna* (Cairo, 1977).
58 Crane Brinton, *The Anatomy of Revolution* (New York: Vintage, 1965), p. 47.
59 Mohamed Heikal, *The Sphinx and the Commissar* (New York: Harper & Row, 1978), p. 50.
60 Ghali Shukri, *Mudhakkirat Thaqafa Tahtadir* [Memoirs of a Dying Culture] (Beirut, 1970), pp. 369–371.
61 Mohamed Heikal, *Hadith al Mubadara*, (Beirut, 1978), pp. 56–57.
62 See Ibrahim, *Urubat Misr*, pp. 127–128.
63 Khairi Aziz, in Ibrahim, *Urubat Misr*, p. 72.

64 Ahmad Baha'a al-Din, in Ibrahim, *Urubat Misr*, pp. 139–140, 144–146.

65 The letter has been reproduced in *al Taqqadum* (an irregular pamphlet of the leftist group the Progressive Assembly of National Unionists), October 11, 1978, pp. 5–9.

66 Mohamed Heikal, "Egyptian Foreign Policy," *Foreign Affairs* 56 (Summer 1978): 726.

67 Ahmad Baha'a al-Din, *Iqtirah Dawlat Filastin* [Suggestion of A Palestinian State] (Beirut, 1968), p. 53.

68 Walid Khalidi, "A Sovereign Palestinian State," *Foreign Affairs* 56 (Summer 1978): 695–713.

69 Tawfic Farah, "Group Affiliation of University Students in the Arab Middle East (Kuwait)," Reports and Research Studies, Department of Political Science, Kuwait University, 1977. I am deeply grateful to Professor Farah for sharing with me his findings and for a helpful discussion of the issues discussed here.

70 Khalidi, "A Sovereign Palestinian State," p. 695.

71 Bernard Lewis, *The Middle East and the West* (New York: Harper & Row, 1964), p. 94.

72 U.S. Senate, Committee on Foreign Relations, *International Debt, the Banks, and U.S. Foreign Policy*, 1977, p. 36.

73 *Al Sharq al Awsat*, March 13, 1980.

74 Abdallah Laroui, *The Crisis of the Arab Intellectual*, p. 177.

75 See Michel Crozier, *The Stalled Society* (New York: Viking Press, 1973); Stanley Hoffmann, *Decline or Renewal: France Since the 1930's* (New York: Viking, 1974).

76 The escape from politics into piety best illustrated by Sadat's revealing "law of shame," proposed to parliament in 1980. Instead of political arguments and the terror of the state, the "law of shame" – an ambiguous doctrine that would seek to shame those who dishonor the "Egyptian family," who disagree with the president, who say things that should not be said about the economy and about peace treaties – would rely on the society's oldest and in many ways most stifling chains: the fear of ʿar (shame), the disapproval of the community, moral prohibition.

77 Albert Hirschmann, *Exit, Voice and Loyalty* (Cambridge, Mass.: Harvard University Press, 1970).

78 The survey and the larger problem of emigration is tackled in Abdel Husayn's essay, "Wealth as an Obstacle to Unity," *Al Mustaqbal al Arabi*, 5 (1979): 28.

79 E. W. Lane, *Manners and Customs of Modern Egyptians* (London: Ward Lock & Co., 1890), p. 272.

80 Jean and Simone Lacouture, *Egypt in Transition*, pp. 29–30.

81 Lewis Awad, *The Seven Masks of Nasserism* (Beirut, 1976), p. 177.

82 Ibid., pp. 154–155.

83 See Jonathan F. Pedersen, "Fighting for Security: Egyptian–American Responses to Middle Eastern Change," senior thesis, Woodrow Wilson School of Public and International Affairs, Princeton University, 1980, p. 24.

84 Ibid., p. 44.

85 William Shawcross, *The Shah's Last Ride* (New York: Simon & Schuster, 1988), p. 353.

86 Lawrence Durell, "With Durell in Egypt," *The New York Times Magazine*, June 11, 1978, p. 46.

87 The account of the conspiracy against Sadat comes from the massive evidence and court proceedings and police records of the Sadat assassination. The documents (in my possession: case number 462, 1981) are a veritable treasure trove of information. My account is drawn from these documents.

88 See Shawqi Khalid, *Muhakamat Firawn* (The Trial of Pharaoh), Cairo, 1986.

89 See note 87.

90 *Al Farida al Ghaiba* [The Absent Obligation] was a fifty-four-page pamphlet written earlier in 1981. A copy is in my possession.

91 A careful study of the social background of the militants who struck down Sadat was made by Hamied Ansari, "The Islamic Militants in Egyptian Politics," *The International Journal of Middle East Studies* 16 (1984): 123–144.

92 Saad Eddin Ibrahim, "Domestic Developments in Egypt," in William Quandt, ed., *The Middle East: Ten Years After Camp David* (Washington, D.C.: The Brookings Institution, 1988), p. 28.

93 Ibid., p. 31.

94 Mohamed Heikal, *Autumn of Fury* (London: Andre Deutsch, 1983), pp. 274–275.

95 Ibid., p. 274.

96 Albert Hourani, "The Decline of the West in the Middle East," *International Affairs* (April 1953): 166.

97 See Yahya Sadowski's *Political Vegetables?* (Washington, D.C.: The Brookings Institution, 1991) for a portrait of political corruption in Egypt.

98 Mohamed Sid Ahmad has covered the phenomenon of political par-

ties in his *Mustagbal al Nizam al Hizbi fi Misr* [The Future of the Party System in Egypt] (Cairo, 1984).

3. FRACTURED TRADITION

1 Joseph Levenson, *Confucian China and Its Modern Fate* (Berkeley: University of California Press, 1968), p. 124.

2 Hanna Batatu, *The Old Social Classes and the Revolutionary Movements of Iraq* (Princeton, N.J.: Princeton University Press, 1978), p. 1035.

3 Levenson, *Confucian China and Its Modern Fate*, pp. xxix–xxx.

4 Hannah Arendt, *Between Past and Future* (New York: Viking, 1968), p. 26.

5 Albert Hourani, *Arabic Thought in the Liberal Age* (London: Oxford University Press, 1970), p. 344.

6 See *Al Mawaqif* 6 (November–December 1969): 5–76.

7 Jean-Pierre le Dantec, as quoted in Albert Bressond and Thierry de Montbrial, "The Ups and Downs of Mutual Relevance," *Daedalus* 108 (Spring 1979): 112.

8 See the thorough and self-critical work put together by the publicists of the PLO Research Center in Beirut, *Al-Muqawamah al Filastiniyah wa Nizam al Urduni* [The Palestinian Resistance and the Jordanian Regime] (Beirut, 1971).

9 Ibid., p. 123. My translation.

10 Ibid., pp. 325–336, 337–360.

11 *Arab Report and Record* 12 (1976): 398–399.

12 Arnold Hottinger, "The Depth of Arab Radicalism," *Foreign Affairs* 51 (April 1973): 504.

13 Sadeq al-Azm, *Dirasah Naqadayah Li-Fikr al Muqawamah al-Filastini-yah*, [A Critical Study in the Thought of the Palestinian Resistance] (Beirut, 1973).

14 Husam al-Khatib, *Fi al-Tajnibah al Thwariya al Filastiniyah* (Damascus, 1972), p. 17.

15 Al-Azm, *Dirasah Naqadayah Li-Fikr al Muqawamah*, pp. 122–123.

16 Hussein Munis, "The Return of the Arab to his Place in History," in Mustapha Amin and others, *Wa Madha ba'da Harb Uktubir?* [What After the October War?] (Cairo, 1974), pp. 69–70.

17 Edmund Burke, *Reflections on the Revolution in France* (1790; New York: Liberal Arts Press, 1955), p. 181.

18 Edward Sheehan, "Step by Step in the Middle East," *Foreign Policy* (Spring 1976): 47.

19 For the text of the interview see Oriana Fallaci's collection, *An Interview with History* (New York: Liveright, 1976), pp. 262–287.

20 Mohamed Heikal, *The Sphinx and the Commissar* (New York: Harper & Row, 1978), pp. 261–262.

21 Fehmy Saddy, "Attitudes of Arab Traditionalists and Modernists toward U.S. Foreign Policy in the Middle East," paper delivered at the Twentieth Annual Convention of the International Studies Association, Toronto, Canada, March 21–24, 1979, p. 2.

22 Joseph Kraft, "A Letter from Saudi Arabia," *The New Yorker*, October 20, 1975, p. 111; see also Salim Daher's essay, "United States–Saudi Relations Since 1973," Department of Government, Harvard University, January, 1978.

23 Maxime Rodinson, "Islam Resurgent," *Gazelle Review* 6 (1979): 6.

24 Albert Hirschmann, *The Passions and the Interests* (Princeton: Princeton University Press, 1977).

25 In *Al-Amal al-Shahri* (Beirut), 2 (April 1977): 71.

26 In *An Nahar al Arabi wa al Dawli*, May 14, 1977, p. 5.

27 Anthony Ashley Shaftesbury, quoted in Hirschman, *The Passions and the Interests*, p. 46.

28 See Eric Rouleau's sensitive report, "Civil War in Lebanon," *SWASIA: North Africa* 2, 41, October 17, 1975, p. 7.

29 Ibid., p. 8. My emphasis.

30 Ray Errol Fox, "South Lebanon's 'Chief,' " *The New York Times*, May 19, 1980, p. A-21.

31 See *Al-Manar*, November 26, 1979, p. 8.

32 Henry A. Kissinger, *White House Years*, (Boston: Little, Brown, 1979), pp. 1276–1300.

33 See Mohamed Heikal's account in "Egyptian Foreign Policy," *Foreign Affairs* 56 (July 1978): 714–727.

34 *Al Ahram*, April 6, 1977, p. 6.

35 See *al Ahram*, December 30, 1977, p. 4 for Saudi worries about Eurocommunism; see also Daher, "United States–Saudi Relations Since 1973."

36 John C. Campbell, "The Middle East: Burdens of Empire," *Foreign Affairs*, 57 (1978): 613–632.

37 "Insignificant nations" was the term used by Irving Kristol in the aftermath of October 1973 to bemoan the way the "significant" nations allowed their power and control to slip. "Where Have All the Gunboats Gone?," *The Wall Street Journal*, December 13, 1973, as quoted in Noam Chomsky, *Peace in the Middle East* (New York: Vintage, 1974); p. 6.

Notes

58 *Al-Nadhir* 3 (October 7, 1979).

59 Ibid.

60 "The Disintegration of Syria?" Beirut, 1979. For obvious reasons, the author wishes to remain anonymous. But he is a most capable and careful scholar.

61 *The New York Times,* December 28, 1979, p. 6.

62 Burke, *Reflections on the Revolution in France,* p. 101.

63 Kamal Junblatt, *Hadah'i Wasiyyati* [This Is My Testimony] (Beirut, 1978), p. 106.

64 The literature on this topic is vast; one exemplary treatment (in the Japanese context) is G. B. Sansom, *The Western World and Japan* (New York: Vintage, 1973).

65 Crane Brinton, *The Anatomy of Revolution* (New York: Vintage, 1965), p. 120.

66 *Al Ahram al Iqtisadi,* February 1, 1977.

67 John Waterbury, "The Opening Part II: Luring Foreign Capital," *American Universities Field Staff,* 20, 3 (1975): 15.

68 Shaykh Abdul Halim Mahmud, *Fatawa'a a'n al Shuiyya* [Opinions on Communism], 1976. The emasculation of official religion and its usage by the political order are revealed in this shallow and cynical work.

69 See *Ruz al Yussef,* August 18, 1975.

70 The research was carried out by collaboration of American and Egyptian scholars under the auspices of the Research Program on Development Studies at Princeton University. See Fouad Ajami, "The Open Door Economy: Its Roots and Welfare Consequences," in Gouda Abdel Khalek and Robert Tignor, eds., *The Political Economy of Income Distribution in Egypt* (New York: Holmes and Meier, 1982), pp. 469–516.

71 See the magazine of the Muslim Brotherhood, *Al-Da'wa,* January, 1979, pp. 52–54.

72 Oriana Fallaci, *An Interview with History,* p. 268.

73 Anwar el-Sadat, *In Search of Identity* (New York: Harper & Row, 1978), p. ix.

74 Hassan Hanafi, "The Historical Roots for the Crisis of Freedom and Democracy," *Al-Mustaqbal Al-Arabi* 5 (1979): 136. This is a most impressive attempt by an independent political philosopher to examine critically the style of authority in the Arab world and, as its title states, the historical roots of the problem.

75 Fadlu Shalq, in *Lubnan al Akhar* [The Other Lebanon] (Beirut, 1976), pp. 51–63.

76 Ibid., p. 61.

Notes

77 Ali Abdel Raziq, *Al-Islam wa Usul al Hukm*, [Islam and the Principles of Government] (Cairo, 1925).
78 *Al-Ahram*, May 10, 1979.
79 Edmund Burke, *Reflections on the Revolution in France*, p. 108.
80 Edmund Burke, *Works of the Right Honorable Edmund Burke* (London, 1803), Vol. 8, p. 255.
81 Sadiq al Azm, "Commentary on Islamic Fundamentalism in the Levant," Proceedings of the Washington Institute for Near East Policy" (Washington, D.C., 1990), p. 24.
82 See Joseph Kostiner, "Shi'a Unrest in the Gulf," in Martin Kramer, ed., *Shi'ism, Resistance, and Revolution*, (Boulder, Colorado: Westview Press, 1987), pp. 173–186.
83 The tale of Musal al Sadr is told in my book *The Vanished Imam: Musa al Sadr and the Shia of Lebanon* (Ithaca, N.Y.: Cornell University Press, 1986).
84 Muhammad Hussein Fadlallah's comments are in a book entitled *Al-Harakat al Islamiyya fi Lubnan* [Islamic Movements in Lebanon] published by *Dar al Shira'* (Beirut, 1984), p. 148.
85 Ghali Shukri, *Al-Turath wa al Thawra* [The Heritage and the Revolution] (Beirut, 1973), p. 23.
86 *The Wall Street Journal*, June 13, 1980, p. 31.
87 Jacques Berque, *The Arabs* (London, Faber & Faber, 1964), p. 290.
88 *An Nahar al Arabi Wa al Dawli*, February 24, 1980, pp. 54–55.
89 Habib Malik, "The Future of Christian Arabs," *The Mediterranean Quarterly* 2, no. 2 (Spring 1991): 72–84.
90 For an astute treatment of Arab nationalism as "covert Islam" see Kamal Salibi, *A House of Many Mansions: The History of Lebanon Reconsidered* (Berkeley and Los Angeles: University of California Press, 1988).
91 Malik, "The Future of Christian Arabs," p. 76.
92 Hani al Raheb, *Alf Laila wa Lailatain* [One Thousand and Two Nights] (Beirut, 1982), pp. 158–159.
93 See my essay "The Battle of Algiers," *The New Republic* (July 9 and 16, 1990), pp. 12–13.
94 Alexis de Tocqueville, *Selected Letters on Politics and Society* (Berkeley and Los Angeles: University of California Press, 1985), p. 296.
95 V. S. Naipaul, *A Bend in the River*, p. 234. See also Bernard Lewis, *History: Remembered, Recovered, Invented* (Princeton: Princeton University Press, 1975).
96 Immanuel Wallerstein, "The Dialectics of Civilizations in the Modern World System," Paper delivered at Ninth World Congress of Sociology, Uppsala, Sweden, August 14–19, 1978, p. 5.

Notes

97 V. S. Naipaul, *India: A Wounded Civilization* (New York: Knopf, 1977), p. 186.
98 Toru Kawajiri, "A Comment," personal communication, April 18, 1980. I wish to note my debt to Mr. Kawajiri for the sensitive parallels he drew between Japan's case and the Arab world's.

Index

Index

Beirut, xiv, xv, xix, xx, 5, 11, 12, 45, 162, 163, 166–7, 240, 241
Ben Bella, Ahmad, 250
Benjedid, Chadli, 248–9, 250
Berque, Jacques, 244–5
Bethlehem, 246
Binder, Leonard, 131
Bismarck, Otto von, 13
Bitar, Nadim, 67, 68, 175
Bolshevik revolution, 38, 234
Boumedienne, Houari, 100, 107
Bourguiba, Habib, 74, 143, 226, 227
Boutros-Ghali, Boutros, 124
Brinton, Crane, 135, 221
Britain, *see* United Kingdom
Brzezinski, Zbigniew, 199
Burke, Edmund, 183, 218, 233–4
Bush, George, 14

Cairo, 5, 119–20, 128–9, 160
Campbell, John C., 201
Camp David accords, xviii, 113, 117, 134, 139, 160, 162, 198
Camus, Albert, 57
Carr, E. H., 83
Carter, Jimmy, xviii–xix, 23, 129–30, 153, 198
Carter Doctrine, xviii–xix, 153
Carter plan, 131, 225
Ceausescu, Nicolae, 25
Chamberlain, Houston Stewart, 57
Chamoun, Camille, 179
Chiha, Michel, 192, 193
Chile, 25
China, 33, 62, 109, 170, 172, 179, 182, 199, 204, 206
Christianity, 75, 107, 117, 127, 246
Lebanon, 192–3, 194–6, 209, 228
citizenry, 39–40
class
Egypt, 103–4, 111
Islam, 72–3, 75, 216
petropower, 187
resentment, 219–20
warfare, 65
Cold War, 25, 223
colonialism, 51, 59, 126, 139, 182, 248
"command economy," 26
Communist Party, xiii

communists and communism, 46, 74, 201
Egypt, 100, 135
Islam, 205
Zionism, 78
community
Islam, 64
revolution, 77
Six Day War, 83
Confucianism, 172
conservative fundamentalism, 74–87
Copts, 109, 159, 228–9
corruption
Ba'th party, 52–3
Egypt, 112, 128, 165
cosmopolitanism, 62, 119, 125, 130
see also modernity and moderniza-tion
Crozier, Michel, 150

Damascus, 77, 162
al Da'wa (journal), 225
dawlat kufr, 158
democracy, 25, 26, 166, 218, 219, 224, 247
de-Nasserization, 18, 110–12
detente, 10, 109
al-Din, Ahmad Baha'a, 81, 139, 141
al-Din Bitar, Salah, xiv, 77
al Din, Fouad Pasha Serag, 155
Dulles, John Foster, 153
Durrell, Lawrence, 154
dynastic states, 237–8

Eastern Europe, 245–6
Egypt, xv, xix, 65, 231
Arab world and (*see* Egypt, inter-Arab politics)
centrality of, 91–4
culture, 125–7, 132
economy of, 105, 187, 224–5
education, 103–4, 151, 188
government spending, 26
inter-Arab politics, 8, 16–19, 84, 91–4, 97, 99–100, 106, 112–15, 120, 121–2, 129, 132, 139–41, 148–9
Iranian revolution, 217
Iraq and, 54, 129

270

Index

Index

Index

Egypt and, 122–3
Faisal and, 125
foreign aid, 131
inter-Arab politics, 11, 148 (*see also* Egypt, inter-Arab politics)
and Islam, 134, 217, 222–3, 226, 233
Jerusalem initiative of, 113, 121, 123, 137–8, 139, 198, 226–7
legacy of, 164–5, 166
Nasser and, 97, 108, 127, 137
October Paper, 114
October War, 110, 113, 115, 143
pan-Arabism, 137–8, 140
Qaddafi and, 143, 144
Revolution, 135
Revolutionary Command Council and, 139
Saudi Arabia and, 118–19
style of, 120–1, 148, 149–50
Syria and, 117
threat to, 154
United States and, 120, 127–8, 130, 152–3, 203
Sadat, Ismat, 165
el-Sadat, Jihan, 127, 165
Sadat initiative, *see* Jerusalem initiative
al-Sadr, Imam Musa, 179, 239, 240
al Sadr, Ayatollah Muhammad Baqir, 237
Safran, Nadav, 126, 133, 212
Said, Ali Ahmad, *see* Adonis (Ali Ahmad Said)
Saladin, 94
Saudi Arabia, xvi, xix, 2, 10, 11, 26–7, 74–5, 83, 115, 119, 120, 152, 153, 172, 173, 197, 229–31, 237
Egypt and, 93, 94, 114, 118–19, 120
inter-Arab politics, 171
Islam and, 199, 201, 229–33
religious extremism, 230–2
Syria and, 179
United States and, 199–201, 203
weaknesses of, 121, 199–200
science, 43–4, 81, 104, 150
shah of Iran, *see* Pahlavi, R. (shah of Iran)
Shaker, Fatna, 148–9
Sharon, Ariel, 12, 163

al-Shati, Bint, 138
Shaykhs, 53
Shiites and Shi'a muslims, xvi–xvii, xx, 12–13, 170, 179, 209, 217, 227, 228, 237–9
Iraq, 27, 235, 236, 237–8
Lebanon, xix, 11, 239–41
Shukri, Ghali, 136, 242
al-Shuqairi, Ahmad, xv–xvi, 4, 34, 99, 180
Sinai accord, xviii, 10, 113, 123
Sinai Peninsula, xix, 161, 162
Six Day War (1967), xvii, 4, 13–14, 157
Ba'th party, 31, 49, 54, 55, 80
Egypt, 90–1, 94, 96, 102, 103, 105, 113, 138
events of, 14
impact of, 5, 8, 16, 30–1, 178–9
inter-Arab politics, 83
Islam, 37, 39, 60–2, 64–5, 72, 74, 75, 81, 83
Nasser and, 14, 32, 39–40, 43, 98, 146
Palestinian movement, 140, 181–2
radicals, 32
revolution, 90, 98, 174–6
society, 37–45
Syria and, 53
United States, 205–6
Smith, Wilfred Cantwell, 71
social contract, 27, 164
socialism, xiii, 42, 75, 104, 234
Egypt, 111, 138
Islam and, 61, 76, 233
military and, 65, 72
morale, 81
Soviet Union, 25, 63, 74, 76, 108, 153, 197, 204, 205, 245, 248
Afghanistan invasion, xviii, 153
Egypt, xviii, 94–5, 117–18
Islam, 78, 201
Syria and, 54
Sudan, 93, 99, 100
Suez Campaign (1956), 14
Suez Canal, xvii, 105, 106, 110, 132, 183
Suez crisis, 98
Sukarno, 109, 146

Index

Sulta, xvi
Sunnis muslims, xvi–xvii, xix, 27, 51–2, 107, 116, 170–1, 209, 214, 215–17, 227, 228, 235, 238, 239, 246
Syria, xiii, xiv, xv, xix, xx, 10, 25, 26, 27, 65, 80, 84, 93, 107, 112, 131, 231, 239
  Ba'th party, 15, 49, 51–2, 141–2, 216
  Egypt and, 115, 116–17, 129, 139
  elites in, 214
  Islam, 71–2, 215–16, 229
  Israel and, 76, 116–17, 141
  Lebanon and, 2, 117, 142, 184, 241
  Libya and, 94
  Palestinians and, 116, 117, 141, 176, 179
  politics of, 117, 171
  revolution, 42
  Saudi Arabia and, 179
  Six Day War, 53–4
  United States and, 203–4

takfir al hakim, 157–8
Tal al Zaatar, 117
Al-Talia (journal), 150
technology, 190, 191, 201, 202, 207, 237, 242–3, 244
Thatcher, Margaret, 153–4
Third World, 18, 26, 47, 68, 70, 146, 186, 251
  detente and, 109
  Islamic fundamentalism, 23
  nationalism, 51
  revolution, 176
  United Nations, 10
Tibbi, Bassam, 35
Tito, 76
de Tocqueville, Alexis, 33, 85, 99, 221, 249–50
tradition, 24–5, 59, 214
  Ba'th party, 72
  dualism, 209
  Islam, 242
  modernization and, 70, 125, 206–7, 208, 224
  myth of greatness and, 55
  Nasser and, 35–6

radicalism and, 44, 228
revolution and, 41–2
science and, 43–4
Six Day War, 78–9
state and, 46
Transjordan, 142, 230
Tunisia, 26, 74, 143, 218, 226

Umayyad Empire, 93
Unionist Movement, 8
United Kingdom, 91, 126, 139, 200, 205
United Nations, xvi, 10, 14, 180, 185
United States, 10, 78, 173
  Egypt and, 94–5, 100, 115, 125, 127, 129–30, 131–2, 157, 161, 162, 203–4
  Iran and, 205–6, 234
  and Iraqi invasion of Kuwait, xix, xx, 13–14, 231, 246
  Israel and, 201–2, 203, 204
  October War, 201–2, 205
  Palestinian question, 196–7, 204
  Sadat and, 120, 127–8, 129–30, 153, 203
  Saudi Arabia and, 13, 199, 200, 201, 203, 232
  World War II, 205
Urabi, Ahmad, 133
Uthman, Uthman Ahmad, 128

Wafd government, 126
al-Wahhab, Muhammad Ibn Abd, 56, 229
Wahhabi movement, 56, 93, 229, 237
Wai, Dunstan, 19
Wallerstein, Immanuel, 208
wealth distribution
  inequality in, 21, 24, 236–7, 238
  inter-Arab politics, 92–3, 121, 144, 147
  Islam, 20–1
  resentment, 221–2
  tradition, 211
  values, 7–8
  warfare, 65
  world-wide, 183, 219–20

278